Privatizing Nature

Privatizing Nature

Political Struggles for
the Global Commons

Edited by

Michael Goldman

Rutgers University Press
New Brunswick, New Jersey

First published in Great Britain 1998 by Pluto Press
345 Archway Road, London N6 5AA

First published in the United States 1998
by Rutgers University Press, New Brunswick, New Jersey

Library of Congress Cataloging-in-Publication Data
Privatizing nature: political struggles for the global commons/
   edited by Michael Goldman.
      p.   cm.
   Includes bibliographical references (p.   ) and index.
   ISBN 0–8135–2553–5 (cloth) – ISBN 0–8135–2554–3 (pbk.)
   1. Global environmental change. 2. Environmental quality.
3. Environmental protection—International cooperation.
4. Sustainable development—International cooperation.   I. Goldman,
Michael, 1960–   .   II. Series.
GE149.P75   1998
363.7'0526—dc21   97–34878
                                                           CIP

Printed in Great Britain

Contents

Notes on Contributors

Giovanna DiChiro is Assistant Professor of Environmental Studies at Allegheny College, Pennsylvania, US.

Antonio Carlos Diegues is a lecturer in Ecological Anthropology at the University of Sao Paulo, Brazil.

Michael Flitner is a Postdoctoral Fellow at Freiburg University, Germany.

Michael Goldman is MacArthur Fellow of Peace and International Cooperation in the Sociology Department, University of California-Berkeley, US.

Samuel-Alain Nguiffo is Secretary-General at the Centre pour l'Environnement et le Developpement (Center for Environment and Development), Yaoundé, Cameroon.

Sanjeev Prakash is an economist/environmentalist in New Delhi, India.

Lynn Stephen is Professor of Anthropology at Northeastern University, Boston, US.

Michael Thompson is an anthrqpologist and Director of the the Musgrave Institute, London, UK.

Acknowledgements

We would like to gratefully acknowledge the support of the Transnational Institute (Amsterdam), especially past and present directors Jochen Hippler and Fiona Dove, for the 'Reinventing the Commons' project; Peter Wahl, director of World Economy, Ecology and Development Association (WEED, Bonn), for organizing and contributing to the 'Reinventing the Commons' workshops in Amsterdam, Frankfurt and Bonn, from which these discussions emerged; the Directorate General for Development of the European Union for generously funding the project; Roger van Zwanenberg and Pluto Press for patiently working with the editor and manuscript; and the many insightful workshop participants who gave their precious time and energy, including Maria Mies, Veronika Bennholt-Thomsen, Wolf Hartmann, Charlotte Hess, Marvin Soroos, Maarten Hajer, Michiel Schwarz, Mariano Aguirre, Rachel Schurman, Myriam Vander Stichele and Susan George.

Chapter 1 was first published as '"Customs in Common": The Epistemic World of Commons Scholars', in *Theory and Society* 26: 1–37 (Dordrecht: Kluwer Academic, 1997). Chapter 5 originally appeared in William Cronon (ed.), *Uncommon Ground: Rethinking the Human Place in Nature* (New York: W.W. Norton, 1996). Both are reproduced by kind permission of the publishers.

Preface

Susan George

One day in May 1875, Karl Marx received a political platform intended to reconcile two antagonistic factions of the German Workers' Party at the upcoming Party Congress. Exasperated, he dashed off the marginal notes which came to be known as the *Critique of the Gotha Programme* – rather a grand title for a quick, irritated, 'will they never get it through their heads?' sort of reaction.

The first sentence of the offending document declared that 'Labour is the source of all wealth and all culture . . .'. Marx shot back witheringly, 'Labour is *not the source* of all wealth. *Nature* is just as much the source of use values . . . as labour, which itself is only the manifestation of a force of nature . . . ' (emphasis in the original).

In these waning days of the second millennium, the war of capital against labour seems, one must hope temporarily, on the way to being won. Globalization pits workers against each other in an international competitive war in which, to use Hobbes' words, 'every man is enemy to every man'. Thus British and American workers are worse off than they were in 1987 and the average CEO of a major US corporation is 'worth' an annual salary 200 times that of his lowliest employee. Workers everywhere are becoming more productive but are mostly penalized for their pains. The rewards flow towards top management and towards stockholders, that is, towards the owners of knowledge and of capital. So far, so familiar.

But capital has not yet won out against nature. Marx, were he to return, would not be in the least surprised to witness the battle now raging over the 'commons'. He would indeed see it for what it is – a titanic struggle for control of the true, primordial source of 'use-values' and of the wealth which underpin labour and life. In such a struggle, because the stakes are high, it is not surprising either to find all kinds of weapons employed: ruse and propaganda, intimidation and blatant violence.

Two problems previously seen as separate have now coalesced under the single heading of the 'commons'. The first concerns the destiny of millions of people dependent on commonly managed natural resources; the second concerns the so-called 'global commons'

– the air, the atmosphere, the ozone shield, the seas, the forests and the innumerable species upon which we all depend.

As for those millions dependent on communal natural resources, capitalism sees no particular reason to incorporate them into the global economy, on any terms. The difference between our time and Marx's is that it's now almost a privilege to be exploited. 'Exclusion' rather than 'exploitation' is the key word, for capital excludes more people than it needs to include in the process of extracting surplus value, more commonly known as profit.

This new situation helps to explain why capital seeks to incorporate the commons on a grand scale, and why now. It has absolutely no use for the people who live by and from these natural (and sometimes urban) resources but it wants their material base. The Enclosure Act in Britain threw farmers off the land to make way for sheep, yes, but also to transform the ex-farmers into workers and thereby supply the mushrooming factories of the Industrial Revolution. The contemporary Enclosure Movement which is attempting massive appropriation of common resources everywhere seeks only control over the resources and has no such secondary goal.

Too many people are already competing for the jobs the global economy can provide, the size of the proverbial 'reserve army' is getting completely out of hand. The uprooted, the dispossessed, the despoiled must henceforward fend for themselves; they are not needed. Nor are they the uprooters', the dispossessors', the despoilers' problem.

Politics is thus no longer about pie-dividing, who gets what resources, when and how; or even about who can give orders to whom, but about the deadly serious business of staying alive. From capital's point of view, it matters little whether the commoners live or die. Where resources are to be extracted and a dollar or a cruzado to be earned, the sheer miracle of the survival, to date, of 220,000 Amerindians, the riches of their 140 separate languages and the range of their Amazonian forest lore are mere feathers in the balance. They are expendable, as the 87 distinct Indian groups already exterminated could inform them, were they still able to do so. Antonio Carlos Diegues describes the forces seeking to take over their resources, but also the Indians' strategies (including astonishing media skills) for overcoming multiple threats. On the whole, a hopeful story.

So too is the well-known one of Chiapas, almost a postmodernist romantic legend. Little romanticism is to be found, however, in Lynn Stephen's account, and a good thing too. Stephen brings out especially well the immediate and dire impact of the global on the   *X* local. In the present case, the North American Free Trade Agreement (NAFTA), and doubtless the International Monetary Fund as well, demanded rural restructuring in the framework of a complete neoliberal overhaul of the Mexican economy. Mexico duly redrafted its Constitution so as to stop government redistribution of land to the landless and to allow privatization of previously communal land.

The change in Article 27 affected half the land in the country, 'slammed the door shut for indigenous people to survive in a legal and peaceful manner' and sounded the alarm which Sub-Commandante Marcos has so brilliantly amplified. The Zapatistas are neither passive, pacifist nor passéiste, but rather looking to integrate their production into the global market, on their own terms. The jury is still out, but the heroic ancestor-figure of Zapata (used, naturally, by the government side too) meanwhile seems to inspire them with an ideology for action and the courage to undertake it.

Conflicts over the commons are not so much questions of public-versus-private as group-versus-individual ownership, with the group asserting the right to determine who is a member of the group and who is not. 'Commoners' are deprived of this right to define their society at the same time they are divested of their traditional property. Samuel-Alain Nguiffo's fascinating close-up of Cameroon forest peoples shows how they must contend not only with predatory private logging companies but also with more or less corrupt state agencies, poachers anxious to bag big game, the World Bank, even non-profit and 'philanthropic' organizations.

The notion of 'rights' and 'law' is manipulated so that the commoners are never judged according to the rules of their own society. Their time-tested processes for 'decision making, arbitration, negotiation and problem solving' become at a stroke illegitimate, null and void. The victims of appropriation are then blamed for deforestation and their social structures are damaged, for instance when some of their number become well-paid employees of the loggers and defend the latter's interests.

As far as the World Bank is concerned, the part of the forest not given over to logging concessions is a biodiversity site to be fenced off according to the Bank's rules of 'conservation', a new variety of enclosure. As Nguiffo points out, 'The interests of "mankind" are opposed to those of local people and they are seen as not being a part of "mankind".' Resistance is beginning to flower but has a long way to go. Ownership rights of local people would first have to be recognized and this the other actors vehemently oppose. One thing is certain: if the local people lose, the Cameroonian forests are done for.

In a book of this sort, one needs to go on full 'noble savage alert' and watch out for the idealizing of 'commoners' as nicer and worthier than the rest of us. They're not. They simply didn't need to read Matt Ridley's *The Origins of Virtue* (1996) to realize which side their bread is buttered on (or which hive their honey comes from, or whatever other metaphor fits the particular commons). Whether or not this is made explicit, cooperative management of common property resources and reciprocity serve enlightened self-interest *whenever one is going to remain a member of the group for the foreseeable future*. You can, perhaps, afford to cheat or be horrid to someone you will probably never see again but you can't if you are going to be dealing with them day in and day out. In that case, cooperation and reciprocity are the only strategies for guaranteeing your own survival, much less prosperity.

Capitalism makes exactly the opposite assumption. In that vein, biologist Garrett Hardin 30 years ago posited 'The Tragedy of the Commons' (1968) in a celebrated and influential article. According to Hardin, each 'rational herdsman' will try to take advantage of all the others by increasing his herd by one animal, then another, then another, until all the herdsmen are doing the same and the resource base – the pasture – collapses (1968:1243–8). Hardin may or may not be a competent biologist but he knows little about history and actual human behaviour. Dozens of historical and contemporary examples – from medieval grazing lands to Maine lobster fisheries – demonstrate that common property is not over-exploited *so long as group members retain the power to define the group and to manage their own resources*. Leaving aside the outright predators (large corporations and the like) it is generally the 'experts' who create chaos and precipitate the 'tragedy' of the commons. This Michael Goldman makes abundantly clear in his two excellent chapters.

Goldman shows how today these experts contribute not only to local disaster but are fast transforming the 'global commons' into private property and a *new object of management*. Just as the Cameroonians dependent on their own forests are not judged to be part of 'mankind', so all common property arrangements are, for the experts, *a priori* objects of suspicion. That people might somehow have managed to survive and to sustain their resource base for centuries without the intervention of the World Bank is a thought not to be entertained. Thus the experts and the development professionals conscientiously try to find the problem and fix it; they endlessly ask themselves what they should do. That the answer might be 'nothing' never crosses their minds. Nor could it: they are paid (by any number of institutions) to intervene. One is struck in this text by the variations on the theme of imperialism and the range of new designer outfits in the Emperor's closet.

'Biodiversity' is another new buzz word facilitating appropriation, not just of physical gene pools but of the local knowledge that goes with them. As Michael Flitner reveals in his lucid chapter, anything non-human and alive – virtually all of nature – is reconfigured under the single term 'biodiversity' as an object of management and regulation in order to expedite 'free' access. When the knowledge of local people is required for the efficient exploitation of these resources, it too may be incorporated; otherwise, the people themselves are dispensable. 'We' should be wary each time 'we' see the pronoun 'we'. Who, exactly, does it designate? When employed by the 'Global Resource Managers' (Goldman's term) one can be sure that the beneficiaries are to be found at the top of the economic totem pole.

People struggling for the well-being of their families and their communities do not necessarily think of themselves as 'environmentalists'. Nor did their predecessors in the nineteenth century when they fought against child labour in the mines or for decent sanitation. Then and now, all these issues ultimately concern the integrity of the human body. Once again, this body is in mortal danger, as Giovanna DiChiro makes clear in her chapter on the 'Convergence of Environment and Social Justice'. A toxics-spewing incinerator in South Central Los Angeles is to the children of that community as rats and adulterated milk were to the children of South London a century ago. The same kind of community organizing is required to oppose these aggressions against both the individual body and the body-politic.

Low-income women of colour are often the outstanding leaders of these efforts. Contrary to many mainstream environmentalists, they understand that at bottom there is no difference between humans and 'nature'. The central political problem is to define what counts as 'the environment'. Sometimes, depending on the community and the culture, it is the inner city or the so-called 'urban wasteland'. The 'multicultural commons' is surely one of the major sites of future resistance movements.

Life in the commons is no more idyllic than anywhere else, quarrels arise and some people refuse to respect the rules. Sanjeev Prakash provides examples, as well as citing everyday acts of opposition to assault from outside and strategies for repairing a damaged commons. He looks in detail at the notion of fairness, also one of the building-blocks of the final chapter by Michael Thompson.

Covering differently many of the questions discussed by Prakash, Thompson ventures a novel and arresting typology of the *styles* of social arrangements and their applicability to various *scales* of human organization, from the local to the planetary. His chapter is surely the basis for another book in itself, opening up a whole new 'Cultural Theory' perspective on the commons which economists and other social scientists would do well to heed. Thompson takes us full circle back to Michael Goldman's chapters at the beginning of the volume, bringing us in a nicely spiralling dialectic to the point of departure, but with everything we've learned from the preceding chapters intact. He gives us a new stepping-stone, the dialectics of *fairness* (definable in four different ways) that actually holds our societies together. This contribution rounds out a remarkably clear, enjoyable and jargon-free book.

So what are the prospects? On the one hand, we know that capitalism can't stop. It is a kind of malignancy which will keep on devouring new resources even as it undermines the very body – nature itself – upon which it depends. Codes of conduct and voluntary restraint are laughably (or lamentably) inadequate to protect common property resources from capitalist confiscation, because that appropriation allows the cancer to spread for a while longer. This is why the stakes keep rising and the subject of the commons, whether in its local or global form, is now so hotly debated.

As for the Global Resource Managers, they know best and no number of disasters will ever convince them otherwise. Nor are the Global Resource Moralizers likely to be of much help. Michael Goldman describes, for example, the well-meaning efforts of the Worldwatch Institute which, having shown with relentlessly accurate factual research that the problem is entirely structural, proceeds to place its hopes in 'consumers' and the inherent wisdom of the 'international community'.

Worldwatch, for all its merits, belongs to what I call the forehead-slapping school, which holds that once individuals and institutions have (thanks to Worldwatch and its ilk) actually understood the situation, they will smack their brows and, in a flash of revelation, instantly redirect their behaviour 180 degrees.

No, I fear we must return to the prosaic square one of democracy, of faith in local people's ability to sort out their own problems in ways best suited not to the Market, not to the Managers, but to themselves. Couldn't they simply be allowed to get on with it? This modest request is an infinitely difficult objective to attain, yet one worth striving for, on their turf, on their terms and on their side.

Introduction: The Political Resurgence of the Commons

Michael Goldman

Around the globe, firms, states and social movements have never been as responsive to the environmental imperative as now. Ecological politics is on the top of many people's agendas, thrust upon even the most reluctant social groups – such as corporate executives – because of the monumental problems that have arisen from its negligence. Ecological politics is not merely a symbolic or rhetorical flourish. Pharmaceutical corporations are actively seeking out countries in the South to which they can donate a percentage of their profits to be invested in 'ecological conservation' in exchange for access to genetic cornucopia 'hidden' in their fertile jungles. Former socialist countries in eastern Europe and the South (e.g. Poland, Vietnam, Nicaragua) are rapidly integrating their economies into global capital circuits by following the ecological preconditions for foreign loans established by the World Bank: 'clean up' old dirty industries, 'professionalize' environmental regulatory agencies, and rewrite property-rights laws, all of which fall under the rubric of 'getting the price right' on nature – that is, making one's natural garden suitably fit for capitalist integration.

Meanwhile, no longer the sole terrain of middle-class Northerners, ecological-political movements are becoming unrivalled in their ability to mobilize disparate strata of society into the streets (Peet and Watts 1996). Although rarely calling themselves *environmentalists*, actors within these social movements are imposing a wide range of demands on ruling governments and classes for alternative strategies of natural resource use and maintenance. 'Right-to-livelihood', ethnic 'identity' and feminist/women's movements are often also motivated by eco-political concerns, as they make claims for more equitable and just access to environments and natural resources.

Take the case of India (Omvedt 1993): in central India, over the past decade, ethnic-minority farmers have been fighting the state's plan to inundate their fertile riverbed fields to build massive dams on the Narmada river. In northern India, Tehri Garhwal women have fought off logging firms and governmental pressures to open up their forested hills to exploitative export production. In southern India, a cross-class coalition of farmers is rallying the state to stop international World Trade Organization (WTO) negotiations on intellectual property rights, which would give Western multinationals increased royalties for farmers' products. And along the southern coast, women of a Kerala fishing community found themselves engaged in two separate political protests at the same time: demonstrating against a recent spate of rapes by policemen and against the new onslaught of mechanized trawling that threatened their fisheries. Hence, their newly formed 'Coastal Women's Front' linked the two issues in a unified political stance as they organized to shield themselves from physical as well as economic violence, protecting themselves, their communities and their coastal waters. India is brimming with *eco-political* movements – diversified social actors that are consciously broadening the scope of ecology, politics and social change.

Although these initiatives from social movements, as well as states and firms, are quite disparate, the common focus is on the question of property rights – rights to land, forests, yields, burial grounds, seeds, intellectual property, ground and surface water, radiowaves, ecosystems, gene transfers, underground minerals, urban space, the village well and pastoral grazing.[1] Whoever controls property rights controls the processes of resource extraction and environmental change. A central metaphor mobilized in these property-based discourses is 'the commons' – a resource-management regime that is perceived of as either *cause* (e.g. the famous 'tragedy of the commons') or *antidote* (e.g. new campaigns to protect 'our common global heritage') of ecological degradation. Different social actors are fighting for different property rights: resource-dependent communities for sustenance and culturally meaningful practices, corporations for commodity and surplus-value production and state agencies for tax revenues and increased jurisdiction – all are fighting for rights to environments on which their power depends.

British historians have shown that in the Anglo-Saxon context the idea of the commons originated with the fields, forest and pasture commons of pre-Industrial Revolution Britain. The commons entered the political realm in debates over how to increase taxes, yields and revenues from the feudally managed countryside. The concept of the commons expanded as the British Empire expanded, attaching itself to pastures, fisheries, forests, deserts, agricultural fields, and village commons of countries in the colonized South.[2]

Today, the commons has become a central metaphor for ecological politics, especially to what many Northern policy makers, scholars and environmentalists now call *the global commons*. Although it may seem an imaginative stretch to extend the everyday practices of pastoralists on their pre-Industrial Scottish pastures to a thoroughly modern notion of the atmospheric commons, the oceanic commons and the genetic commons – its advocates disagree. On the threshold of the twenty-first century, as the globe and its resources seem to be shrinking, local environmental problems are now presented as fundamentally global problems. According to the prevailing global-commons perspective, the world is becoming small and interconnected very fast, and we need to develop a global science to match these changes. One only needs to look at the 1986 nuclear catastrophe in Europe to see why. The technical failures at the Chernobyl power plant were catalytic in changing people's awareness throughout Europe and western Asia as to what nuclear energy proliferation means in terms of basic rights to non-radiated livelihoods, food supplies, water, soil, animal and plant life. Global nuclear politics temporarily eclipsed all other political concerns once the devastating effects of the nuclear plant explosion became painfully evident, through the contamination of food supplies, soils, livestock and people's bodies. Overnight, this environmental crisis was no longer merely a Ukrainian problem, a Soviet problem or even a European problem. Self-righteous 'not-in-my-backyard' vigilance suddenly lost its thunder as downwind populations thousands of miles away were not spared the agony of the disaster.

Hence, today we find that although *good* ecological politics of local communities matters for the so-called global human community and ecological commons, those who can affect 'local' commons are no longer necessarily based in the locality. In the case of Chernobyl, one would be hard-pressed to 'blame' the surrounding community of Ukrainians for the Chernobyl eco-catastrophe. A genealogy of responsibility shows that the destruction was rooted in distinctively *non-local* communities, especially the key players in the extended Cold War – in the Kremlin and US Congress, in complacent scientific institutes, and in the aggressive world-wide nuclear industry.

Because local commons are never completely under the control of locals, local institutions, and local ethnosciences anymore, and because ecological trouble spots can erupt anywhere with downstream or downwind consequences, many global-commons advocates mistakenly conclude that a new breed of 'global experts' is required. What follows from this twist of logic is the need for *global science* to understand these new transboundary problems and *global institutions* to manage them. Indeed, from US military scientists who spent half a century wastefully concocting hundreds of 'what-if' scenarios of the potential downwind effects of nuclear bombings, to the earth-conscious Club of Rome scientists who continue to conduct high-tech, global modelling in order to quantify the absolute ecological 'limits to growth' of industrial expansionism, the discourse of global scientific problem solving is fast becoming hegemonic.

Universalizing the Commons, Eclipsing Divergent Interests

In the process of universalizing the commons, this 'hot' new worldview creates some very troublesome political shortcuts. For example, is all knowledge common, generalizable and universally accessible, as the global discourse assumes? Are heritages, histories and interests necessarily common? Are the dynamics of ecosystems, and natural-social relations embedded in a commons site, really transferable, replicable or generalizable? In discovering or inventing the *global ecological commons* and its fragile future, elite Northern scientists and policy makers also gave birth to the appropriate methods for their understanding (i.e., *global science*) and the character of its inhabitants (i.e., *the global citizen*). What use do these apparati of globalization serve?

In the 1980s, when elite Northern scientists established that the Amazon is the 'lungs of the world', they were directly challenging the rights of forest dwellers against the rights of metropolitan populations around the world who supposedly depend upon forest preservation for their daily dose of oxygen (Hecht and Cockburn 1990). If the Amazon *is* the lungs of the world, then shouldn't Northern urbanites have the right to dictate production strategies in the Southern forest? Non-Amazonian policy makers, scientists and activists argue that the fate of the world's oxygen supply should not be left up to irrational 'slash-and-burn' peasants. Consequently, elite-based environmental groups and global institutions have intervened in the Amazon, under the premise that more rational management skills *by forest dwellers* were required to ensure continuous oxygen supplies and 'sustainable' extraction in the world's rainforests.

These late twentieth-century discoveries/inventions of the fragility of the globalized commons have created more than new scientific evidence: they have created new demand for global regulatory institutions and sciences, staffed by global technocrats and scientists.

The creation of this global-commons discourse justifies the conditions for their problem-solving tools: global experts unconstrained by provincial traditions, metaphors, politics and local ecosystems. For the global scientist to be able to function, they require access to the whole globe and its data. No longer constrained by national or local politics, the global scientist uses the *local* as a site for data collection and *the global* as a site for knowledge production, legitimation and dissemination.

Distinct from local-knowledge producers or ethnoscientists, global-knowledge producers or technoscientists are not limited by local tradition or culture. Global technoscience is believed to have become, therefore, 'a culture of no culture', a science unshackled by politics (Traweek 1988). Despite the persistence of the commons metaphor, local conditions and local cultures conveniently disappear from view. When locally distinct ecologies are left in the hands of transboundary scientists, and politics is left in the hands of global 'anti-politics' technocrats (Ferguson 1994), the terrain of struggle moves from the grass-roots to the technoscientific laboratory, from commons activists to technocratic boardrooms.

The point here is not to dismiss the validity of technoscience and cherish the people's ethnoscience, but rather to deflate the public notion that science is autonomous, progressive, value-free and all-knowing, and to send out warning flares to illuminate the fact that this new turn in elite-based ecological politics – to globalize, depoliticize and scientize – is a deeply political act. Why is it that when grass-roots social movements raise the flag of radical environmentalism – that is, make strong demands for greater control over their environments – powerful institutions join in with triumphant calls for a depoliticized, delocalized, 'serious' science of ecology and resource management? What does it mean when scholars, policy makers and the media shift their attention to the global playing field, and rally behind a new set of global care-taking institutions, such as GEF, the World Bank, WTO, NAFTA, and UNCED?[3] Where are the ballot boxes for the global citizens of these new global institutions?

We argue that all of these disparate processes having to do with the environment, are, first and foremost, profoundly political acts. In general, struggles over nature, and over the meanings of nature, are inherently political. So, too, are the natural sciences. Science is not a terrain of no-culture or no-politics; science is a thoroughly contested social process. And ecological politics is a mixed bag of struggles over science, knowledge, culture, capital, property, gender, race, nation, natural resources and more. The more socialist forms of existing ecological politics are concerned with democratizing science and other local/global institutions of power, whether they be institutions that manage natural resources, social groups, scientific knowledge, commodity-producing organizations, or public policy.

Globalization is the buzz word that describes the capitalist world system at the end of the twentieth century. Yet, hidden behind the obfuscating rhetoric of globalization are different political situations and strategies across the globe. The authors of this book highlight some of the more provocative strands of ecological politics practised and contested throughout the world. Ironically, we learn that the most vociferous calls for reinvigorating the commons are not just coming from grass-roots commoners trying to take back control over local resources and production practices from non-local predatory forces. Some of the most persuasive arguments actually come from Northern academics, World Bank policy analysts, and even logging, pharmaceutical and fish-farming firms.

These 'defenders' of the commons (many of whom are none the less in the business of expanding access to private property and surplus-value production) argue that the sustainability of private-property regimes is actually completely *dependent* upon the maintenance of non-private property such as the commons. Without commoners and the state assiduously working, protecting, managing and reproducing the world's watersheds, forests, coastal waters, mountainsides and healthy communities, the *use-value* of privatized nature would dramatically diminish, yet another dimension to a changing global division of labour.

For example, the production of exportable commodities from the Amazon forests in Latin America comes from less than 2 per cent of the forest's 'products'.[4] The future of commodity production, however, depends upon the sustainable maintenance of the remaining 98 per cent of the Amazon forest. No single logging firm (or state agency) wants to pay for the upkeep of the whole forest and its forest-dwelling communities – the costs would be prohibitive. Yet if community institutions diligently nurtured the Amazon as a commons, they would ensure a healthy ecosystem from which to extract the forest's most market-valuable products for surplus-value producers. The more support common-property institutions can get from state and transnational agencies, the more 'sustainable' capitalist mining, farming and logging can be. But on whose backs?

Less than ten years ago, small producers in the Amazon were calling for the expulsion of the World Bank, as it was recklessly financing road construction, logging, colonization and livestock production in their fragile forests. By contrast, today the World

Bank is the main financial supporter, along with the Brazilian state, of 'extractive reserves' managed by rubber tappers and other small extractors. Has the World Bank made a radical change in the way it promotes capitalist expansion in the Amazon? How are we to distinguish among the many calls for 'managing' the commons? What are the local manifestations of global ecological problems and vice versa? How do these ecological changes reflect the global division of labour? The authors of this book offer a road-map of the history and politics of the world's commons to help decipher the multitude of current environmental claims and actions. After all, to understand ecological politics today, one needs to appreciate how and why the Amazon rubber tappers and forest activists mobilize the metaphor of the commons differently than the World Bank. Our book serves as a guide down this rocky path of ecological politics, explaining confrontations at the crossroads between radical social movements and neoliberal institutions.

Perhaps our most salient observation is that this renaissance of the ecological commons marks a turning point in ecological politics. On this cluttered discursive landscape, many of our worst fears regarding capitalist triumphalism have *not* come true. Strong states are not simply being replaced by markets, tradition by modernity, the local by the global, environmental ethics by rapacious capitalisms. Globalization has not snuffed out politicized ecological practices on the ground. Instead, across the map, hybridities have emerged. For example, new transnational capitalist interventions into natural-resource abundant sites in the South (e.g. forests, mines, fisheries, farmlands) are being met with new social movements articulating alternative development paths that defy oppositional Cold War-type thinking. That is, they are neither anti-capitalism, *per se*, nor pro-authoritarian state socialism. They are not necessarily pro-subsistence, anti-modern, completely local or allergic to all forms of capitalist market relations. Moreover, locally rooted visions of the environment and natural-social relations are not simply being supplanted by Northern professional-class panda-lovers or tiger-park planners. The real world of radical ecological politics is not unfolding in such black-and-white ways.

We find that transnational tendencies in ecological politics have two interrelated sides: powerful incursions from transnational corporations, Northern states and global finance institutions, and powerful linkages among social movements in solidarity across national boundaries. By the mid-1990s, it has become quite evident that disgruntled fisherfolk, forest extractors or women right's activists actually have the power to stop a World Bank steamroller – and this transnational dynamic is emblematic of radical ecological politics today. To many people in these dynamic social movements, the term *local* does not mean provincial, limited or unscientific, but *located, situated and partial*. As well, the term *global* does not reflect the universal, general or apolitical, but *distributed, layered and also partial* (Haraway 1997:121). Social movements are overturning the discursive strategies of dominant social actors and institutions. Although the book's authors do not argue for a meta-explanation for what is unfolding, we do find that these multiple meanings, interests, scientific claims and movements add up to something quite powerful.

Radical Ecological Politics in Practice

Coming from diverse country and professional backgrounds, the book's authors compare notes on the politics of the commons and the extent to which the ideal behind the metaphor – that is, the notion that local communities are in the best position to decide for themselves how to manage natural environments – is or is not valid for a transboundary political agenda. Each of us brings to this collective endeavour a story and a message; together these chapters work to reveal the complex and dynamic nature of ecological politics around the world. In no way is our treatment comprehensive or even in agreement. Instead, we have sought to show how environmental issues are often at the core of current political expressions, a point that women's movements have been making for some time. That is, we make our own environmental conditions, and our environments make us. The common myth that *nature* and *culture* are somehow distinct is false; our definitions, perceptions, and senses of *the natural* are so deeply mediated by our historically specific experiences that it is not meaningful to talk about nature in abstraction from social forces. All knowledge is contextual, and all knowledge producers are situated in ecological-social experience. Scientific views on nature can be understood as *ethno*sciences, as all scientific sites – from the National Academy of Science in Washington, D.C. to the common-property regimes in the Cameroon forests – are *known* through thick cultural lenses.[5] The process of privileging certain knowledge producers is indeed a political act. We need to rethink the power we give to global institutions to whom we have endowed, symbolically at least, the future of the Earth. We need to rethink how we explain the dialectic between local and global ecological problems and how it reflects transnational divisions of labor – in political, economic, and scientific realms.

In Chapter 1, I review the major debates on the commons amongst (mostly Northern) scholars and professionals. I find it useful at this historical moment – when the commons is being touted as an 'efficient' institution to manage our troubled global environments – to focus closely on the assumptions, arguments and discontents of the commons debates. There, the commons has become a unifying metaphor rallied for the cause of both 'environmentally sustainable development' and 'modernization', two powerful concepts that are taken for granted by those who are engaged in these debates. The main literature on the commons lacks serious consideration of active social movements and their counter-hegemonic strategies that challenge the very same development and political institutions that many of these commons debaters represent. Therefore, I invoke a call for more reflexive and historical inquiries into the commons, which are precisely the aims of the rest of the book's authors.

Antonio Carlos Diegues, in Chapter 2, takes us to the heart of the Brazilian Amazon to show how a number of recent events have helped ignite vibrant social movements there. These movements are sufficient evidence that the history of the Amazonian commons cannot be told as simply capitalist triumphalism over weaker, traditional institutions and actors. Forest dwellers are actively responding to external interventions by *creating* new commons, in the form of new worldviews, political institutions, markets and ecological management strategies.

Faced with two powerful discursive strategies over the past few decades – the Amazon as *geographical vacuum* waiting to be filled, and as *economic panacea* that would reverse Brazil's deteriorating economic conditions – small producers have had to self-organize to survive. Diegues introduces us to autonomous fisher communities that are strengthening their control over lakes and rivers to thwart access to outside extractors who refuse to follow communal use-right rules. He explains how small extractors have linked up with non-local NGOs to fight state colonization projects for land clearing, logging, mining, and livestock production that are destroying huge swathes of forest. He demonstrates how, long before receiving international support, the well-known rubber tappers created powerful common-property regimes called 'extractive reserves' through conventional strategies of rural-union organizing.

A similarly diverse terrain also exists in Mexico, as Lynn Stephen reveals in Chapter 3. Today, with political victories claimed by both the pro-NAFTA neoliberal state and the revolutionary Zapatista Army of National Liberation, one of Mexico's key political contests is over the right to Mexican commons: the *ejidos* created through land redistribution after the Mexican Revolution and the communal holdings of indigenous communities known as *comunidades agrarias*. In the 1990s, the Mexican government pushed through a series of 'land reform' policies aimed at supporting the North American Free Trade Agreement and affecting almost 50 per cent of Mexico's national territory. Most importantly, these legal and policy changes end the government's obligation to redistribute land to those who need it and regularize landholdings through measuring, mapping and assigning individual certificates of use rights which can be converted to private titles – all paving the way for privatization.

These radical changes represent, among other things, a battle over the Mexican commons, and Stephen reveals how indigenous peasants in Chiapas and Oaxaca interpret this terrain of contentious ecological policies. Through the eyes of those who work the land in two distinct Mexican communities, Stephen demonstrates why state and social-movement agendas can be alternatively embraced and rejected by indigenous farmers striving to protect their landholdings.

From Cameroon, Samuel-Alain Nguiffo presents in Chapter 4 the complex conditions under which forest dwellers and others are struggling over Cameroon's precious forests. The forest represents *the* major site of political confrontation in Cameroon where many actors are pitted against each other – semi-nomadic (Baka) forest dwellers, settled (Bantu) farmers, logging firms, state agencies, international developers such as the World Bank and nature conservation organizations such as the International Union for the Conservation of Nature and its Resources (IUCN). These forest commons are the perfect exemplar for the confusion and destruction being waged on tribal communities in rainforests, ironically in the name of protecting 'Africa's' common heritage.

Major state agencies represent Cameroon's environmental problems as caused by warring tribal factions, particularly between the Bantus and the Bakas. With these people's histories and worldviews reduced to a postcolonial cliché – *traditional* peoples caught in a *modern* world – the state legitimates its own strategy to expropriate the forest commons from the forest dwellers, transferring the commons into state property. As the state's interests are more closely aligned with big exporters, especially French logging firms, the facts of declining forests have to be carefully produced. Through Nguiffo's rendering of the local-national-transnational forces at play over the commons, we learn that most international and national 'remedies' for fixing Cameroon's forests are simplistic and ill-conceived. By contrast, Nguiffo offers strategies that emphasize the needs of the forest dwellers as a way to reduce the destructive social and ecological tendencies in Cameroon's repressive political situation.

We then travel to the United States, where Giovanna DiChiro shows us in Chapter 5 the urban neighbourhoods and workplaces of working-class environmental activists. DiChiro finds a remarkably salient political discourse in the cities in which these activists organize: nature as community, and community as multicultural. The most pressing environmental problems of US cities – toxic contamination of air, water, streets, schools, housing complexes – most adversely affect working-class people of colour. Over the past two decades, when mainstream environmental organizations refused to take up urban toxic issues, working-class Latinos, African Americans, Native Americans and Asian Americans mobilized themselves into what has become a dynamic environmental justice movement. They learned quickly that they had to confront not only governmental agencies and private firms, but also environmental groups whose philosophical tenets were based on what DiChiro calls 'colonial nature talk', or discursive strategies that separate people's 'colonized' histories from their natural environments. By contrast, people-of-colour activists are bridging ecological with social-justice concerns, working to stop polluters through the organizing of fragmented and alienated communities. As a consequence, the 'urban commons' are being redefined as rooted in biophysical, built and social environments, and the political terrain of the commons expands to include struggles over social justice, and race, ethnic and class inequalities.

In Chapter 6, shifting from the urban to the global, Michael Flitner directs us to the crossroads of bio-tech business and species extinction by deconstructing the seductive idioms of 'biodiversity' and the 'global commons'. On the one hand, biological diversity across the world is under imminent threat, as species become extinct every day. On the other hand, the major focus of efforts around reversing this trend is rooted in both bio-technological innovations and global-commons discourse, a focus that may only exacerbate the problem of species extinction. While this focus is quite effective in creating consensus amongst leaders of industries, governments and mainstream environmental groups, the movement to make 'biodiversity' into a global commons may actually mask, and support, ongoing practices to privatize and capitalize sites of biological diversity.

Biodiversity conservation, Flitner informs us, is currently an act of coercion as well as redemption, *protecting* the wild and unknown of nature from local human intervention while at the same time *domesticating* the wild and *patenting* the unknown for greater integration, and private profit, in the globalized economy. These are the worrisome tendencies dominating biodiversity practices. But biodiversity also remains firmly rooted in local livelihoods, so that this hegemonic discourse creates new spaces for political participation of local and indigenous communities. Flitner guides us through the mine-field of texts and practices concerning species extinction, gene-altering technologies, bio-commodity production, the new politics of the global commons and their relations to ecosystems and resource managers in the South.

Our last two chapters reflect back on the questions of how and why commons institutions work. Sanjeev Prakash and Michael Thompson argue that prominent Northern scholars debating the pros and cons of the commons – whether they're interested in *developing* village commons in the South or *inventing* global institutions to regulate global environmental commons – fail to grasp how existing commons institutions actually work in coordination, or not, with other social institutions and actors. Sanjeev Prakash (Chapter 7) uses the concepts of social capital, fairness and collective action to explain how commons institutions thrive and change through historical relations of interdependence and from valued cultural norms. Thompson (Chapter 8) invites us to use a nuanced 'cultural theory' framework to better appreciate the complexity and dynamisms of commons institutions, whether they be local or global, large or small.

The Power of the Commons

In the current ecologically degraded maelstrom of dying state socialisms and rising neoliberal capitalisms, we find fertile political flowering in everyday struggles over nature that remain unrecognizable by the radar of many scholars and mass media. Today, activists represent the vanguard in articulating both a *critique of theory* as well as a *method for praxis* of radical ecological politics. This section makes an attempt to highlight some of these innovations.

First, ecological politics is not a marginal constituency issue mobilized by middle-class romantics and ascetics. On the one hand, transnational corporations and international financial institutions (IFIs) such as the World Bank are fast becoming leaders in constructing powerful and seductive discursive strategies on everything from 'managing the global commons' and 'bio-prospecting' to 'environmentally sustainable development' and 'getting the price right' on nature. Nature has become front-and-centre in transnational debates on land reform, free trade, structural adjustment policies and the new frontiers of national sovereignty, global scientific endeavours, and flexible forms of capital accumulation. On the other hand, there is a wide range of dynamic and potent social movements making demands for more democratic control over jungles, river valleys, hillsides, industrial wastelands and inner-city landscapes.

Second, at the core of ecological politics, be it radical or neoliberal, is the issue of proprietary rights to nature. Unfortunately, most observers have inadequately described it as a battle between two property regimes – common versus private property, with its neocolonial assumptions about tradition and modernity. In this debate, false dualisms are imagined that muddle the politics being played out over environments. North is pitted against South, global versus local, economic growth versus subsistence, abundance versus scarcity and rational science versus irrational beliefs. Our studies reveal that Himalayan producers, Cameroonian forest extractors, and US urban survivors do not present themselves as essentially anti-modern or solely dependent on either private property or community-controlled commons for their survival. They demand that their worlds be recognized as situated within multiple (albeit contradictory) linkages that can be empowering while also running the risk of being exploitative.

Third, ecological politics is not a singular, globalizing discourse. We find that the *ecological* refers to the many scientific discourses (techno- and ethnosciences), the multiple meanings and imaginaries, and the many ecosystems as well as natural-social relations, deployed in its name. The *politics* refers to the range of actors, policies, institutions and worldviews. The politics of nature has come to dominate state, subnational and transnational politics, but that does not mean all eco-political impulses are the same. To deconstruct this essentialized 'truth', we could do well by starting with the mobilization of the concept of the commons, as it is being simultaneously utilized by everyone from Mexican *ejidatarios* to World Bankers.

Fourth, radical elements of new eco-political movements possess many of the following characteristics:

- They *organize* for socialized control over use-values without being solely anti-commodity form or pro-subsistence.
- They *challenge* dominant technosciences for being partial and situated knowledge.
- They *work* as internationalists while being located.

- They *mobilize* to gain control over ecological use-values for livelihood and social justice rather than for more efficient ways to reproduce the production conditions for capital expansion.
- They *transcend* the most depoliticizing discursive dualisms – local/global, traditional/modern, capitalist/non-capitalist market relations, ethnoscience/technoscience and nature/culture (O'Connor 1998).

Anti-dam activists in Thailand, Chile and India; inner-city housing/squatter activists in the US, Brazil and Germany; activists in the Indian-controlled lowlands of Ecuador fighting the petroleum state, and activists in Indonesia battling destructive gold- and copper-mining projects currently understand their environmental struggles along multiple axes. Radical commons movements are as much about struggles over what counts as nature as they are struggles over class formation, nation building, gender forging and race boundary-making. That is, just as men and women living in the tropical forest define themselves in part by their natural environments, their forced resettlement by 'national' projects for electrification and rural modernization become political battles over more than forest management, but also, to varying degrees, over nation, class, gender and ethnicity.

This type of praxis emerges from what Antonio Gramsci called 'the organic intellectual', who is scientist and activist, naturalist and socialist, integrated into a site-based community as well as part of a larger, universal community. The most vibrant, empowering, democratic and revolutionary movements of ecological politics are those that engage the organic intellectual in all of us. Ultimately, the radical elements of existing ecological politics are dominated by passionate – even revolutionary – feelings about the ecological and social commons. The commons – a material and symbolic reality, always changing, never *purely* local or global, traditional or modern, and always reflecting the vibrant colours of its ecological, political, cultural, scientific and social character – is not at all disappearing into the dustbin of history. To the contrary, we find that the commons are increasingly becoming a site for robust and tangible struggles over class, gender, nation/ethnicity, knowledge, power and, of course, nature.

These movements also reveal the pitfalls of traditional socialist analysis and show how to approach the politics of nature from a green-feminist-materialist perspective.[6] Simply put, the problem that both traditional socialist and contemporary neoliberal perspectives suffer from is defining complex socio-ecological forces in terms of 'economy'. Disembedded from its socially entangled and environmentally situated dynamic form, and separated from actually practised economic exchanges, 'economy' has become a universalistic metaphor for what 'industrial man' does. He – and the model is based on a sexist and Eurocentric sense of the hard-working industrial man in the privately owned European factory – works for wages that enable him to rise upwardly towards greater comforts and skills based on his increased productivity. That is, the more he produces for the commercial market, the better his household conditions – and this is generalized to global human conditions – become. This has been the worldview of both traditional socialists and capitalists alike. Women, nature, peasants, etc., become valorized in society only as they enter this formal world of economy, work and value. Today, as many actors acknowledge the existence of widespread ecological crisis, nature is now coddled for being a precious and scarce commodity, but only as it enters and exits the formal economy. Similarly, nature, just like its reified counterparts of women, peasants and informal sector workers, is deemed relevant only in its commodified form (or, as Polanyi argued, 'fictitious commodity' form) imputed with value useful to the economy.

This obsession with increasing value, however, ignores the reality of most people struggling for their basic rights of livelihood and community. Most people exchange their produced goods in 'informal' markets and for household and village 'economies'; most labour and live for more than just (meagre, formal market) wages. Hence, the traditional socialist emphasis on *formal-market* labour struggle typically neglects more pervasive 'labour and more' struggles occurring outside 'traditional' wage-labour markets. In other words, women, men and children who work in the household, the community, the informal sector and in the lower rungs of the formal sector, are not 'valued' by hegemonic discursive strategies. The value of whole populations working the community-managed forests, fisheries, pastures, public spaces and the household, add up to 'zero' in this economistic worldview.

Under 'modernization', many were promised good industrial wage jobs that were to come with greater integration into the global economy. But after decades of modernization, most people have found that *more* economic growth never simply translates into more food, more marketplace freedom, more social justice. More economic growth, as it is being articulated through neoliberal politics (the political flavour of the day), is leading to widespread ecological destruction and greater threats to people's livelihoods, survival and social justice.

According to leading eco-social theorists, the reason lies in the way 'economy' is discursively framed. That is, the prevailing definition of economy in dominant political, scientific and cultural institutions is in fundamentally quantitative and objectivist terms. How else can we compare, measure and judge these 'objects' of life across space and time except through such alienating (and, as Foucault argued, disciplining) practices? How else can we measure the 'wealth' of nations except by adding up commodities produced, wages distributed, products purchased? The problem, of course, is that when wealth is defined in purely economic/quantitative terms, most social labour, ecological processes and cultural worldviews become devalued. Although wealth production under capitalism depends upon this reservoir of support, knowledge, labour and synergy of unpaid social labour and natural processes, these efforts remain outside an economic calculus.

Most importantly, by privatizing these devalued 'conditions' of production – disembedding and thrusting them into the formal-market sphere – existing forms of capitalism end up destroying the support system on which surplus production is based. This, James O'Connor (1998) argues, is the most profound contradiction of capitalist practices today. That is, without the unpaid labour from the commons, the household and the community, and without tapping ecological processes, there could not be any surplus-value production for capitalist industries. Maintenance of the commons is thus one of the legs on which commodity production stands.

On the flip side, however, the worldviews, knowledges and labours of these invisible populations are precisely where alternative political visions and practices arise, as this book demonstrates. In each chapter, note how the commons struggle is a qualitative struggle, not over 'how much' commoners should be compensated, 'how much' resources should be redistributed, or 'how much' value should be imputed onto one's labourpower or resource base. These are conventional political-economic measures and they fall short of representing people's realities. Commoners' movements are not demanding – as traditional labour movements (and, for their own gains, business/capital interest groups) do – a quantitative shift in their hours of work, share of the profits, share of state subsidies and resources, or share of environment ownership. Struggles over the right to sustenance and livelihood, the right to healthy and socially just forms of land use and intergenerationally sustainable relations of production (whether for the production or reproduction of commodities, use-values, cultural institutions, etc.) are distinctly qualitative questions broached by new social movements. The struggle to transform one's urban neighbourhood into a safe, non-racist, non-violent living, working and playing space cannot be 'valorized' for profit-making, and often works against such economic imperatives. Moreover, the right to use and protect indigenous knowledge systems without the threat of global patent lawsuits or corporate poachers is not an issue that can be 'solved' through 'suitable monetary compensation' or redistribution of profits (i.e., distributional justice). Indigenous people's demands for rights to their biodiverse environments are direct challenges to the way in which hegemonic political discourses of capitalism, and traditional critiques of capitalism, are framed.

Political strategies to regain control of production and reproduction can be described in a number of ways, including what O'Connor (1998) calls 'ecological socialism' and what Mary Mellor (1997a) calls 'materialist ecofeminism'. These perspectives are reflected in social-movement praxis, that is, their theories and practices. The power of the commons, we collectively argue, is the nexus for many of today's political challenges. Struggles against dominant forces working to privatize nature *and* culture are being framed in terms that challenge economistic ideologies. Power struggles over the commons reflect the qualitative character of community, social justice, and nature-social relations. As Karl Polanyi (1944:163) argued forcefully in *The Great Transformation*,

> To separate labor from other activities of life, and to subject it to the laws of the market was to annihilate all organic forms of existence and to replace them by a different type of organization, an atomistic and individualistic one.

Social movements across the world are trying to overturn the notion that their labour, lives and worldviews are, as Mellor (1997a) argues, parasitic on the 'wealth-creating sector' of the formal economy. What we learn from these movements is that, in fact, the reverse is true. 'To separate basic provisioning from the "wants" of the capitalist market economy would expose the ecologically and socially destructive basis of the latter,' Mellor explains:

> The importance of making women's [and others whose labours are devalued, such as 'commoners'] work and care throughout life central to provisioning is that this is easily achievable by the use of direct human labour, there isn't a resource implication over and above basic subsistence. This is the work women have done for free for most of history, it can therefore be organized for free again,

although not to be done exclusively by women . . . [A]n ecosocialist politics would look to the deeper materialism of communal security and subsistence. (Mellor 1997a:6)

Neoclassical economic theories, Mellor writes, are always working to bring those outside of the mainstream from 'here' to 'there' through dramatic social and institutional change (e.g., privatizing or retooling common-property regimes for capitalist practices). By contrast, social movements are making the case for reclaiming 'the "here" of people's lives' and starting from the premise of people's, not the market's, needs (Mellor 1997a:6).

Through our survey of struggles over the privatization of nature, we find reinvigorated political debates on the commons. The questions that movements raise are more pervasive and profound than those typically discussed in the scholarly and professional literature, which are often narrowly posed as (more or less) technology transfers, institution tweaking and resource allocation. In fact, in writing this book, we discovered that struggles over the commons reflect a widespread phenomenon to transform existing nature-society relations into non-exploitative, socially just and ecologically healthy relations. Despite strong oppositional forces, the power of the commons is flourishing.

Notes

1   Of course, nation-state politics is also firmly rooted in contending definitions of property – control over territory, the propagation of certain property regimes over another, i.e., state-owned or privately (or corporate) owned. Many of our modern wars are fought over such differing property regimes, and how they affect interpretations of 'other' ethnic groups or nationalities.

2   In fact, the existence of common-property regimes did not originate with the English, even if the semiotic sign may have. Moreover, colonial practices were a critical factor in the destruction of many different resource-management practices in 'the colonies'.

3   Global Environmental Facility (of the World Bank), World Trade Organization (formerly GATT), North American Free Trade Agreement, and the United Nations Conference on Environment and Development.

4 The ratio is conceptual; despite the exhortations of World Bank economists, such phenomena cannot be realistically measured (Myers 1984).

5 This is not an epistemological relativist approach, rather one that calls for Sandra Harding's 'strong objectivity' and Haraway's 'situated knowledge' – culturally sensitive critiques of the nostalgia for 'pure research' and ahistorical/non-ideological ivory towers.

6 A wide range of literature has emerged on a materialist/eco-feminist perspective, from Kate Soper, Vandana Shiva, Donna Haraway, Mary Mellor and many more.

1

Inventing the Commons: Theories and Practices of the Commons' Professional

Michael Goldman

In the early 1990s, I lived in the Rajasthan desert of northwest India, along one of the world's largest irrigation canals and resettlement projects which was financed and organized by many of the major international finance and development organizations – the World Bank, Canadian, Japanese and Swedish aid agencies, UNICEF and the Ford Foundation. Two million hectares of the desert commons were privatized in the name of development. While I was doing ethnographic research, the place was abuzz with these developers and aid experts speaking in the most hopeful terms about *revitalizing* and *improving* the commons of the Rajasthan desert. They wanted to create canal outlet users' associations, joint forest management practices, common markets for pastoralists, women's producer cooperatives and more of what they called 'new institutions of commons management'. At one meeting in which these ideas were being aired, low-income canal users, one by one, stood up and denounced these imported ideas: 'What's the point of a water's user association,' one man demanded, 'when all the water decisions have already been made. You just want us to fight amongst ourselves for the little water you deliver. You take away our desert and give us a water outlet.'

The latest professional literature on the commons had been consulted, but the historical reality of the desert had not. Twenty years ago, under the promise of more productive land and more plentiful water to the desert poor, development professionals had designed an enormous project that privatized the water supplies, pastures, forests, village space, burial and cremation grounds and markets – all sold off in the name of efficient profit-making and modern living. Now, 20 years later, in the midst of growing ecological and social problems, the latest crop of development scholars and professionals has arrived, briefcases in hand, proposing to create new and improved 'desert commons' in India's desert. The World Food Program is doling out food; UNICEF, medicine; Japan, 'afforestation'; Canada, 'water efficiency', and the Ford Foundation, research. And quietly, after each harvest, the government of India sets up its famine relief camps and work-for-food projects. The dispossessed commoners are now working for low wages on export-oriented, irrigated and elite-owned farms. Like Marx's observation that English child-labour laws came into effect precisely at the historical moment when child labour became superfluous for English industry, so too have concerted efforts to 'preserve' and 'remake' the world's commons come precisely at the time when our major development and finance institutions have worked to destroy the commons, discarding them into the dustbin of history.

In this chapter, I offer a homily on the literature debates on the commons, for among many of the well-established (and mostly Northern) scholars and commons professionals, there is a fundamental tension between knowledge production and historical consciousness, a tension between casting a blind eye towards the destructive forces of capitalist expansion onto the commons and a broad smile that beams at the 'underskilled' local commoner who defies all odds by protecting the commons. But what at first appears as a cacophony of voices on the world's commons is actually a monotonal 'epistemic community' amongst many scholars and professionals, one that deploys a singular set of discursive modalities and practices rooted in the famous argument of the 'tragedy of the commons'.

Despite the fact that this model of natural-resource use espoused by biologist Garrett Hardin, the 'tragedy of the commons', has been thoroughly challenged by social scientists and activists of most stripes, the model's assumptions – e.g., that selfish individuals using a common-pool resource will overconsume to the detriment of all – have not only survived but fruitfully multiplied, as if driven by higher laws of natural selection.[1] Its seeds have sprouted, for example, in works of natural scientists who apply biology's behavioural laws to complex social realities. It thrives deep in the soul of most commons theorists, even those fervently opposed to Hardin's model, who ply their trade by identifying, protecting, managing, saving, developing and making efficient commons throughout the world.[2] This commons-tragedy discourse has also shaped the thinking on the new 'global commons', led by academicians and policy makers striving to direct supranational decision making on the grey areas of global real estate: the earth's ozone, deep seas, 'biodiverse' reserves (e.g. the Amazon), the North and South poles, the air waves and so on. In other words, an old, dubious framework once applied to questions of the local commons (i.e., how to stop self-interested shepherds from destroying community pastures) is now being applied to saving our global commons.

Through a review and critique of the commons literature, this chapter makes one central point about the various positions engaged in the debate: although they may have divergent views on the social nature of property and resource use (e.g. academic distinctions among open access, state-owned, and kin-, caste-, tribe- and village-controlled property regimes), they converge in their essential definition of development and modernity, i.e., why this topic matters in the first place.

To be sure, the empirically based findings and prescriptions vary in content. Some studies show that particular cultural institutions (e.g. forest-dwellers' slash-and-burn practices, animal-herders' nomadism) have become obsolete in their capacity to manage the natural-resource base of communities and should be retooled to reduce degradation.[3] Others find that the commons would be better managed by a more global, market-driven logic of resource use that increases productivity, and therefore, human and nature's well-being. Despite these variations, all commons debaters are motivated by the prevailing question: what should external agents do? Should they (development professionals, international finance institutions and scholars) invest in 'women', in their sons, in skill development for wage work or in subsistence strategies? Should local forests be better managed, more highly diversified, contained by fences, equipped with fees, fines or subsidies? How can we transform macroeconomic policy to 'develop sustainably' fisheries that are depleted? Do the Bantus have the capacity to effectively manage Cameroon's forest resources? What economic and political incentives would entice tradition-based commoners to see the trees for the forest, the domestic goods for the exportable, their provincial needs for Merck's?[4] These questions reflect the search for the holy grail of successful commons models. Whether implicit or explicit, their prescriptions are meant for the ubiquitous professional-class 'we', recommending that development professionals get investment portfolios right, for the benefit of development's alleged client, the world's commoners.

This chapter argues that the commons metaphor is an important icon of the 'development world',[5] with instrument-effects resulting from professionals unreflexively engaged in the real world of Third World commoners and First World structural adjustment loans.[6] At a moment when the commons model is being heralded as an effective and nuanced mechanism to rationalize supranational institutions managing both local resources and global environments, this chapter hopes to situate these debates in a critical, discursive context. That is, why intervene on behalf of the commoner's commons? Why development projects? Why the World Bank (IBRD), World Trade Organization (WTO), UN Environment Programme (UNEP) and World Resources Institute (WRI)? Why should Northern commons experts and developers work so hard to help Southern locals define their own property relations, and conversely, why should locals follow the prescriptions of Northern developers? In the path created by these experts scurrying to 'clarify' property relations in Third World sites, I would argue that significant artefacts (e.g. institutions of power) are being left behind that undermine commoners' rights to control the knowledge produced, and ultimately – because this knowledge helps determine the role of capital, the state and development institutions on that site – the realm of what is defined as the commons. If this is so, then the commons debate is worth mining, not for insights into strategies for improving social and ecological conditions (however meaningful these strategies may be to differing interests) but for explanations of new forms of social control that can lead to intensified exploitation of all forms of nature, human and non-human. In other words, this body of literature can best teach us about 'the commons project' as a hidden and not-so-hidden institution of domination and imperialism in North–South relations. If we are to learn anything from the 1992 Earth Summit in Rio – the Greatest Commons Show on Earth – it is that the objective of the Summit's major power brokers was not to constrain or restructure capitalist economies and practices to help save the rapidly deteriorating ecological commons, but rather to restructure the commons (e.g. privatize, 'develop', 'make more efficient', valorize, 'get the price right') to accommodate crisis-ridden capitalisms.[7] The effect has not been to stop destructive practices but to normalize and further institutionalize them, putting commoners throughout the world at even greater risk.

The following sections present the distinctions in the commons debates, starting with the 'tragedy of the commons' school, and then moving across the spectrum to three 'anti-tragedy' positions, noting their discontents as well as their assumptions.

First, the Tragedy

The tragedy of the commons develops in this way. Picture a pasture open to all . . . As a rational being, each herdsman seeks to maximize his gain . . . The rational herdsman concludes that the only sensible course for him to pursue is to add another animal . . . and another, and another . . . Therein is the tragedy. Each man is locked into a system which compels him to increase his herd without limit – in a world that is limited. Ruin is the destination towards which all men rush, each pursuing his own interest in a society that believes in the freedom of the commons. Freedom in a commons brings ruin to all. (Hardin 1968:1244)

Although Hardin did not invent the perspective of the self-interested individual posited against nature and society, he certainly touched a responsive nerve. This tragedy perspective blossomed within the context of an elite intellectual feud among natural scientists active in the US environmental movement of the 1960s and 1970s. The politically conservative camp of conservation biologists argued that blame for the wildfire of post-World War II ecosystemic destruction should be attributed to the selfishness of people.[8] Their call was, and still is, for replacing communal institutions (in which footloose individuals reign) with private ownership and stronger state interventions in order to reverse the actions of the world's majority who blindly think they can have the freedom to overgraze, overconsume and overbreed.[9] This is a political discourse with its roots in the predominant Anglo-American critique of community and common property, dating back to the fourteenth century: that the 'sloth, idleness and misery' of serfs in feudal England represented the biggest obstacle to the productivity of agriculture (Rockham, cited in Peters 1994:8). Only through the enclosures of common land and forced removals of serfs could vast swathes of communal landholdings be consolidated into private holdings. The communal culture of shared land use was attacked on the basis of being 'anti-progressive'. As Jeremy Bentham believed, 'The condition most favourable to the prosperity of agriculture exists when there are no entails, no unalienable endowments, no common lands, no right of redemptions.'[10] To Bentham, the road to individual liberty and societal wealth is paved with the individual's freedom to convert land into a commercial good; for the individual to have rights to land, traditional institutions that bind people to the commons must be destroyed, and the land must be privatized (Bentham, quoted in Polanyi 1944:180). The leap from Bentham to Hardin is not so great as it may first seem.

In response to this thesis, the 'anti-tragedy' school emerged as a disparate group of political scientists, ecologists, anthropologists, sociologists and economists who challenge Hardin's *magnum opus* with a litany of counterfactuals, mostly from in-the-field empirical research. They argue that the tragedy thesis is remarkable for its lack of historical, theoretical or cultural veracity.[11] Within this school, one can observe three tendencies, which I identify as the Human Ecologists, the Development Experts, and the Global Resource Managers. The Human Ecologists, I argue, demonstrate the complexity of the commons from a local culture- and territory-based perspective; the Development Experts programmatically show how to restore the degraded commons, strengthen weakened social institutions and 'modernize' the Third World poor, and the Global Resource Managers explain how the commons are not just local or the problem of the poor, but contribute to global ecological crisis. Although their collective self-image is one in opposition to the facile tragedy model, in fact, their assumptions and instrument-effects are quite similar.

The Human Ecologists: The Question of the Commons

The Human Ecologists are field-based scientists who use case studies to identify the surviving features of commons tenure systems and resource-management institutions throughout the world.[12] In the Swiss mountains, Maine lobster fisheries and Ethiopian pastures, these researchers have found overlapping and complex property-resource regimes that defy the simplified modelling that defines what they ascribe as the dominant, Western view of public and tribal land and resource uses, of which the 'tragedy of the commons' thesis is the most well-known manifestation.[13] According to McCay and Acheson in *The Question of the Commons* (1987:22), common property is conventionally and erroneously viewed as 'amorphous, diffuse, ephemeral, and unspecified in comparison with private property, and this view, when it is successful in the political and legal process, plays a role in the enclosure of the commons'.

Just as they suggest, this debate is not merely an academic exercise: the tragedy interpretation of the commons can be a powerful influence in state development policy. Indeed, tragedy proponents persuasively argue that enclosures of the commons is the first step to successful modernization. World Bank policy makers, for instance, have recently increased pressure on their project managers to promote both 'privatization' and 'sustainability' of common lands and resources, as this strategy is considered the ticket to economic and ecological prosperity for the Third World poor. The Human Ecologists warn, however, that these policies must be modified to accommodate distinctions among sites, as no global template can apply to the multiple forms of the world's commons. When seen from the ground, no two commons look alike. It is only in the field, recording everyday cultural practices and ecological cycles, that one can understand the true complexity of historically evolved and socially sculpted land and resource tenure arrangements.

For example, Patricia Vondel (1987) finds that though rice is considered by the development world as the prototype crop of the Green Revolution – a revolution in land privatization and use intensification – productive relations are anything but typical in the province of South Kalimantan in Indonesian Borneo. In the swamps, rice is grown under private tenure when swamp waters recede. When swamp waters flood the rice paddies, however, common-property rules prevail; the community manages the paddies for duck and duck-egg farming. Same site, different property-rights regimes, high degree of diversity in production, depending upon the season. One finds subsistence and commercial production side by side – for barter or export – depending if it is rice, duck meat or duck egg. Similarly, in semi-arid regions of Asia where non-intensive agriculture is practised, some communities of landowning farmers open their fields to pastoralists during fallow seasons so that the neighbours' or transhumants' herds can graze on nutritious crop waste; in exchange, the farmers receive free animal labour, animal dung and milk products.

By and large, this literature's emphasis is on the social complexity of territory. It frames the debate as between an unimaginative Hardin model and, at the other extreme, the overimaginative romanticization of pre-modern life. In an effort to establish a middle ground with good empirical evidence, much of this terrain is covered by biologists and anthropologists in the field, asking questions, turning over stones. Consequently, the science of locality and territoriality is promoted; culture is introduced as a complex set of institutions that mitigates the worst disasters, and will continue to do so until external forces intervene or human populations outpace old institutions. In some cases, the burly state ruins local harmony, extracting rural resources for a voracious urban crowd; in other cases, it's the regional elite who displaces the commons-dependent poor, with bigger fishing boats, costly borewells reaching deeper groundwaters than hand-dug wells and so on. The Human Ecologists argue that to maintain economic and biological benefits, commons resource sites must be 'strongly defended'. For wild fish and game depletion, 'open access' resource regimes (or *res nullius*, Latin for 'no one's property') are the main source of the problem and restricted use is viewed as the rational solution.[14] The logic of communal user rights is typically more appropriate, according to these academic observers, than the logic of distant state or short-sighted private actors. The Human Ecologists' attraction to local conflicts and activities, however, is also their fundamental shortfall: they are unable to see beyond territoriality and locality.

As is discussed later, the commons exist not only in a specific place, but also on a microscopic (e.g. plant germplasm) and macroscopic (e.g. the earth's atmosphere) scale. Social relations on local sites can be either the point of departure or return for inquiries into ozone depletion or germplasm expropriation, air pollution or groundwater contamination – all not necessarily locality- and territory-based. But the Human Ecologist's lens does not focus well on the dialectic relations between local and nonlocal and consequently the complexities of the 'outside' world become blurred.[15] The role of extensive structures and institutions such as the state, capitalist production relations and ecosystemic changes are only relevant in this literature as they exist in or near 'the site'; consequently, these institutions, forces and power relations are reduced to mere artefacts. Such dynamics, as well as the specific sites and cultures under study, tend to be reified by the commons scientist. Later in this chapter, we see why an analytical framework on the commons must not take the fundamental pillars of societies so lightly. First, however, we will turn to a more policy-oriented, utilitarian perspective on the commons. Rather than have the world revolve around the commons, as it does for the Human Ecologists, the next group of authors sees the world turning around the concept of 'growth', asking how the commons can be made more productive.

The Development Experts: Making the Commons Work

A recent World Bank Discussion Paper that focuses on *development* as an institution of modernization exemplifies the latest thinking from this camp of the anti-tragedy commons literature. As many authors note, the World Bank is at the heart of international development; its activities, plans, reforms and reports tend to be quite influential in professional development and scholarship communities, as well as in elite government and business circles. Less discussed, however, is the fact that the Bank is also deeply engaged in, and on the cutting edge of, commons discourse. The Bank's Discussion Paper is a self-critical review of Bank work; the two authors, Daniel Bromley and Michael Cernea, are not only well-known commons experts, they are impetuous reformers in the development project, for which their anthem is 'putting [the common] people first'.[16] In this case, the people are the commoners who depend upon common-property resources for their livelihood; the authors are concerned that development planners, scholars and practitioners are putting the people last, or at least consulting them late in the project-planning process. Consequently, project effectiveness suffers. Convenient for our purpose, the authors are both participating in the latest round of commons scholarship as well as situating it within a larger debate on how to improve development efforts to make the commons, and the commoners, more productive and efficient. These Development Experts, most of whom are employed by the World Bank, Western policy institutes or environmental non-governmental organizations, can be distinguished from the Human Ecologists by their self-described task.[17] Their job is 'development' and not simply discovery; their goal is to find the problem and fix it.[18] After reviewing their main concerns, I try to situate their work in a discussion of their objectives as development experts producing scientific knowledge about the commons.

In their well-circulated paper, 'The Management of Common Property Natural Resources: Some Operational Fallacies', Daniel Bromley and Michael Cernea (1989) challenge conventional Hardin-esque approaches to the concepts of the commons, property and development-project design. They argue that most academic scholars and Bank project managers have misunderstood the fundamentally social nature of common-property regimes and resources. According to Bromley and Cernea, in spite of its currency among analysts and practitioners, the metaphor of the commons being destroyed by self-interested small-scale producers is inappropriate for explaining most cases of environmental degradation. In agreement with the Human Ecologists, they argue that the commons have always been managed through local institutions, and alternatives at the state and regional levels have rarely been capable of accomplishing the task. They conclude that development projects cannot succeed without working through existing resource-dependent communities to rebuild undermined local institutional arrangements.

Bromley and Cernea believe that the fundamental logical error of the tragedy view is that property is misconstrued as an object, such as land, when in fact property represents 'a right to a benefit stream'. The particular type of right depends upon the actual property regime in effect, which can change over time. Four regimes are conceivable:

state, private (individual), common and open access. Each has its distinct characteristics of resource management and social institutions. To understand the processes of resource degradation or sustained use, one must start with an understanding of the historically specific nature of property and institutional arrangements at the site.[19] The authors express concern that this straightforward agenda has been missing from development work at the World Bank and throughout the development world. They recommend that development's agenda for action in the 1990s focus on building rural managerial capacity as the first step toward 'sustainable productive use of natural resources' (1989:59). Although they acknowledge that the World Bank and its colleagues regularly initiate jazzy new fads – 'end poverty', appropriate technology, basic human needs, integrated rural development, 'women in development' – they expect this one, because of its intrinsic logic, to stick.

These authors note that the conventional tragedy literature fails to focus on the negative externalities of private and state property regimes, even though processes of environmental degradation are not unique to a specific type of property relations. Here, the authors find an asymmetrical logic in the tragedy literature, where blame for resource abuse is unequivocally attributed to the property structure of the commons; yet when resource degradation is found elsewhere, such as on private property, the cause is attributed to external and cultural circumstances, such as taxes or rent seeking.

This is their general critique; a more nuanced set of arguments emerges from their discussion of the shortcomings of World Bank projects seeking to improve the commons. Good and bad examples are discussed. In Somalia, the Trans-Juba Livestock Project was an unmitigated disaster because, like so many other Bank-financed projects trying to develop common lands, developers 'proceed in the absence of a clear understanding of the sociological context and institutional arrangements (including property rights) on the ground' (Bromley and Cernea 1989:27). Bank staff and development consultants, they find, have little or no knowledge of the local conditions, which is a recipe for dismal project failure.[20] But, as Bromley and Cernea are quick to note, Bank staff are not the only ones with a 'knowledge problem':

> The lack of adequate sociological understanding and competence is often common among local government officials and technical specialists, who mistakenly assume that simply belonging to the local culture automatically gives them the skills needed to manipulate and change it. (1989:28)

When they looked further into World Bank staff reports, they were surprised to find a whole series of fallacious assumptions, half-truths and generalizations regarding the status of local land tenure, land use and economic behaviour.[21] Bromley and Cernea conclude from this internal evaluation that many projects are designed with a 'lack of solid data base', insufficient input from local participants and inadequate skills to bring about productive change. What to do? They advocate a shift in emphasis, from *things* to *processes*: rather than design a project to improve a forest or grassland (i.e., things), design one to strengthen local managerial capacity (i.e., process). They criticize development assistance, which 'has, for too long, been predicated upon an assumption that money and some technical assistance . . . would facilitate the process of self-help at the village level' (p. 58).

Despite their acknowledgement of past errors, it appears that this newly sensitized version of development assistance is not so different from the old: peddling money (i.e., the Bank loan, without which there could not be a project) and technical assistance (i.e., imported goods and services) based on the development experts' calculations of the local situation and needs. Under revised conditions, apparently, the experts would be better prepared.

Bromley and Cernea's report is less a challenge to conventional wisdom, on the development community's understanding of the commons, than it is a call to step up the process of acquiring local data and knowledge. Indeed, this call reverberates throughout the 'anti-tragedy' and development reformers' work. Whether the knowledge is of one's research subject or development client, these reformers argue that international experts are misunderstanding the world's poor commoners. With piecemeal knowledge, the commons – and their restoration – will remain in crisis. This serious claim, however, begs for an explicit, and reflexive, declaration as to what this knowledge is, what it is for and whom it will serve.

Contextualizing the Debate's Silences

Overall, the intellectual boundaries inscribed by this debate are quite narrow: they fall within the very small time and space frame of a project, local clients and a development team. The discussion is silent on other relevant actors and larger time horizons. To expand the context, one would need to ask of the Somalian pasture development project, for example, what are the World Bank's macroeconomic policies for Somalia? What are the implications for property relations nationally and across social classes, as well as the uneven economic effects of Bank loan disbursement and repayment conditionalities? How do *these* 'processes' affect the local commons, user groups, project design and Bank staff constraints? Neither Bank staff nor Bank 'clients' are as ignorant or inflexible as they are perceived and portrayed. Both act within sets of constraints that remain unexamined by this literature. Perhaps Bank staff do not bother to obtain local data because it would be irrelevant to their policy objectives. Or perhaps their job requirements do not allow for time- and labour-intensive data collection in regions where electricity and safe drinking water are extremely scarce, not to mention in places where there are no 'qualified' cultural anthropologists and Western-trained field researchers who speak the same scientific language. Although scientific shortcomings on the commons is defined simply as a lack of knowledge, the authors erroneously assume that a lack of knowledge on H Street at World Bank Headquarters equals a lack of knowledge, period. Can it be that 'locals' are ignorant regarding their own affairs, property relations, rights, social relations? It could be more accurately asserted that the world's population is truly ignorant as to how to encapsulate life experiences and social conflicts into concise Bank data for project promotion and normalization of development practices. Could these scholars be suffering from the biases of ethnocentrism?[22] No, the problem is far greater than a case of misinformed reformers.

Why do Bank staff, as the authors assiduously claim, have insufficient databases from which to work? Perhaps, the answer is self-evident: if social scientists from around the world have yet to 'know' local conditions, as the Bromley-Cernea critique rightfully suggests, how can we expect perpetually rotated, Washington, DC-based Bank staff to pick up the slack within the time frame of a project's handling period, and in project sites dotting the world map? If it takes a decade, to be generous, for the 'classically' trained anthropologist to gain a limited knowledge of a village community, how many lifetimes would it take for a Bank anthropologist to know hundreds, as their heavy project load, spanning whole continents, requires?

For all the lack of self-reflexivity that Bromley, Cernea, and others claim to have found amongst developers, the same can be said of them.[23] They fall prey to tendencies that one astute observer, Majid Rahnema, notes of the post-World War II concept of 'poverty':

... almost all the definitions given to the word are woven around the concept of 'lack' or 'deficiency.' This notion reflects only the basic relativity of the concept. What is necessary and to whom? And who is qualified to define all that? (Rahnema 1991)

Debates about accuracy of data and utility of knowledge are not new to social science, not even to those who study development. One example is the controversy on the condition of the commons in sub-Saharan Africa. In the midst of heated debates (and much human misery) about 'the food crisis' in Africa in the 1970s and 1980s, analysts found fundamental flaws in data on which scholarly arguments were built regarding its existence, extent and cause.[24] If the data on food production yields are dubious at best, from province to province, nation to nation – as many scholars on Africa argue they are – how can the 'continent's food problem' be uniformly explained and transcontinental development action plans be drawn up? In spite of its own acknowledgements of poor government data, the development world did not hesitate to draw simplistic and reductive conclusions: production yields have dropped, agriculture in Africa has stagnated and greater external intervention (e.g. financial loans and grain, chemical inputs and equipment sales) is necessary to end the crisis (World Bank 1981, 1994). Since the development community has guided the world through the Green Revolution, it finds itself with, as Africanist scholar Sara Berry ironically notes, a 'comparative advantage in providing the material means, as well as the financial and organizational capability, to achieve the breakthroughs in agricultural output and productivity which Africans have apparently failed to produce for themselves' (Berry 1984: 65).

There are many reasons why data would be problematic: on the collector's side, it is hard to identify the characteristics of the population from which to draw a representative sample; on the provider's side, rural producers have been reluctant to be informers for production data when such data lead to higher taxes. That is, as African governments have increased regulation and taxation of market transactions, producers have shifted their goods to non-regulated parallel markets. Hence, market-based data in Africa have failed to measure true food production. Consumption, trade and social reproductive behaviour of self-sufficient, non-exporting rural households have been ignored by statistical inquiries depending upon formal market data. Furthermore, these phenomena cannot be measured by economistic methods. Despite the paucity of meaningful data, World Bank officials none the less concluded that there existed a dire 'food crisis', and called for rapid agrarian change through multi-billion dollar loans tied to major structural adjustments of national economies and governance institutions. Without a scientific leg to stand on, the development world brought in the era of structural adjustment with a bang, and its resonance is being felt throughout Africa.

Critics of these 'development-fix' practices take great pains to demonstrate that the only global explanation one can make about property relations and regimes across the African continent is that none can be made. What constitutes social production and reproduction on the pastures, watersheds, forests, planted fields of Africa? Sweeping claims about common, village, private or household property cannot capture the variation and dynamics of social, cultural, political and cultural relations. For development experts to assert they have a game plan for making productive relations on common property 'better', 'more efficient' and 'sustainable', they have first to construct a world of values and property relations which befits an imagined reality. To do so, they must agree to a definition of property – as well as appropriate mechanisms for interpreting the 'true value' of property and natural resources (e.g. prices) – however far removed these definitions are from the irreducible material activities of highly diverse, resource-dependent communities. When the development world ignited a fire of structural adjustment activities under the skins of Africans, it insisted that social reproductive capacities (e.g. morals, norms, forms of cooperation, kinship networks) would adjust accordingly. In fact, a well-oiled sea-change of material life in rural Africa did not occur as planned. Instead, these interventions have reversed macroeconomic trends of the previous decades with increasing net capital flows to the North, steadily falling per-capita income, decreasing welfare expenditures and deteriorating public infrastructure and goods (Barratt Brown and Tiffen 1992, Campbell and Loxley 1989, Woodward 1992, Watts 1994).

Global Resource Managers: the Commons Catastrophe, the Global Solution

We have thus far established two types of commons experts: the Development Expert and the Human Ecologist. The conundrum of the disintegrating commons is also studied and maintained by a third category of expert, whose focus is global. Unlike the human-ecology scholars who have criticized the tragedy literature for misunderstanding local institutions, knowledges and cultures, and different from the development planners and scholars whose concern is refining the institution of development in its efforts to restructure the commons, this third literature is produced by expert 'worldwatchers'.[25] They have their fingers on the pulse of the earth and are in the process of drawing up and quantifying a new global map of incalculable risks, shortfalls and disasters. For these worldwatchers, the commons is neither an isolated pasture nor a continent's capacity to produce food. Their concerns rest with a set of global commons whose degradation threatens to imperil all life on earth – the earth's ozone shield, the deep blue seas, terrestrial biomass, the world's atmosphere and climate, and toxic-contaminated communities. Representative of this perspective are the Worldwatch Institute's *State of the World* annual reports, the World Resources Institute's studies, follow-up work from the 1992 Earth Summit in Rio and so on. These texts are not just available to small segments of the academy: Worldwatch's products alone are translated into 27 languages and distributed free to world leaders in politics, media, business, academia and development. Global Resource Managers (GRMs) are global in their knowledge, reach and impact.

The data on the global commons are indeed quite compelling.[26] The air: one in five breathe in air more poisonous than WHO basic standards, leading to a range of health ills, including severe lung and brain damage. The atmosphere: seven billion tons of carbon are released into the atmosphere each year, affecting the world's climate. The ozone shield: holes are beginning to show in the Southern Hemisphere, which are being associated with rising rates of skin cancer. Land: humans today appropriate 40 per cent of the net primary product of terrestrial photosynthesis by harvesting the earth's biomass; in 35–40 years, when the human population doubles, our survival will require 80–100 per cent appropriation of the earth's biomass – a practical impossibility. The oceans, rivers, forests, and subsoil aquifers have become victims of open-access strategies and are consequently being over-mined and over-contaminated. Switching our gaze from local phenomena to the global, these commons experts show us widespread deforestation, carbon overload in the global atmosphere, climatic changes, elimination of biological populations, erosion of watersheds, polluted air, diminished habitats for wild animals and reduced spaces for productive human use.

Although these planetary concerns are not practically relevant to the work of most traditional commons researchers, they are integral to that of the newest commons marshals, who are spearheading the effort to define and more efficiently manage the global commons. Though the atmosphere, oceans and public common space are often thought to be open-access regimes, in fact, formal international organizations have been constituted to regulate access and monitor their (mis)use. The oceans are regulated and monitored by a number of supranational entities: the International Whaling Commission passed a moratorium on whaling in 1985; the London Dumping Convention of 1972 manages the ban on ocean dumping of highly toxic pollutants and radiation waste (by 1983, low-level radiation waste dumping was also banned); the Law of the Sea enables states to regulate access to a 200-mile zone from their coasts, the Commission for the Conservation of Antarctic Marine Living Resources controls mining of the Southern Ocean. Agenda 21 of the Earth Summit is negotiating stronger laws to better protect the seas; the Global Environment Facility of the World Bank has begun to fund Black Sea restoration and other clean-up projects. These organizations and their professional consultants are equipping themselves to gather the data and are uniquely situated to become, in a sense, the modern stewards of these global commons. As they do, they constitute public spaces and resources as the new commons to be monitored, measured, regulated and administered. In this world of global resource managerialism, worldwatching has become essential (Luke 1994). As it turns out, GRMs have replaced the barefoot peasants as the 'experts' on the commons; now, within the new discourse, it is their knowledge, rules, sciences and definitions that have become paramount for explaining ecological degradation and sustainability.

By shifting the commons inquiry from local to global, pastures are no longer simply defined as sites of conflict between or amongst pastoralists and farmers, but are rationalized as small fragments of terrestrial biomass whose misuse negatively affects not just local or regional populations, but us all. In other words, local commons-use patterns in the South are also a problem for the North. Yet, in an effort to generalize about the cumulative impact of local patterns, this epistemic community of GRMs has tried to operationalize the problematic tradition of the local commons model. From the lowly commoner to the powerful nation-state, they find that all act based on a rational set of rules, making decisions based on a restricted menu of economic choices. The problem that most perplexes GRMs is: what are the most rational, professional, informed and efficient commons institutions available to facilitate these decisions? This question suggests a context and epistemological framing that has been left unexamined by the commons literature; the following discussion highlights two aspects of this lacuna.

Global resource managerialism becomes the authority on the commons

> World economies are depleting stocks of ecological capital faster
> than the stocks can be replenished. Yet economic growth can be
> reconciled with the integrity of the environment. (MacNeill
> 1990:110)

Implicit in the handling of local-commons problems by global actors
is that these concerns are no longer local; hence, they require global
intervention. Indeed, new institutions are being formed to manage
these problems: global-climate treaties, multilateral trade pacts,
chemical-use bans, international review panels. They use multilateral
legal procedures, Northern-based think tanks, high-flying economic
theory and development-bank capital to identify the source of these
new problems, develop the tools and perform social experimentation
to pursue the elusive solutions to managing Planet Earth while not
compromising 'the integrity' of the growing world economy.

The handling of the case of the atmospheric commons exemplifies
this discursive shift away from the local and into the hands of GRMs.
The rapid degradation of the earth's atmosphere by carbon dioxide,
chlorofluorocarbons (CFCs) and nitrous oxide is a scientific and
empirical indictment of the dominant path of industrialization. The
United States, western Europe, and Japan produce almost 50 per cent
of the world's carbon dioxide; in the United States, the carbon
dioxide comes primarily from smokestacks of electric utilities and
other industries, from commercial and residential heating and from
motor vehicles.[27] Seventy per cent of the CFCs that eat away at the
earth's ozone layer has been manufactured and released from
refrigeration, air conditioners and solvents from Western capitalist
countries. Nitrous oxide is a by-product of the petrochemical-based
fertilizer industry, fossil-fuel burning and deforestation. Over the past
ten years, global warming and destruction of the earth's atmosphere
has been described as the 'ultimate' global commons problem. That
the earth's climate is being engineered, and warmed, by the worst
effluents of this century's industrialization does offer hope that an
ozone-friendly re-engineering is also possible. But, according to
some experts, a 60 per cent reduction in fossil-fuel use is necessary
to stabilize global climate.[28] How do GRMs perceive the solution?

With respect to the carbon dioxide problem, GRMs advocate that
the rapidly industrializing countries of the South (e.g. Thailand,
Mexico) use unleaded gasoline, equip vehicles with the latest
pollution-reduction equipment and build new factories and power

plants following the stricter regulations of Western-based facilities. If GRMs had their way, every new car on every new road throughout the South would meet the world's highest standards for efficiency and pollution reduction. But the question remains: what effect will these 'green' industrial policies have on the commons, both global and local?

Director of Washington, DC-based Worldwatch Institute, Lester Brown, argues in his *tour de force, Building a Sustainable Society*, that many global consumption habits cannot be construed as local creations. Brown recounts how the collusion of giant US corporations such as Standard Oil, GM and Firestone (oil, auto, rubber respectively) in the post-World War II period effectively led to the replacement of rail-based urban transport systems with their own, ecologically destructive brand of transport: the gas-guzzling, carbon-emitting car (Brown 1981). Despite his structural description of the problem, he finds the solution to rest in the hands of individual 'consumers': If US consumers were better armed with the facts (i.e., that their obsessive driving habits are destroying the planet), they would change their behaviour. In turn, private corporations would be forced to retool their research-and-development capacities, responding efficaciously to a sea-change in consumer demand.

World Resources Institute (also based in Washington, DC) warns that if current trends continue, cars and trucks will become 'the world's dominant consumer of energy and the largest source of both global and local air pollution within 35 years' (WRI 1990:141). WRI concludes that pollution reduction and energy efficiency can be greatly enhanced by technological advances being invented by private oil and auto multinational corporations, such as unleaded gasoline and stratified-charge engines. Thankfully, these technological innovations may not only save the atmospheric commons, they may do so without much inconvenience to Northern consumers. As WRI sees it,

> Energy conservation was once unfairly linked to the need for drastic cutbacks in living standards. Although some changes in human behavior are clearly appropriate, conservation efforts are now strongly focused on introducing new technologies for producing and using energy more efficiently and on improving energy management. By increasing energy efficiency, demand can be reduced without adversely affecting personal lifestyles or a country's economic growth. In fact, increasing energy efficiency can even enhance them. (1990:145–6)

This position of the GRMs, however, contains a fundamental contradiction: that carbon dioxide emissions can be reduced with greener technologies and selective user fees, introduced within the context of an expanding industrial capitalism. GRMs' plans for Third World transport systems reveal this quite clearly. First, though GRMs advocate that each new car or truck to hit the South should include a pollution-reduction device (capable of reducing carbon monoxide but not carbon dioxide), the quantity of pollutants emitted into the atmosphere would continue to increase rapidly in the aggregate, thus imperilling the atmospheric commons. Second, most capital goods (e.g. auto plants) originate in the North; hence, this narrative explains more about the expansionary demands of the North's industrial base than it does about the demand in the South to rapidly industrialize with the latest technologies.[29] But the North's industrial base will continue to expand, and pollute, as it caters to the expanding 'needs' for capital goods by the South – demand stimulated by Northern finance capital and development banks. Third, each industrial expansionist project requires more raw materials extracted from the earth, rivers, forests, aquifers and from workers. Industrial production requires a site, and most production sites have an impact on local commons; yet *their* despoliation and transformation are never discussed in the global commons discourse. Ironically, the 'local' has been completely expunged from the GRM commons exegesis and replaced with an undifferentiated logic of global resource managerialism. For the GRMs, 'sustainable development' is just another way of saying that world economic growth rates can be sustained without destroying the earth.

Globalizing the commons discourse
In their reform-minded article, 'On the strategy of trying to reduce economic inequality', Nobel Laureate Trygve Haavelmo and Stein Hansen argue that there are three prerequisites for 'good' development solutions in the context of globalizing tendencies: good knowledge as to how to change the world's destructive development path, 'an addressee to receive this knowledge', and an 'internationally accepted body [with] the authority and power to choose the future path of development and enforce it' (Haavelmo and Hansen 1991). This statement typifies the collective denial in the GRM literature of the history and nature of this type of authority and power currently accountable to no popular community. In this literature on the global commons, the experts have decided the problems are so complex, so catastrophic and so immediate, that there is no time or political space to make these decisions collectively

or varyingly, based upon the historical needs of different social groups and the ecosystems on which they depend. Worse than in the works of the site-based Human Ecologists or the project-based Development Experts, the Global Resource Managers have completely spliced out the local, the vitality of the commons and the activity of the commoner. Only 'docile bodies' and subjectless sites remain (Foucault 1979). As Haavelmo and Hansen imply, development is a singular discourse, to be 'received' by one (docile) community and to be authored by another.

This lack of epistemic reflexivity can also be found in a special issue of the development world's main scholarly journal, *World Development* (Streeten 1991). The authors – all certified GRMs – construct a world full of cooperation and 'institutional innovations that transcend the state': global institutions that can manage global resources and trouble spots in a world of ill-equipped national and regional institutions. Their call is for a global central bank, debt facility, industrial board, energy policy, environmental protection agency, progressive income tax, etc., with greater powers to negotiate international disputes. In managing the global commons, GRMs have replaced case studies of local conflicts over scarce resources (e.g. the Human Ecologists' parable) with 'a global *human* commons' regulating

> access to the global *natural* commons in a way that (1) minimizes and/or mediates conflicts among nations and other interest groups; (2) insures increasing equity of access among those groups; and (3) moves toward sustainable resource use so as to balance the needs and wishes of the present generation against those of future generations. (Goodwin 1991:2)

In these utopic revelations on how the world could become a better place through global board meetings, GRMs do not seriously examine the Third World's experience with existing institutions. After all, the IMF has been a *de facto* central bank for the world economy for years, the World Bank the central planning agency, and GATT the central trade agency. While GRMs insist that the biggest problem with global bodies such as the IMF is they do not have *enough* power, their historiography of international institutions masks the hegemonic activities of these interstatal agreements, multinational corporations, international banks and business cartels. The end of the Cold War does not mark the end of hegemony, as some GRMs would believe (see Keohane 1984);[30] it can, however, mark the moment where the real interests and unequal power relations of existing international institutions are laid bare. Yet, instead of a reality check on commons institutions and crises, the local and the global are interpreted through a discursive lens in which GRMs see an exciting new world of rational cooperation and modernization aimed to enhance the collective good.

This discourse, of course, does not go unchallenged. As a leader in global resource managing, WRI slipped slightly from its high horse after publishing a report that framed the global warming problem in terms of the behaviour of the Third World poor.[31] The report argued that one simple step towards reduction of methane gas production, a global warming gas, is for Asian households to keep fewer methane-producing cows and cultivate fewer methane-releasing rice paddies. Everyone can play a role in saving the planet, the argument went, poor commoners and rich profiteers alike. However attractive, rational and populist the report's conclusion may have seemed, the Centre for Science and Environment in New Delhi accused WRI of practising 'environmental colonialism'.[32] By neglecting to distinguish between 'luxury emissions' such as air conditioners and automobiles in rich capitalist countries and 'survival emissions' from rice and milk production in poorer capitalist (e.g., India) and socialist (e.g. China) countries, WRI, according to its Indian critics, has been caught gazing primarily at Asia's poor producers while trying to find a sound solution to the world's atmospheric problems. According to the WRI report, India will be increasing per capita emissions by an estimated 400 per cent from 1990 to 2024, as compared to the US's 70 per cent. The fact that most of the carbon dioxide emitted since 1900 still exists in the earth's atmosphere, that this build-up represents the main source of the problem, and that it has been mostly produced by a handful of industries within Western capitalist countries, is neglected by the GRMs (Cameron 1992).

Critics argue that this ecological discourse has conjured up a series of 'Orientalist' spectres that miscast the South as rapidly reproducing Third Worlders who have become uncontrollable consumers, polluters, and unaware global citizens, à la Hardin's worldview. Implicit in this thinking is that global resource experts consider the world's most numerous resource users, Third World peasants, as subordinates:

> In other words, the change that must happen [as advocated by this commons discourse] requires unprecedented action carefully guided by the experts of the West. Because the Third Worlders do not have this knowledge – but instead are caught in a chronic pathological condition – the scientist, like a good doctor, has the

moral obligation to intervene in order to cure the diseased (social) body . . . [In this message] one can discern the authorial stances of a father/savior talking with selfless condescension to the child/native. (Escobar 1995:159)

Instrument-effects of the Anti-tragedy Perspectives

What is at stake in these [development] strategies . . . is an entire biopolitics: a set of policies regulating a plurality of problems such as health, nutrition, family planning, education, and the like which inevitably introduce not only given conceptions of food, the body, and so on, but a particular ordering of society itself . . . The biopolitics of development continues the deployment of modernity. (Escobar 1995:143)

In spite of the apparent fecundity of the scholarly literature and its robust challenges of the famous straw-man 'tragedy of the commons' position, this survey has sought to show that these literatures are anything but oppositional. In practically no instance do the commons experts of any school engage in an analysis of modernity, development and its institutions, and the way in which they, as strategically situated Northern actors, actively construct the knowledge/power relations they have with their subjects/clients. On the contrary, their work affirms and legitimates the latest round of World Bank edicts on modernity and development, which propose that 'the achievement of *sustained* and equitable *development* remain the greatest challenge facing the human race'.[33]

Despite the fine-tuning of plans developed to help the commons – from valorizing mineral reserves and urban real estate to adopting international trade agreements and population control policies – projects, programmes and processes fail time and time again. One only needs to look at the World Bank's self-funded evaluations to learn how dismal its 'success' rate is, even by its own standards.[34] These auto-critiques send development scholars and planners back into their laboratories to recast ways to fund and intervene into more sites with the hopes of succeeding, at last. My argument is, as anthropologist James Ferguson finds from his own research, 'that what is most important about a development project is not so much what it fails to do but what it does do'.[35] Access for domestic and foreign capital to more remote zones of resource- and labour-rich sites is being accomplished through social experimentation and state expansionism in the name of 'making the commons work'. In most cases, Third World state development agencies become the guardians of a relatively large influx of foreign capital intended specifically to restructure social-natural relations in 'undeveloped' areas so that projects, and the state itself, can set root and capitalist relations can grow.

The science of development is further refined based on this process of increased intervention into new sites and bodies. Today, both sides of the commons literature (tragedy and anti-tragedy) argue, with equally feverish pitch, that a new science of resource managerialism is required, with themselves at the helm. Whether it be rapidly eroding coral reefs off the coasts of the South Pacific, famine in the pasturelands of sub-Saharan Africa, rainforests in Latin America, or another failed World Bank development project, they are unified in their belief that the crisis on the commons must be universally tackled and rationalized by well-trained teams of international experts sensitive to local needs and ecological capacities. This most recent round of problem solving, however, should be understood within the context of the historical practices of these imperialist processes. According to Escobar,

> What must be analyzed is how the peasant's world is organized by a set of [externally contrived] institutional practices. One must also investigate how the institutional practices and professional discourses coordinate and interpenetrate different levels of social relations; that is, how the relations between different actors (peasants, mothers and children, planners, international agencies, agribusiness corporations and so on) are rendered accountable only through a set of categories that originated in professional discourse; and, finally, how the latter implicate other types of relations, such as class and gender. (1995:109)[36]

Over a period of more than 40 years, a seamless series of detailed projects have been deployed by elite institutions, universities and professional organizations, in newly carved careers of sustainable development, commons management and anti-poverty policy, producing new idioms, standards, performance schedules and evaluative procedures. These professions have been mostly self-referential – plans, tools, methods, evaluations performed for the satisfaction of professionals themselves – and wholly unrelated to the worldviews and ideas of the so-called beneficiaries whose perceived 'lack' is the key signifier for this discourse. The full array of development enthusiasts view the trouble of the commons similarly: the global commons crisis is still attributed to the actions or inactions of the preconceived individual subjects – most of whom live in the South and are resource-poor. Solutions rest with private actions and global organizations flush with money to transform and regulate; global agencies mobilize a whole range of financial, intellectual and political resources to transform expeditiously the world's commons as a project of modernity. Yet these agencies are driven by discursive practices of privatization, production intensification, integration and capitalization. Each process, alone, runs the risk of degrading local commons, institutions, and ecosystems; in combination they have proved to be disastrous.

The flip side of the common's resource-degradation argument is the overpopulation card, or the argument that there are 'too many people' for the planet's carrying capacity. Reformers consider the 'overpopulation problem' as a commons problem that can be solved with more social control of the commoner's (social) body.[37] This, of course, is the final terrain of state intervention, with serious racial, class and gender implications: the preconceived subjects of population policies are uniformly poor darker-skinned women who are otherwise completely voiceless and invisible in decision-making apparatus. In this discourse, their only *visible* decision is the one that is purportedly destroying the world; it defines them uniformly within the discourse as (reckless) reproducers. The last terrain of social control in the late twentieth century is one's body, physical desire and manifestations of love, and these are the last uncolonized sites that dominant discursive practices have sought to control, in the name of saving the global commons. The rationale for such problematic interventions, i.e., sterilizations (usually by coercion or force), is that the commons is also 'ours' to save, and no longer just the realm of the culturally enigmatic and undisciplined subject, the Third World commoner. Once physically re(-)formed (i.e., without functioning reproductive organs), the commoner will learn to live, labour and behave on the public commons more rationally; but if she doesn't, at least her ability to reproduce will have been deterred. One can see the parallel motives of distant global resource managers implementing bio-social plans to regulate both the commoner's body (and capacity to reproduce) and the commoner's natural resources (and capacity to produce). These are a few instrument-effects of the commons/development world, tragedyists and anti-tragedyists alike.

Why So Much Interest in the Commons?

The topic of 'reinventing the commons' has regained currency amongst development planners not simply because of their slow learning curve – as Bromley and Cernea note – but for more substantive reasons. First, the commons crisis has ignited social movements that threaten the workings of development, state and economic institutions; and second, the rapid and large-scale degradation of the world's air, water, forest and biogenetic resources threatens the reproduction of capital (M. O'Connor 1994). It is in response to these challenges that many elite scholars, international finance institutions and state agencies bother to search out local sites of ecological stress, and then send in their high-priced professionals to 'fix' them.

Although tragedyists and anti-tragedyists alike acknowledge the commons are in crisis, they collectively observe the problem through a particular lens in which they see local institutional breakdown, communal disintegration, social apathy, but not social action and conflict. This perspective ignores the fact that over the past few 'development' decades, marginalized populations in the South have been organizing anti-development and anti-state movements and insurrections. In India, every corner of the postcolonial map finds a radical movement seeking to reclaim power over land and resources. In Mexico, the Zapatistas and other indigenous peoples' movements are mobilizing communities who have unsuccessfully competed for resources with large landholders and industries, and have gained numerical strength precisely at the moment when the *ejidos*, Mexico's common lands, were robbed of their legislative protection from real estate markets (Foley 1995; Stephen, Chapter 3, this volume). Similar processes are occurring in Brazil, the Philippines, Indonesia and most nations where international development institutions (professional and financial) have thrived. Moreover, the same could be said of urban, feminist, labour, race/ethnic and environmentalist movements in the North (see DiChiro, Chapter 5 this volume). These struggles are, in part, being fought over the commons, and are challenging the legitimacy of elite discursive practices of capitalist development and expansion.

Secondly, as expansion is constrained by the degradation of healthy production conditions world-wide, scholars and professionals alike have taken to search for the universal 'logic' of the commons. In contrast, though, to the prevailing epistemic discourse, some critical theorists maintain that nature is socially produced, and scarcity of healthy environments can be largely attributed to two historically specific tendencies: capitalist *overproduction* (e.g. loggers unselectively clearfelling to keep costs down and 'survive' global competition) and *underproduction* (e.g. refusing to do 'costly' reforestation of denuded sites) (J. O'Connor 1988). In times of extreme scarcity, the state – and social movements – inevitably intervene. Hence, processes of ecological degradation and repair become politicized, that is, thrust back into the public domain. From this perspective, questions of scarcity cannot be simply answered by calculative scientists, as utility and value can be measured from many conflictual positions. To timber, mining and ranching enterprises, perhaps only 2 per cent of a tropical forest offers marketable commodities, and the rest, marked for destruction, is post-production waste (Altvater 1993:226). To some forest producers, the trampled 98 per cent may represent use-values; this is why tropical forests such as the Amazon can be seen as at once 'overexploited and underutilized' (Myers 1991). Many commons analysts, by contrast, understand scarcity as the defining moment of the decline of the peasant mode of production – the pre-progressive and pre-scientific stage of social and economic development. Scarcity becomes a discursive trope to invoke the well-worn tragedy parable and prescription, as well as to mask contradictory interfaces between capitalist and noncapitalist processes. The post-scarcity world awaits us on the other side of economic/market rationality.

By viewing ecological limits as social limits, however, the causes and repercussions of environmental crisis become clearer: 'Acid rain destroys forests and lakes and buildings and profits alike. Salinization of water tables, toxic wastes, soil erosion, etc. impair nature and profitability. The pesticide treadmill destroys profits as well as nature' (J. O'Connor 1988:25).

In this way, scarcity of the ecological commons is operationalized as an eco-Marxist and not neo-Malthusian (or Hardin-esque) concept. As production conditions become degraded, contaminated and scarcer for the purpose of valorization, there is greater competition amongst capitalist sectors and communities for diminished access to healthy resources. This competitive terrain is expressed in ideology – in masking or normalizing sources of destruction – and materiality, in struggles over land, vegetation, fauna, minerals and water. A survey of the commons literature reveals that activities *and* analyses of common property regimes are notably abstracted from such historical rhythms. Ironically, with perhaps the exception of the Human Ecologists, these experts overwhelmingly conclude that the global logic of the market – or what Elmar Altvater (1993:217) calls 'capitalist socialization' – is the instrument that will revitalise the threatened and enigmatic commons.

Conclusion: Hegemonic and Successor Sciences

Amongst scholars and professionals, the world's commons are invariably defined by a set of epistemological norms. Natural and human processes are expressed in terms of their valorized contribution to a nation's GNP. Although many culturalists and localists (e.g. Human Ecologists) express their concern for neglected cultural and ecological variables, these are also judged in terms of capitalist norms of economy, efficiency and competition. Hence, they ask how commoners could produce more for less under different circumstances, such as with imported skills, capital, technologies and management institutions. Meanwhile, globalists work to overcome the parochialism of focusing only on local conditions, but fail to acknowledge the complexity on which their preferred globalized social and natural world is based. All work within their situated knowledges to show that the actors they study are either rational or irrational, adjudicated by the discursive parameters of development.

Ultimately, not only are conflicts over property viewed purely in developmentalist terms, but so are their 'remedies', i.e. intervention and valorization. These development strategies, however, are not merely economic interventions: they are political, cultural, social and ecological interventions with multiple effects on the way people organize their social worlds. Under existing power-knowledge relations, for commons scholars and practitioners to interpret the social reproduction of labour power, ecological conditions, worldviews and knowledge through rational modelling is tantamount to subverting meanings, silencing voices and annihilating popular institutions. In the debates over whether the commons are in crisis, commons tragedyists and anti-tragedyists alike ignore the temporal and spatial dialectics of the lifeworlds they claim to know, and those they inhabit. Consequently, these intellectual sparring partners have developed, perhaps unwittingly, their own ideological 'customs in common', and become, despite their avowed differences and disputes, the strangest of bedfellows.

This chapter is not so much a critique of the findings of studies on the commons, *per se*, as it is a critique of the instrument-effects that dis-embed their subject matter from dominant sites of power and knowledge. In this respect, the commons enterprise avoids what

Bourdieu calls 'epistemic reflexivity' or the process of grappling with the eminently political basis of scientific-knowledge production (Bourdieu and Wacquant 1992). As long as the commons is perceived as only existing within a particular mode of knowing, called development, with its unacknowledged structures of dominance, this community will continue to serve the institution of development, whose *raison d'être* is restructuring Third World capacities and social-natural relations to accommodate transnational capital expansion.

By contrast, a successor science situates the commons within the contested hegemonic culture and political economy of expanding modernization and capitalism. It reflexively grapples with colonial and imperial practices, including historical relations between dominant and colonized social groups, and the multiple places where the scientist-inquirer stands in the context of the development world's conveyor belt of social experimentation and scientific discursive practices. Finally, a successor science engages alternative science-for-the-people scientists/activists and helps translate situated knowledges across very diverse communities with explicitly acknowledged power-differentiated relations (Harding 1986, Haraway 1989, 1991, Levins and Lewontin 1985). Pleading innocence – as many detached scientists and don't-look-back development practitioners do – does not keep the instrument-effects of their work from fuelling undemocratic interventions into, and exploitative relations with, the social and ecological lifeworlds of the commoners.

In other words, to begin to understand the context and content of struggles over the commons, one needs a critical and self-reflexive analysis of the institutional practices of development, modernity and imperialism, and the way powerful agents (e.g. IFIs, developers, NGOs and scholars) discursively reduce and rationalize human behaviour to a common metaphor.

Notes

1   Garrett Hardin's (1968) parable imagines a set of pastoralists who destroy the future viability of their pastoral commons by each of them selfishly deciding to increase their herd size for individual short-term benefit, until the commons becomes overgrazed.
2   As Feeny et al. (1990) argue, Hardin's perspective 'has become part of the conventional wisdom in environmental studies, resource science and policy, economics, ecology, and political science'. One finds it as a foundational assumption in new

institutional economics, game theory and rational choice and action theories. Anthropologists such as Pauline Peters (1993, 1994) find it the basis of resource-use policy in many parts of the South (for Peters, livestock and range policy in Africa).

3   'Institution' is defined as 'both supraorganizational patterns of activity through which humans conduct their material life in time and space, and symbolic systems through which they categorize that activity and infuse it with meaning' (Friedland and Alford 1991).

4   In 1991, the US-based pharmaceutical company Merck paid the Costa Rican government $1.1 million and a promise of future royalties in exchange for rights to collect biological specimens for commodity development from state forest commons.

5   Some authors locate the origin of 'development' in the interwar period when 'the ground was prepared for the institution of development as a strategy to remake the colonial world and restructure the relations between colonies and metropoles' (Escobar 1995: 26). The development 'world' comprises organizations such as state departments, foreign aid and relations agencies, charities, missionaries, think tanks, international NGOs and universities, that are heavily engaged in the institutional practices described in this chapter. The phrase 'development industry' is used to emphasize the accumulative aspect of this world's practices (Sachs 1992). Others date the birth of development in nineteenth-century European state practices, as a counterpoint to the devastation of 'progress' – the social disorder of poverty, unemployment and urbanization (Cowen and Shenton 1995). Most critics understand the origins of the institution of development as Eurocentric.

6   Foucault (1979) conceived of the term 'instrument-effects' to explain what gets served by the endless failures of prison systems, i.e., exercises of power through prisons. James Ferguson (1994:255) uses the idea to illustrate 'failures' of development projects: 'If it is true that "failure" is the norm for development projects in Lesotho, and that important political effects may be realized almost invisibly alongside with that "failure", then there may be some justification for beginning to speak of a kind of logic or intelligibility to what happens when the "development" apparatus is deployed – a logic that transcends the question of planners' intentions. In terms of this larger unspoken logic, "side-effects" may be better seen as "instrument-effects"; effects that are at one and the same time instruments of what "turns out" to be an exercise of power.'

7 See O'Connor (1988, 1998) on 'production conditions' (ecological, human, and public).

8 The politically progressive camp – Rachel Carson, Barry Commoner et al. – attributed the North's environmental problems to changes in post-World War II industrial production, which dramatically increased chemical and fossil-fuel consumption. They implicated large polluting corporations and *laissez-faire* governments in poisoning rivers, air, water supplies, soils, ecosystems and worker's health. They argued for bans of the most pernicious toxic inputs and outputs, and strong regulation of the most polluting enterprises.

9 One of the implications of Hardin's argument can be understood by the following subhead in his tragedy article, 'Freedom to Breed is Intolerable'. Here he replaces the common pastoralist with the common human breeder, planting the seeds for inquiries into the actions of individuals, such as sexual intimacy, asking whether they improve or destroy the 'global commons'.

10 Polanyi's is perhaps the most brilliant analysis of these issues. He understood the enclosures of the commons – starting in the fourteenth century in England and France and eventually practised in colonized territories abroad – as a critical process in the subordination of social institutions to the market economy, and rooted in the ideological contradictions of the 'liberal creed' (e.g. Bentham, Malthus).

11 The literature includes *The Ecologist*, special issue, 1992; Ciriacy-Wantrup and Bishop 1975; Berkes, ed., 1989; Wade 1987; and Ostrom 1990. An extensive bibliography of case studies is being catalogued at Indiana University, published thus far in three volumes (see Martin 1989 and 1992, and Hess 1996).

12 Influential authors include James Acheson, Bonnie McCay, Fikret Berkes, Evelyn Pinkerton, E.N. Anderson, Elinor Ostrom, C. Ford Runge and Margaret McKean.

13 James Acheson on Maine, Dan Bauer on Ethiopia, and Robert Netting on Switzerland, in McCay and Acheson 1987. The collection is considered a classic in the field.

14 'Rights have no meaning without correlated duties, and the management problem with open-access resources is that there are no duties on aspiring users to refrain from use' (Bromley 1992:4).

15 'Difference is now encountered in the adjoining neighborhood, the familiar turns up at the ends of the earth . . . The world is increasingly connected, though not unified, economically and culturally. Local particularism offers no escape from these

involvements. Indeed, modern ethnographic histories are perhaps condemned to oscillate between two metanarratives: one of homogenization, the other of emergence; one of loss, the other of invention . . . Everywhere in the world distinctions are being destroyed and created' (Clifford 1988).

16   Michael Cernea's publications, written primarily at the World Bank, include the edited volume *Putting People First: Sociological Variables in Development* (1985), and dozens of World Bank Reports, Discussion Papers, and articles in professional journals. Daniel Bromley's publications include the edited volume *Making the Commons Work* (1992) and reports and papers written as a Bank consultant. He is also a co-founder of the International Association for the Study of Common Property and editor of *Land Economics*.

17   See, for example, N.S. Jodha (1992b), the works of Robert Chambers at the Institute of Development Studies (Sussex), Robert Wade, David Reed at World Wildlife Fund, Robert Repetto at World Resources Institute, the editors and writers at *World Development*, and numerous World Bank-financed publications.

18   Many authors, such as Bromley, wear two hats – in his case, within the academy as a property and economic institutions scholar, and as consultant with the World Bank, where consultants are obliged to skip the theorizing and offer ready-to-eat pragmatic and programmatic advice. The Bank has been described by many inside and outside as anti-intellectual and it has little tolerance for drawn-out anthropological findings or abstract social theory. Hence, it is quite easy to distinguish between the more scholarly Human Ecologist and the pragmatic Development Expert in their publications.

19   This is an assumption shared with the Human Ecologists.

20   Indeed, their concerns are shared by Bank project evaluators, as the following passage indicates: 'By all accounts little was definitely known at the time of appraisal about the [population's] way of life, grazing rights, motivation, etc. Only the scantiest literature exists on these matters and not even that was examined either at project preparation or appraisal, since neither team had included a social anthropologist' (Somalia: Trans-Juba Livestock Project, PPAR, World Bank, 1983:10, cited in Bromley and Cernea 1989).

21   Just as their title suggests, they found 'operational fallacies' as well as ill-conceived assumptions on which Bank staff and consultants based their project design, implementation and evaluation. Cernea has since written an internal evaluation of

Bank resettlement operations ('Resettlement and Development: The Bank-Wide Review of Projects Involving Involuntary Resettlement, 1986–1993' April 8, 1994), and there, too, he found system-wide institutional dishonesty in regards to displacement and resettlement of populations negatively affected by World Bank loan projects.

22 A vibrant literature on this question exists, though it is hardly discussed amongst the commons scholars. See Clifford and Marcus (1986); Clifford (1988); Haraway (1989).

23 Though lacking self-reflexivity, this industry is remarkable for its self-referential tendencies. Most Bank reports, for example, reference almost solely works by Bank staff and consultants – a compelling discursive practice (Escobar 1995; Smith 1987).

24 The long list starts with a seminal piece by Berry (1984). See also Bernstein (1990); and extensive debates on the science, methodologies, data collection, and statistics of development institutions making claims about Africa, authored by Ardeshir Sepehri, Eboe Hutchful, Lucy Walker, Giles Mohan, Ankie Hoogvelt, and others in *Review of African Political Economy*, especially volume 62 (1994).

25 For a humorous and thoughtful critique of the Worldwatch Institute, see Luke (1994). With appreciation, this section borrows the main word play and some ideas from Luke's article. See also Beck (1992).

26 These statistics have been culled from our only 'global' sources: UN and World Bank publications, and Worldwatch's annual *State of the World* series (1991, 1992, 1993, 1994).

27 While carbon monoxide production from autos can be reduced through improved technology (15 years ago a US car produced about one pound of carbon in the form of carbon monoxide for every gallon of gas burned; today, it's closer to one-half a pound), carbon dioxide – invisible and odourless – is an inevitable by-product of fossil-fuel consumption. Although scrubbers and catalytic converters can reduce smelly and irritating smog by reducing carbon monoxide, no technology can prevent the release of carbon dioxide from fossil-fuel consumption. Hence, the problem is structural not technical.

28 According to a 1995 report by the UN-supported Intergovernmental Panel on Climate Change.

29 According to a 1996 UNDP lobbying booklet for US Congress, the United States receives about $1.50 in sales and services for every dollar contributed to UNDP. The returns are better at the World Bank: though the US has only invested $1.9 billion in the

World Bank (excluding IDA transactions) *over the past 50 years*, US corporations received approximately $5 billion in contracts from World Bank loans in the past two years alone. In general, 40 to 60 per cent of the Bank's lending capital passes through the hands of Southern governments and into the coffers of Northern corporations, making development lending practices critical for Northern corporations' expansionary needs. One senior Bank official estimates that $10 billion of Bank loans translates into $250 billion in Northern investments in the South (staff interviews, 1995). Other data come from former Bank treasurer, Eugene Rotberg (1994), and the US Treasury Department (1995).

30   This school defines the term 'hegemony' narrowly and contrary to the Gramscian usage. They simply find that since the Cold War is over, since the United States is no longer the military and economic hegemon, and since none else exists, the moment lends itself to global cooperative tendencies.

31   WRI is financially supported by UNEP and UNDP, as well as other sources, and its higher-level staff fluidly travel from one development agency to another (e.g., the World Bank, US State Department, environmental NGOs). WRI co-publishes reports based on work from these agencies and has become the world's premier NGO source for data on national resource consumption, publishing reports called *Global Trends in Environment and Development and World Resources, A Guide to the Global Environment* (published bi-annually).

32   See Hammond (1990, 1991) versus Agarwal and Narain (1991).

33   The opening line from the *1992 World Development Report* (Washington, DC: World Bank, 1992), the momentous statement on the World Bank's changing stance on the environment and development, cited and eloquently critiqued in George and Sabelli 1994 (emphasis added).

34   Numerous Bank self-studies in recent years include The Wapenhans Report, The Morse Commission Report, India Agriculture Operations Division Report, Irrigation Sector Review, and the Arun III Dam (Nepal) decision from the Bank's Inspection Panel.

35   Ferguson studied development agencies' work in Lesotho and found the following: 'The "instrument-effect", then, is two-fold: alongside the institutional effect of expanding [non-local] bureaucratic state power is the conceptual or ideological effect of depoliticizing both poverty and the state' (Ferguson 1994:256).

36 Escobar researched development's nutrition and hunger projects in Colombia. Although these projects had practically no effect on reducing hunger or malnourishment, he argues, the instrument-effects of these interventions profoundly transformed the conditions under which people live, in particular their integration into external market relations and into the new terrain of class-dominated power relations this integration entails (1995:109).

37 Most arguments on the 'population problem' promote (sometimes inadvertently) coercion of the South's majority, especially females. By and large, arguments that do not focus on North–South, gender, race and class power dimensions of human history typically find simple technological and elite-scientific 'solutions' to the complex social reality that produces densely populated communities forced to compete over too few resources. For an alternative view, see Lappé and Schurman (1988) and Hartmann (1987).

2

Social Movements and the Remaking of the Commons in the Brazilian Amazon

Antonio Carlos Diegues

In Brazil, common property regimes do not exist like artefacts from an archaeological dig, existing today as time-worn versions of their distant past. Although typically made 'invisible' by the state and other elite actors, rubber tappers, artisanal fisherfolk and forest harvesters have successfully struggled to reaffirm and rebuild their commons as vibrant community-based institutions of natural resource appropriation and land and water management. Under constant threat by land speculation, urbanization and capitalist expansion, the commons none the less survive in the hands of diverse social groups who, up until recently, have been politically weak and geographically isolated.

This chapter tries to show that contrary to the conventional view of the ecological commons in the Brazilian Amazon, resource-management institutions are not moribund, and resource-using commoners are not passive in the face of powerful actors eager to transform the Amazon into a profit-making machine. Recent attempts to occupy and deforest the Amazon have unleashed new social movements that are rebuilding and creating new common property regimes as a strategy for democratizing production and social institutions in the Amazon. It is from these forest-based social movements – typically portrayed as backward and in 'need' of modernization – that we see some of the more positive efforts to transform Brazil into a more democratic and ecologically sustainable society. As they strengthen their ties with regional, national and international movements, commoners from the Amazon appear to be one of the more serious challenges to the current neoliberal policies of the state. Their success in rebuilding the commons in the Amazon, however, is ultimately linked to political strategies elsewhere in Brazil. But, their efforts to build social institutions of equality, justice and sustainability may become the catalyst for progressive

54

political change, starting from deep within the Amazon and extending outwards to Rio and beyond.

'The commoners' thrive in marginal but biologically rich ecosystems, such as the Amazonian humid forest. Their communal social institutions have existed in many forms and places, and are characterized by a common utilization of renewable resources such as fish, forest and medicinal plants, cattle and products of shifting agriculture. Common appropriation regimes typically exist alongside, and benefit from, sites where families 'privately' grow, raise and/or produce vegetable gardens and domesticated animals, hunt and gather, and make craft products. Access to these marine and terrestrial resources and space is dependent upon participation in the social kinship life through *compadrio* (kinship/godparent) ties. These appropriation regimes continue to prosper in part because of the strongly held view that renewable resources must be conservatively managed and not overexploited.

These traditional institutions contradict, in practice, Hardin's 'tragedy of the commons' theory (1968). In his highly influential writings, US biologist Garrett Hardin argued that commoners would necessarily overexploit communally owned resources, destroying everyone's natural resource base, as well as profitability. But the Brazilian experience reveals that Hardin's universal remedy for resource management – privatization – does not necessarily lead to a more rational use of natural resources, as private appropriation schemes for cattle raising and large-scale agriculture in the Amazon over the past 50 years have demonstrated. In Brazil, instead of talking about the 'tragedy of the commons', one should consider that there is a 'tragedy of the commoners' (McCay and Acheson 1987), as they have been consistently expelled from their traditional territories through land speculation, large state-owned hydro-electric plants, and wildly irresponsible development schemes.

From the 1960s onwards, common property regimes have been under tremendous pressure and commoners all over Brazil have been stripped of their rights of access to renewable resources, often through violent expropriation. Many rural communities have mobilized in response, forcing the state to formally recognize their rights, including those whom the state refers to as 'squatters' or people without property titles. For example, in the 1980s, the state reluctantly agreed to set-up 'extractivist reserves' (*reservas extrativistas*) for rubber tappers and for fisherfolk along estuaries, rivers and bays in the Amazon. Thus, sprinkled across the Amazon, one finds social movements articulating a national political agenda to *rebuild the commons* in some places and establish new common property regimes in others. Remarkably, movements have forced the state to legally recognize their common property regimes as national models for 'sustainable development' and for conservation of biological and cultural diversity.

In the Brazilian case, the rebuilding of commons has been possible only after the rebirth of democracy, after the long years of military dictatorship (1966–84). The military regime promoted 'economic modernization' or rapid colonization of Brazil's frontiers (e.g. the Amazon) through massive fiscal incentives for cattle raising, mining operations and large power plants that ultimately have led to rapid devastation of natural resources and expropriation of traditional local communities of Indians, rubber tappers, and riverine fisherfolk (Diegues 1992b). The social reaction against these processes was at the same time cause and consequence of the opening of new democratic spaces in Brazil, through the creation of rural unions, local movements, non-governmental groups and progressive political parties. In this context, the emergence of collective actions at the local level (Ostrom 1990) was only possible because they were backed by large social mobilizations, the rise of a powerful political consciousness and the creation of new cultural symbols.

Collective actions concerning the commons have erupted across Brazil's vast landscape, motivated by a number of social forces. First, extensive environmental degradation throughout the Amazon and Atlantic forest has cultivated an ecologically conscious populace. Second, non-governmental organizations (NGOs) linked to international activist organizations have offered their support to local collective actors, mobilizing their capacities to exert pressure on multilateral banking institutions, industrial countries' parliaments and the Brazilian state. The successful campaign to find Chico Mendes' killer and to support, in part, his organizing plans, is one such example. Third, some Indian and non-Indian cultures have become more socially visible and better organized. Often these peoples' organizations have received the support of important national institutions, such as the Catholic Church. In the late 1980s, local movements, NGOs and research groups were able to establish important alliances around issues such as forest conservation, marine resources conservation and social participation in rural areas because of these strategic alliances. These social and ecological practices and processes are crucial factors in the movements to rebuild common property regimes in Amazonia.

Deforestation and the Conditions for New Social Movements

The recent occupation of Amazonia must be seen in the context of modernization politics and capital accumulation and not simply in terms of so-called development. Because of its possibilities for rapid capital accumulation, over the last few decades, Amazonia – the last significant frontier in Brazil – has been catapulted into the national economy. This massive appropriation of the region's renewable and non-renewable resources by national and international capital has resulted in unprecedented depletion of the natural resources and the marginalization of the local population. These rapid changes were fuelled by two critical ideological constructs: Amazonia as *geographical vacuum* and as *economic panacea*.

First, the ideological dimension in effect during the 20 years of military rule (from 1964 to 1984) was the 'geographical vacuum'. Half of the Brazilian territory had to be occupied at any cost. Since the 1970s this strategy had a clear geopolitical dimension, expressed in huge economic programmes such as the National Integration Program. Long and costly highways such as the Transamazon and the Northern Perimetral Highway (running close to the northern frontiers of the country) were initiated and partially completed. In order to occupy the region with Brazilians, the government encouraged the arrival of landless peasants from the northeast and from areas with land conflicts in the south. Hundreds of thousands of peasants poured into the region, most of whom lacked the farming experience and capital necessary for survival in a totally different, aggressive tropical environment. Some of these newcomers arrived spontaneously, attracted by the publicized availability of cheap land, while others came in groups to set up organized settlements, as was the case in the State of Rondônia.

Most settlements quickly failed, principally because of land conflicts, but also because of the low fertility of the forest land, lack of services (marketing, extension-work and social infrastructure) and an unfamiliar environment (Diegues 1992b). In fact, the recent occupation of Amazonia has resulted in the highest number of land conflicts, proportionally speaking, in Brazilian history. It opposes, on the one hand, the traditional dwellers (the Amerindian tribes, the riverine and forest extractive populations) and, on the other, the newcomers, such as farmers and Brazilian and multinational cattle-ranching and mining interests.

By the mid-1970s the military government's strategy had changed. Replacing agricultural settlements of small farmers were grandiose mining projects (Grande Carajás), large dams (Tucuruí and Balbina), industrial centres (São Luís do Maranhão and Manaus) reliant on mineral processing and free zones, and large agribusiness projects. These projects benefited not only from a number of tax incentives, but also from the plentiful cheap labour available, composed principally of those farmers who had abandoned their plots of land.

The second ideological dimension to the recent widespread occupation is the fallacious assumption that the Amazon could be an instrument for solving overall structural problems brought about by the failed 'Brazilian economic miracle' of the 1970s based on uneven capital accumulation in the southern regions. In fact, in the mid-1960s, the already highly concentrated land-tenure system became even more unequal as the result of the labour-saving technology (called modernization) implanted in the south, which forced the labour force off the fields. Many of the small farmers and tenants in the wealthy southern states were forced to sell their plots as intensively mechanized soybean production expanded, which required larger areas of land and less labour input. Many farm workers, especially sharecroppers and other tenants, lost their sole source of income. As a result, 2.5 million peasants migrated from the rural areas of the state of Paraná alone during the 1970s. Many migrated to Rondônia, where they began clearing the forests.

Attempts to introduce land reform met fierce opposition from big landowners. The federal government's modest attempt at land distribution in 1985 was also a failure. Opposition to land reform has also increased deforestation in Amazonia, as many big landowners, fearing land reform, burned large tracts of forest to 'improve' the land, as a means of escaping agrarian reform in their latifundia. According to Brazilian legislation, clearing of a forest is a sign that the landowner is using the land productively, and thus should not be expropriated.

The ideology of occupying Amazonia at any costs was backed up by a series of incentives for large livestock-raising and agricultural schemes in the region, since latex extraction and nut harvesting by traditional populations were considered backward economic activities which failed to effectively occupy, or sufficiently utilize, the territory. Since 1966, when special subsidies and incentives were created, 581 projects have been approved for agriculture and cattle raising (Oliveira 1989). These projects cover an area of over nine million hectares, the average area per project being 16,300 ha in Pará and 31,400 ha in Mato Grosso. A study carried out by Yokomizo (1989) concluded that of 92 projects analysed, only three were profitable. Multinational enterprises not only bought land in the region, but benefited from incentives as well and from the infrastructure established in the region by the government. One study (Eglin and Thery 1982) identified 19 multinational groups in Amazonia, owning approximately 7,342,000 ha of land, used for logging, cattle raising, agriculture and speculation.

Pasture for cattle is the main use of the deforested land in Amazonia and the impact of this cattle raising on the forest environment is much more severe than that of small farming activities. According to Hall (1989) less labour-intensive forms of land use have the highest impact on the Amazon forest, as is the case of logging and ranching. Many studies have shown the non-sustainability of cattle ranching in the region (Hecht 1982, Fearnside 1989). These studies show that the initial enrichment of soils (from cutting and burning of biomass) is basically detrimental to the total available supply of nutrients in the ecosystem. Lacking the defences of the diversified natural system, within a few years many pastures were invaded by pests and weeds. Many ranchers overgrazed in some areas and then abandoned the deteriorated pastures. The high costs of chemical fertilizers (Amazonia has no known phosphate deposits) and of weed control meant that ranchers found it more profitable to clear new forest than to recuperate old pastures (Goodland 1988). It is clear, then, that large agricultural and cattle-raising projects (combined with land speculation) were responsible for most of the deforestation, as compared with forest cutting by small farmers or slash-and-burn agri-culturalists. In fact, large projects have often expanded their holdings by buying out or forcing small farmers off their lands. Small farmers were frequently used by large companies to clear the forest, plant food crops for one or two agricultural seasons and then grow pasture (Gall 1978). Logging companies also received special incentives in the lumber-extracting areas of the State of Pará. In the State of Pará alone, lumber extraction grew 4,000 per cent during 1970s (Schmink 1988) and logging roads opened up access for clearing the forests.

The failure of the previous strategy is reflected, for example, in the large number of small farmers who abandoned farming to become gold placer miners (*garimpeiros*) often roaming from one of these open mining sites to the other. Today this quasi-nomad population comprises over 600,000 people. Gold prospecting, undertaken by both placer miners and firms is a widespread practice along many river areas of Amazonia, causing serious health and environmental problems.

From these state-instigated migration flows, the region's population rose from approximately 2.6 million inhabitants in 1960 to 8.6

million in 1989 according to the IGBE (Brazilian Geographic and Statistical Institute). Between 1970 and 1980, the annual population growth in Amazonia was 5 per cent compared with 2.5 per cent for the country as a whole. This high increase in population, however, was unevenly distributed and is now concentrated in the capital cities in the north (notably Manaus and Belém), in the State of Rondônia and in southeastern Pará. There is a generalized 'pull' effect on populations of poor farmers and traditional peoples attracted by large economic projects. The increase in the urban population has been higher than that in the rural regions and more than 65 per cent now live in urban centres. The slum areas in and around the cities have increased dramatically, even though job opportunities and most of the social services are highly deficient. The rush of migrants to the 'attractive' Free Trade Zone of Manaus has been met with the availability of relatively few jobs.

The impact of 'modernization' has resulted in the indiscriminate depletion of the forest in many regions. By 1989, as much as 8 per cent of the total Amazon had been deforested, an area almost the size of France. Recent studies show that the rhythm of deforestation decreased in 1992, but increased again in 1993 and 1994, particularly in Rondônia, southern Pará and in the newly created state of Tocantins (INPE 1995). The impact of forest clearing is serious, not only in ecological terms (loss of biodiversity, aggravation of the greenhouse effect, soil erosion, etc.) but also in social and cultural terms. The livelihood of the traditional populations has been deeply affected. As enormous numbers of rubber and nut trees have been felled, income and employment opportunities have been lost, forcing people to migrate to the urban areas. As productivity decreased, after a few years of land cultivation, small farmers also abandoned their plots and migrated farther north. In many cases the land was sold to speculators from the south or to large neighbouring cattle ranches. Many migrants then became wage earners on large plantations or else they ventured out to the placer mines in search of gold. Native Indian reserves are being invaded by these individual miners as well as large logging and mining companies, making them the most vulnerable communities in the Amazon.

By the end of the 1980s there were signs that the government was intending to change some of the most damaging policies leading to deforestation in Amazonia. In April 1989 President Sarney announced a new programme for the region, called Our Nature (*Nossa Natureza*). This initiative came at a moment when the federal government was under heavy opposition due to a number of different events. A few months before, the well-known leader of the rubber tappers, Chico

Mendes, was murdered and his death brought about a major national and international reaction. It is likely that the government was concerned with the possible suspension or cancellation of a number of multilateral loans, including the follow-up of the North-western Development Program (POLONOROESTE), due to pressure from environmentalists at home and abroad.

The Our Nature programme had a very nationalistic tone, reaffirming Brazilian sovereignty over Amazonia and deep concern for what sectors such as the army called the dangerous 'internationalization of the region'. The programme instigated broad environmental protection and research activities and established national forests and parks. Some investments by SUDAM (the government's supervising organ for the Amazon) were suspended and limits were placed on round-log exports. By 1990, it was also clear that no money had been allocated for the programme and nothing important would come from it, except for the creation of IBAMA, Brazil's major environmental institute.

In March 1990, the newly elected president, Fernando Collor de Mello, took office in the midst of a political crisis, an annual inflation rate of more than 4,500 per cent, high foreign debt and a fall in the GNP. Collor appointed a highly respected environmental activist, Dr Lutzemberger, to head a new environmental secretariat, known as SEMA, with the president's support to addressing the most pressing environmental questions, particularly in the Amazonia. A total ban on incentives and on the export of hardwood logs was established. There was also a commitment to remove gold miners from the Yanomami reservation and to halt the construction of new pig-iron smelters along the Carajás Railway. From the beginning, Lutzemberger fought for a new style of development for Amazonia, and attempted to halt the paving of the highway extending from Rio Branco, in the Brazilian State of Acre, to Pucalba in Peru. He favoured forest management and extractive reserves. By that time, deforestation was actually slowing down, more due to the deepening financial crisis than to a sea-change in governmental action.

Lutzemberger soon ran into enormous opposition from various social sectors, including the environmental movement, who began criticizing him for being more active outside Brazil than inside, where crucial environmental problems were being ignored. Lutzemberger's strongest opposition came from the newly elected governors of the states which comprise Amazonia, most of whom favoured development of the region at any cost. These governors, backed by the same social conservative forces that had benefited from the previous incentives, also received support from sectors of the army, which believes Amazonian NGOs are directed by Northern governments in order to diminish the sovereignty of Brazil over the Amazon region. Lobbying by these governors and members of the Congress is very strong, and it appears that some of the destructive incentives which had been eliminated are now making a return.

Deforestation and the Extractivist Populations

In Amazonia a large rural population relies on the forest and its products for survival. Approximately 1,500,000 people, or 33 per cent of Amazonian rural population, harvest forest products in combination with subsistence agriculture and fishing (Allegretti 1987b). In addition, the Amerindian population, of approximately 220,000 persons, also rely on forest products such as rubber, oils, fruits and fibre. While extractive production has declined in terms of the share of the total dollar-value income generated in Acre, Amazonas and Rondônia from 1970 to 1980, it is still of substantial economic importance and its value continues to increase in absolute terms. In Acre, while the area occupied for extraction decreased from 1970 to 1980, and the areas of cattle ranching and agriculture increased dramatically, the per hectare value of extraction increased much more than either meat or crop production. At the same time, rubber exports increased as a share of overall state exports. The business of extraction, therefore, has become an attractive development alternative to cattle or agriculture for small producers. Whereas almost half of the small producers in the Amazon earn less than the minimum wage, the average annual income for forest extractors in the early 1990s was US$ 1,500, or twice the minimum wage (Allegretti 1987a). Moreover, the greater sustainability of extractive activities – they do not destroy forests – makes it a more attractive long-term alternative.

Rubber tappers typically live in *colocações*, which are both living areas and productive units in the forest. In the centre of *colocações*, *seringueiro* families build houses made of *paixiuba* (a palm tree). Most of the *colocações* are established at the side of an *igarapé* (small river). This production unit is customarily around 300 to 600 hectares in area. The latex is collected from the rubber trees and transformed into rubber through smoking over a fire. In the *colocação*, shifting agriculture, hunting and fishing are also essential livelihood activities. Every day, the *seringueiro* walks several kilometres through a path called *estrada da seringa*. In order to earn a minimum income, the *seringueiro* has to extract latex from 100 to 150 trees daily, producing around 500 kilograms of rubber. In order to survive, each *seringueiro* has to work some 200 to 300 rubber trees (Allegretti 1987a). There is no division of labour in the rubber extraction process. The tapping and transformation into latex is done individually by the *seringueiro*, who stays the whole day in the forest. Under these conditions, each *seringueiro* family is very isolated as *seringueiros* are dispersed throughout the forest. As explained above, the main outside contact of the *seringueiro* is with the *barracão*, a warehouse belonging to the rubber baron, where he buys what he needs at a high price. The free producer deals with the middleman (*regatão*) from whom he buys the goods he needs.

The impact of deforestation on the *seringueiros* has been disastrous. From the beginning of the 1970s, with the state policies of encouraging occupation of Amazonia based on cattle raising and fiscal incentives, the situation of the rubber tappers worsened dramatically. These policies contributed to changes in land ownership and use that deprived the rubber tappers of access to their traditional sources of livelihood. Since the 1970s, there has been an increasing concentration of land in the hands of a few large owners, most of whom come from the south. At the same time, the number of smaller holdings has increased. In Acre, for instance, between 1960 and 1970, the area predominantly devoted to extraction fell by 65 per cent, while the area devoted to agriculture increased 410 per cent and cattle ranching by 132 per cent. During the same period, the number of holdings devoted to extraction increased by over 1,000 per cent, implying that the traditional rubber-producing estates were fragmented as rubber barons withdrew or sold out and independent rubber production was taken by free rubber tappers. In 1970, the number of holdings smaller than 500 hectares represented 57 per cent of the total number of holdings while in 1960, these were only 9.5 per cent of the holdings (Schwartzman 1989). Consequently the number of small producers, particularly renters and occupants, increased. This reflects the emergence of autonomous rubber tappers who are largely occupants with precarious tenure or, in some cases, renters.

Consequently, large rubber tree and Brazil nut-tree areas are being transformed into cattle ranches. Although these trees are protected by law and should not be cut, all other trees are usually cut and burned. This hinders the survival of the protected trees which remain semi-burned and isolated in the middle of new pastures. One of the areas of widespread destruction of Brazil nut and rubber trees is the southern part of Pará where many large cattle-raising farms have been established. In the same area, pig-iron plants are being developed and, as a consequence, large areas of those valuable trees are being cut and burned for charcoal. At the same time, logging activities also responsible for the destruction of Brazil nut trees, are increasing dramatically (Allegretti 1987b). The expansion of cattle ranches and other large (usually speculative) holdings is responsible for the expulsion of the *seringueiros* from their traditional lands and activities. Many of them became wage earners on the ranches or have migrated to the outskirts of the new towns of Amazonia. Often they become temporary workers, migrating from one place to another, or have entered gold-mining activities as *garimpeiro*.

Not only are the rubber-tapping areas being reduced but deforestation is also affecting the availability of fish in the *igarapés* and game from the forest, which deprives forest extractors of their main sources of protein. Rivers are also being polluted by mercury used by the *garimpeiros* (Petrere 1989). River fishing is still the most important source of protein for the Amazonian population and fish consumption there is highest in Brazil, over 35 kg per person per year. (Diegues 1992a). Fishing also employs a large number of people either for subsistence or for commercial purposes. But in recent years, larger farmers are putting fences close to the rivers, creating serious conflicts with traditional fisherfolk. At the same time, people coming from urban areas using predatory fishing gear are depleting the fish supplies in the area. As a result, riverine fisherfolk are organizing themselves to manage the lakes – the biologically richest areas – on a communal basis (Hartman 1989, Loureiro 1991).

The Indian population in Amazonia is the single human group suffering most from deforestation and related large development projects such as mining, dams and road construction. Since the European colonization of Brazil began 500 years ago, the number of indigenous people has declined from six million people to its current level of about 220,000. These survivors speak more than 140 languages and dialects. Prior to the arrival of the Europeans, the indigenous population was widely distributed across Brazil, consisting primarily of hunter-gatherers, many of them living in the Amazon forest. These Amazonian peoples were the last indigenous groups to be destroyed by contact with the colonizers, mainly because they lived in isolated forested areas. The progressive displacement of indigenous people resulted from physical extermination, enslavement and especially the spread of new diseases to which they had no resistance. Some 70 per cent of the remaining indigenous population lives in the north and central-west regions where Western-style 'civilization' has only recently appeared (CEDI 1987).

After 1910, the Brazilian authorities adopted measures designed to protect native people from the most extreme forms of violence and other conditions leading to long-term population decline. Some institutions like FUNAI (previously SPI) were created to protect Indian communities, but their activities were often ineffective in checking continuous aggression by outsiders, and sometimes even abetted it. During the first half of the twentieth century alone, some 87 distinct Indian groups were exterminated (Farren 1989).

The main policy to protect Indians has been to establish 'reserves'. By 1990, some 27,000,000 hectares of land had been set aside as reserves; almost half of this area was included in the last four years. Many of these reserves, however, have not been physically delineated. As their limits are not clear, invasions by loggers, *garimpeiros*, large companies, ranchers, speculators and others are common and frequently lead to open conflicts. The extension of these reserves is often criticized by large agricultural and mining interests with the argument that too much land has been allocated to too few Indians. Other Brazilians, however, suggest that these Indians have inhabited those areas for centuries and that they require access to large areas of forest in order to survive. Moreover, they point out that in Brazil, the land controlled by only a few latifundiarios is far more than all that has been set aside as Indian reserves. Overall, the threats to Indian lands come from a number of sources, including invasions of gold- and cassiterite-mining operations, commercial logging, landless peasants and large dams. Together, they threaten to completely undermine Indian social institutions and the ecosystems on which they depend.

As a consequence of these invasions, Amazonia is at present the region with the highest rate of land conflicts in Brazil. The unplanned occupation of the area has led to many heated and often violent disputes throughout the region between squatters or other occupants with precarious tenure and landholders. Those claiming legal titles to the land are often the much feared *grileiros* (land speculators) who commonly engage *pistoleiros* (hired gunmen) in order to drive small farmers off the land they occupy. Land tenure, especially access to land for cultivation and housing, is currently the most conflictive social and political issue in that region. These conflicts have been aggravated by the government's retreat in 1988 from proposing long-promised programmes of agrarian reform. Human rights abuses in the Amazon region are all particularly centred around land tenure issues (Farren 1989).

Violence, however, is not limited strictly to land title issues but is also used by landlords to obtain cheap labour. Most of the workers in the *fazendas* (livestock and agricultural estates) are hired through middlemen (*gatos*) to clear the forest. Most of the workers are financed by the *gatos* and as a result are in debt to them. In many cases they are stuck in the *fazendas* without being able to leave as they are not in a position to pay their debt. This debt peonage is made effective through use of force. Many rural union and Indian leaders have been killed in conflicts over land and labour. So too have several progressive Catholic priests who took positions in favour of the rural poor. During the last 20 years, over 150,000 people were involved in land conflicts in the region, resulting in thousands of deaths of rural leaders, particularly in the states of Pará, Maranhão and Goiás.

Rebuilding the Commons through New Social Movements

Until the 1960s, social conflicts in the region were not as acute as they have been since, and local populations were not as well-organized to oppose domination and exploitation. During the last two decades, however, the local population has been deeply affected by the violent processes of land and natural resources expropriation. Many negatively affected groups have started to react and to organize.

By the end of the 1980s, a series of national and international events and situations placed Amazonia in the public spotlight. First, when the military dictatorship ended, several social groups and political parties seeking constituencies were instrumental in organizing a politics of protest and resistance amongst rubber tappers, homesteaders (*posseiros*), Indians and small-scale miners (*garimpeiros*). In the 1970s, agencies of the Catholic Church (e.g. Pastoral Land Commission (CPT) and the Missionary Council on the Indigenous People (CIMI)) publicized incidents of violence in the region, openly criticized the military and assisted in the creation of rural unions and other local institutions. Soon after, the *seringueiros* and indigenous communities started a number of political organizations, such as the Union of Indigenous Nations (UNI).

Internationally, too, the Amazon hit the spotlight. First, in the late 1980s during a severe drought in the US, some scientists and environmentalists started to make the links between large-scale deforestation in the Amazon and the 'greenhouse' effect caused by increased forest burning. Several networks were established between Brazilian and US NGOs denouncing deforestation and violence in the Amazon. US NGOs such as the Natural Resources Defense Council, the Environmental Defense Fund and the National Wildlife Federation started lobbying the US Congress to pressure the World Bank and the InterAmerican Development Bank to stop funding large projects that were carving up the forest, particularly in Rondônia and Acre (POLONOROESTE).

Due to these pressures, the World Bank halted disbursement of the POLONOROESTE loan, pending compliance by the government with new loan conditionalities that superficially, at least, covered forest and indigenous people's protection issues. These political pressures provoked surprise and resentment amongst Brazilian politicians and the military, stirring up suspicion that foreign agents were behind these environmental concerns. Many believed that the sudden appearance of Amazonian leaders, such as Chico Mendes and Indian chiefs (*caciques*), in foreign capitals was actually a media strategy to mask imperialistic designs on the Amazon's natural resource base. But as one observer points out:

> The danger of internationalisation of Amazonia evoked by the Brazilian Government is a myth, to the extent that society has long been part of a national/transnational world. Moreover, it is a myth that can be used to cover up the perversity of the national policy for regional occupation. It does not, however, exclude the reality of political pressure by governments and international corporations brought to bear under new form. Planet-wide awareness is real and it is active, which does not preclude, however, formation of a form of ecological ideology favouring those very forms of pressure. (Becker 1992:95)

By the end of the 1980s, particularly after the assassination of rubber-tapper leader Chico Mendes, forest dwellers rallied to form a national coalition to protect their interests. In 1989, the Kayapó Indians, after expanding their international public campaigns, hosted a six-day First Encounter of Native Peoples, in Altamira, Xingu, in which over 600 indigenous leaders, Brazilian and foreign supporters, journalists and a few celebrities participated. They condemned the invasion of the Yanomami Indians' land by new ELETROBRAS plans to build several large dams in the Amazon. Meanwhile, protest forced the World Bank to withdraw loans from Brazil's energy sector and, instead, provide (very small) funds for energy conservation, which further enraged Brazilian authorities.

One government strategy to control deforestation in the Amazon is the establishment of protected areas, such as national parks and ecological stations. These areas are also created to meet the requirements of international institutions, such as the World Bank, when large development programmes such as the POLONOROESTE are funded. One of the contradictions in this process is that such protected areas follow the North American model of creating wilderness in which no dweller is allowed to stay (Diegues 1996). Brazilian legislation on protected areas unequivocally states that rubber tappers, riverine groups and artisanal fisherfolk are not allowed onto their own territories in order that certain places can be 'preserved'. This environmental policy has sparked numerous conflicts as local populations have refused to leave their land.

By the late 1980s, resistance to land eviction became so strong that a new form of protected area was proposed, commonly called 'extractive reserves'. The creation of this new category of protected area – in which locals can actually continue to live and work – was a direct result of sustained protest movements by 'commoners', especially rubber tappers and artisanal fisherfolk, often with NGO assistance. Today, there are nine extractive reserves covering two million hectares on which more than 28,000 people live (CNPT 1994). The economic activities in these reserves include small-scale fishing, babassu and Brazilian nut-tree harvesting and rubber tapping. The most remarkable aspect of these reserves, however, is that they represent a resurgence of locally managed common property regimes. That is, social and political confrontations over the past two decades between traditional populations and both large landowners and the state have led to innovative, practical and democratic reconstruction of threatened common property regimes as well as the creation of new types.

In this vibrant political landscape, three distinct strands of activism thrive in the Amazon. First, autonomous local movements unrelated to broader social movements are responding, protesting and organizing around aggressive and unjust state actions. Above all, they are fighting to defend their territory and social institutions against external interventions. Although they appear as the weakest of the three types, they are more dispersed across the map, more spontaneous and perhaps more abundant. Second, local movements with incipient alliances with non-local NGOs are working to fight projects, legislation and other oppressive state activities. They appear to be better organized, with more facilities and non-local support to sustain forms of resistance. Third, the rubber tappers have organized the extractive reserves movement. They are well connected to larger social movements, but their strategies, skills and tools come mostly from within their local ranks. The rubber-tappers movement emerged in the 1970s during the height of conflict over land grabs in Acre;

at that point, they organized the first rural union in Brazil. By 1985, they had organized a national council as well as a constructive plan for extractive reserves. Only by the mid-1980s did they start to link up with other national and international social movements. As we will show below, these three types of commons-based movements collectively reflect the diversity of practices, politics and worldviews of Brazilians dependent upon the commons for their livelihood.

Brazil has two types of social movements of traditional communities living in protected areas – local movements with and without direct links to broad national movements. Those without links can be considered as local reactions against the administration of conservation or protected areas that curtails traditional forest harvesting, hunting and agricultural practices. They are also local spontaneous reactions against territorial invasions by outsiders, a process that can result in the unofficial declaration of an 'exclusive resource use unit' by the environmental authorities. They have succeeded in pressuring park administrators to open up negotiating channels on the alternative use of natural resources. These local movements or institutions are, however, incipient and weak and still subordinate to state administrations.

Spontaneous local movements are local instances of resistance and organization of small-scale local extractivist producers, in defence of their traditional territory. They have the objective of gaining control over access to natural resources, and which in some instances came to be recognized by IBAMA (Instituto Brasileiro do Meio Ambiente) as legitimate (or tolerable) forms of action. One example is the case of the fishers of Rio Cuiabá, near Santo Antonio do Leverger, who traditionally fished with canoes and hand-lines in deep pools in the river that were rich in fish. They would *sevar* the fishing sites – that is, throw corn or other types of food in the water regularly to attract fish. Recently, amateur fishers from southern Brazil have began to appear with motorboats and have preyed on the fishing resources, without using the *sevar* method. In reaction, locals formed river patrols and only permitted the 'Southerners' to fish if they used the traditional way of the region. This method, however, demands great ability, because the local fishers do not use weights to anchor their boats. Rather, they use one hand to paddle and the other to hold the line, which turned out to be impossible for the southern sport fishers. IBAMA later recognized this location as an area for the exclusive use of local fishers, giving it the character of natural resource conservation.

Another autonomous movement of fishers are the ones who have collectively closed off lakes in the Amazon region. These lake communities have assumed control of the territories that they have traditionally occupied but which now were threatened by commercial fishers coming from the cities. For example, many *vargeiros* and riverine communities of Amazonia have had access to their local fishing sites reduced by the fences of large landowners. Commercial fishers from the cities are also employing predatory fishing equipment to overfish the waters. The *vargeiros* from many rivers of Amazonia spontaneously closed lakes for the sake of their survival and to protect the natural resources. IBAMA eventually expressed some support for these fisherfolk through the establishment of fishing reserves in Amazonia. This struggle has produced more than new rules of access to the lakes. According to one observer:

> The closing of the lakes has brought together a movement to delineate their territories, which in practice amounts to small community ownership. The affirmation of communal ownership is, in this context, an affirmation of communal responsibilities and rights shared by consent of the community members, who depend for their subsistence on the use of a specific territory, without, however, having any legal basis for this affirmation. (Ayres and Ayres 1993:3)

These processes of communal appropriation have been met, however, with extensive physical violence. In one conflictive situation, IBAMA's protected area officials joined up with the Federal Police to harass *quilombo* communities (originally established by escaped African slaves as places of refuge) of the Trombetas River area for their extractivist activities of fishing and nut collecting. In 1979, the IBDF (which became IBAMA) created the Ecological Reserve of Trombetas, in an area long used by the inhabitants of Trombetas. IBAMA, assisted by the Federal Police, took hunting and fishing equipment from the residents, in a manner similar to the repression by mining companies that had become established in the area, such as Alcoa, Mineração Rio Norte and Eletronorte, who were considered by the Afro-Brazilians from Trombetas as 'foreign' in opposition to the local populations. The establishment of the ecological reserve on the left side of the Trombetas River, and the later creation, in 1989, of the National Forest on the right side of the same river, made the way of life of these people unviable. Those who insisted on staying on their land were not allowed to hunt, fish or plant crops. For these Afro-Brazilians, the restrictions imposed by IBAMA were considered as a new slavery, destroying their way of life, and threatening their cultural connections with the falls and the waters, which they consider sacred. Some old residents were expelled three times from their homes, by three different entities — Mineração Santa Patrícia, IBAMA and Alcoa. For most of the old inhabitants, this 'new slavery' meant misery and an unacceptable life in favelas and *beiradões* (shacks built along the river-bank) to where they moved after being displaced by the large projects and protected areas.

This case shows an alliance of the private forces (mining companies) and public (IBAMA) is physically and culturally destroying a population that until now had lived in harmony with the forests and rivers of Amazonia. In the view of these institutions, the action is legitimated by the appeal to 'economic and ecological modernity', according to which the expulsion of the Afro-Brazilians of Trombetas is considered fundamental to the establishment of 'ecological modernity', characterized by the need to separate humans and nature through the constitution of protected natural areas. This will ensure the 'economic modernity' needed to obtain high profits for the mining companies, according to the plans of the military regime for the occupation of the 'vacant spaces' of Amazonia (Acevedo and Castro 1993).

The second type of local movement in isolated regions are those supported by NGOs and research institutes. One example is the project of the Mamirauá Ecological Station, in the State of Amazonas, administered by the Mamirauá Civil Society and supported by several international environmental non-governmental organizations, among them the World Wildlife Fund (WWF). The EEM (Mamirauá Ecological Station) covers more than one million hectares, having been created to protect a large part of the floodplain between the Japurá and Solimôes rivers. In this huge area live 4,500 *vargeiros,* spread over 50 small communities, with an average of 14 households in each. These communities live from fishing, hunting and gathering forest products. Along with these traditional activities, however, there is logging for sale to the sawmills in the cities.

Contrary to what is required by legislation – expulsion of the population of the area – the project administrators decided to allow the *vargeiros* to remain in this territory where they have always lived. During the floods, water covers millions of hectares, making law enforcement an impossible task. The administrative team, belonging to a local non-governmental organization, believed that only with community participation could the biodiversity and culture of the region be protected. This type of management, however, is different from the establishment and imposition of 'management plans' by scientists and bureaucrats. It requires a longer time for development, since it depends on continuous consultation and a constant dialogue with local populations, inclusion of social scientists in research teams and more flexibility in planning. It places more value on the process of decision making than on the establishment of rigid conservation objectives. The experience of this project has demonstrated, however, that once a decision is taken by the local population, it has a much greater chance of being followed. This is demonstrated, for example, in the consensus that was reached by the local population in regards to the conservation and sustainable use of lakes, which had extreme biological and socio-economic importance.

In these discussions, the communities decided to define six categories of lakes, including totally preserved areas, such as lakes for reproduction of fish (untouchable, with the shoreline included in the area of total preservation), 'subsistence lakes' (for exclusive use of the community for subsistence fishing), 'market-oriented lakes' (for exclusive use of the community, with the fish to be sold), and 'lakes for use of the nearby urban centres' (where fishing is permitted to satisfy the needs of municipalities). The communities, in an assembly, also decided on the types of sanctions to be applied to those community members who disobeyed the decisions. The administrators of EEM concluded:

> With the definition of the limited areas for professional fishing, it is hoped to create some kind of 'social responsibility' between the fishermen, of the urban centres and local fishermen that leads the community members to defend, almost in unison, the preservation of lakes and non-predatory fishing . . . The consensus reached means that there is a good chance that the decisions taken will be carried out, thereby reducing the requirement for additional effort in implementing these decisions, and was judged by the Mamirauá Project Team as being very satisfactory from the biological, geographic and conservationist point of view. (Ayres and Ayres 1993:10)

The third type of local movements concerning the commons is typified by the rubber-tappers' extractive reserves – locally initiated and recently supported by national and international coalitions. Created in the 1970s, during the height of conflict over land in Acre, this movement organized the first blockade *(empate)* in which rubber tappers confronted the machines that were cutting down the forest and threatening their way of life. In 1975, when the first rural union was created in Basiléia in Acre, in one of the centres of high density of rubber trees, the reaction of the landowners was violent, and in many cases the houses of the rubber tappers were burned and the leaders assassinated. The National Council of Rubber Tappers, established in 1985, responded with a strategy of pursuing the creation of 'extractive reserves'.

The extractive reserves are administered communally. Although not allocated in individual lots, families have the right to exploit the resources along their traditional extractivist tapping routes (the *colocações*) within the reserves. The land cannot be sold or transformed into non-forest uses, except for small areas that are allowed to be cleared for subsistence agriculture (not more than five hectares per family, or approximately 1–2 per cent of the area of the reserve). The creation of these reserves is also based on the local organization of rubber tappers and on programmes of education, health, cooperativism, marketing and research into alternative systems of forest management.

The community members of extractivist reserves are aware, through their representative organizations, that a legal guarantee against aggression by large economic interests is not enough. It is fundamental that their extractivist production has economic viability, since they currently depend primarily on only a few products, such as rubber, nuts or babassu palm-trees. Rubber production is precarious because of the high cost of production and an external market unfavourable to primary products, and also because of the lower price of latex produced by monoculture plantations in the south of the country. The rubber-tappers solicit government subsidies to maintain prices for rubber on the internal market, while they look for alternative markets for products of Amazonia on the international market. To this end, a few cooperatives are organized to eliminate the middlemen (Schwartzman 1988) and facilitate marketing.

The National Council of Rubber Tappers also created a Centre of Training and Research that, together with Brazilian universities, looked for ways of diversifying production through research and the establishment of systems of management of natural forests, agroforestry, neo-extractivism and genetic conservation (Viana and Kageyama, quoted in Diegues 1992a).

The extractive reserves gained international notoriety after the assassination of the rubber-tappers' leader, Chico Mendes, in 1988. The first extractive reserve was officially created in 1988, and was called the Project of Extractivist Settlement, being part of the National Plan for Agrarian Reform of INCRA (order # 627/INCRA). In 1990, the extractive reserves became part of the protected areas system under the authority of IBAMA (Government Decree # 98897). Based on a movement to support their land rights and their traditional way of life, the rubber tappers began to count on the support of environmental groups and national and international non-governmental organizations. Also, in 1986 the Alliance of the People of the Forest, which also included the indigenous populations, was created. The joint effort of the indigenous leadership, the rubber tappers, and those adversely affected by dams, supported by environmental organizations both within and outside Brazil, made possible, for example, the creation of the Encounter of the People of the Forest, in Altamira in 1989, to protest against the construction of hydro-electric dams on the Xingu River, where many indigenous reserves are located (CEDI 1989). This joint effort was responsible for the suspension of plans to create large dams along the Xingu River.

The rubber-tappers' movement, despite the organized reaction of large landowners through UDR (Democratic Rural Union), expanded not only into Acre, where 60 per cent of the municipalities had rubber-tapper organizations, but also into other states such as Amapá, Rondônia and Amazonas, including ten extractivist settlements and four extractivist reserves covering three million hectares and benefiting around 9,000 families (CIMA 1991). In 1992, IBAMA created CNPT (National Council of Traditional Populations), for the purpose of technical support for the reserves in Amazonia and expanding the idea to other regions of the country. Currently there are other extractivist reserves outside of this region, based on extractivism of babassu, a natural resource of the *cerrado* (savannah vegetation in semi-arid areas), and on fishing resources in Santa Catarina State. The establishment and reinforcement of extractive reserves continues in the Amazonian region and in other areas of the country, not only in the tropical forests, but also along the coastline, as is the case of Pirajurubaé in the State of Santa Catarina and Mandira in São Paulo.

The movement to establish extractivist reserves is an example of defending, reinforcing and recreating threatened ways of life. Furthermore, in Amazonia it is an alternative that can enable the sustainable use of natural resources, which respects both biological diversity and the traditional way of life of populations. As Silberling stated (1990), official and public recognition of these reserves was only made possible by the strong social movement that worked together with the National Council of Rubber Tappers, looking for national as well as international legitimacy, especially in their struggle against other forms of ownership, in particular the large landholdings. They managed, through social mobilization, to raise the levels of consciousness and education of their members, creating and re-creating values of group solidarity fundamental to the continuity of the creative process. The frequent meetings of the leaders of the National Council with the rubber tappers in many regions of Amazonia helped them to organize associations that will propose new reserves. Their ideological and symbolic role has been based on the creation of solidarity involving the support of other groups, social forces and policies within and outside the country, and on obtaining financial and technical resources, along with contributing decisively to the growth of the power of local associations of rubber tappers, who feel linked to a larger movement that transcends Amazonia.

Conclusion

As this chapter illustrates, communal appropriation practices in Brazil is not an issue of the past, but a very critical political strategy of the present. The interest in reviving commons institutions is spreading, as more communities are responding to predatory enclosures of their territories by landlords and investors driven by the political momentum of the expansion of the economic frontier. Commons activism coincides with other social processes aimed at maintaining threatened livelihood of certain traditional communities. It can be seen as a process of social reconstruction of livelihoods that have been partially disorganized by the expansion of the market economy and the encroachment of large private businesses into communally managed sites. In this process of social reaction, it is clear that environmental protection issues related to sustainability play an important role, as some social actors, including government and non-government agencies, see these experiences as 'case studies' leading to the search of 'sustainable development'. It is hard to foresee the outcome of these social experiments, as they contradict the current neoliberal policies of the Brazilian state. The success of these social experiments will clearly depend on their socio-economic sustainability and on the capacity of the support movements to counteract the tremendous strength of powerful latifundia and conservative social forces in Brazil. The success of these social experiments is ultimately linked to the possibility of the establishment of a long-living democracy and the recognition that biological diversity can only be ensured through the empowerment of the resource-dependent commoners who maintain both the biological *and* cultural diversity of Brazil.

3

Between NAFTA and Zapata: Responses to Restructuring the Commons in Chiapas and Oaxaca, Mexico

Lynn Stephen

Indigenous peoples and states in Mexico have a long history of common lands. Well before the arrival of the Spanish in 1519, ruling states such as the Aztec permitted conquered peoples to maintain ancestral territories and common lands. During the colonial period protection of common lands diminished (particularly with a 90 per cent decline in indigenous population), but common lands were preserved in some parts of New Spain. With independence and a series of laws aimed at promoting individual property titling and the disentailment of lands held by the Church, Mexico's indigenous peoples began to lose their common lands at a rapid pace. State development policy during the 'Porfiriato' period (1889–1910) encouraged foreign investment, measuring and purchase of so-called vacant land – an expropriation process that resulted in a landlessness rate of 96 per cent among rural Mexican households (Cockcroft 1983:91). By 1910, Mexico's indigenous population was deprived of 90 per cent of its land (Bartra 1982:36).

Without a doubt, the most enduring legacy of the Mexican revolution has been the agrarian reform constituted under Article 27 of the constitution (and formally in a 1920 law) that allowed for the formation of *ejidos* as collective entities with a legal stature, specific territorial limits, and representative bodies of governance (Baitenmann 1995). *Ejidos* were created to satisfy the demands of landless peasants who had seen their communal village lands eaten up by large agricultural estates and/or who served as labourers on these estates. An *ejido* is a communal form of land tenure to which members have use rights, usually in the form of an individual plot of land. The formation of *ejidos* since the Mexican Revolution has involved the transference of more than 70 million hectares from large estates to slightly more than three million peasant beneficiaries

(Stavenhagen 1986:262). In addition to *ejido* lands, another important part of the rural sector is made up of agrarian communities that hold indigenous common lands based on historical claims usually dating back to pre-Columbian and colonial times (Barry 1995:5).

The amount of land transferred from large estates to *ejidos* varied regionally. In the State of Oaxaca, for example, large landed estates were not the norm. There, haciendas were confined to the central valleys and the coast and indigenous communities managed to hold on to significant amounts of land. Private land was also held by the state's large indigenous population (Taylor 1972). Nevertheless, in these areas where communities had lost land, the formation of *ejidos* marked a significant improvement in the lifestyle of landless day labourers and sharecroppers.

In other areas of Mexico, such as some regions of Chiapas, the Mexican Revolution was tardy in its arrival and, due to entrenched resistance to land redistribution, fewer *ejidos* were formed. Most *ejido* land in Chiapas was transferred in the 1930s and 1940s (Collier 1994:41). The primary source of *ejido* land was opened through colonization of unused forested areas of the jungle. Colonial land, labour and social relations remained intact in many areas of Chiapas until the 1970s when a series of forces including Christian liberation theologists, independent peasant organizations, brutal styles of government and grinding poverty combined to instigate the formation of new *ejidos*, regional organizations of *ejidos* and regional peasant organizations.

In the 1980s, a series of measures aimed at privatization of government enterprises, a loosening of federal regulations to permit and encourage foreign investment and ownership, and the individualization of property and social relations between the state and its citizens have found their logical conclusion in agrarian policy which followed in the wake of the reformation of Article 27 of the Mexican Constitution in 1992. The reformation of Article 27 is part and parcel of a series of policies designed to support the accords reached in the North American Free Trade Agreement. This change in the Constitution ends the government's obligation to redistribute land to the landless and permits (but does not require) the privatization of land held in non-alienable corporate status as *ejido* or communal land (Stephen 1997, Harvey 1994). The change in the law affects almost 50 per cent of Mexico's national territory.

In the 1990s, there has been a wide range of responses to the North American Free Trade Agreement (NAFTA), the structural adjustments of the 1980s and 1990s and the reform of agrarian reform. These range from government programmes designed to regularize *ejido* and common lands, to armed rebellion by indigenous peasants. In this chapter I examine two different responses to the government's move to end land redistribution and regularize existing landholdings. I contrast the case of the Zapatistas' call for land reclamation (commonly called 'invasions' in the press) with the decision of a Zapotec *ejido* in Oaxaca to participate in the government's programme of land regularization known as PROCEDE.

My theoretical point of departure is that rather than trying to understand reactions to state policy about common lands and the globalization of capital from either a macro or micro perspective, we do better to look at the multiple discourses concerning land, the state and its agents, and historical figures of the Revolution such as Zapata, as competing elements in an unstable hegemony. Hegemony is a lived process and is profoundly altered by competing discourses which emerge in response to it (Williams 1994:598). Counter-hegemonic discourses such as that of the Zapatistas thus come to coexist and dialogue with, and become incorporated in ever-changing dominant hegemonies. Because both the Mexican state and the Zapatistas have successfully incorporated the revolutionary symbolism of Zapata in their respective programmes, a wide range of meanings is attached to the figure of Zapata at local levels (Stephen 1997). From this range of meanings emerge two very different responses to common land policy.

In the first section of this chapter, I outline the restructuring of Mexico's rural sector and current programmes and laws aimed at ending the government's obligation to redistribute land and to encourage the regularization of existing landholdings on an individual basis. Then I outline the reaction of the Zapatista Army of National Liberation to the reforms and discuss their plan of action for rural development and land reform. By way of contrast I discuss the reactions of Zapotec indigenous farmers and wage workers to the reforms in order to delineate the logic of their incorporation into government land regularization programmes. I conclude by suggesting how regional variation in combination with the use of historical symbols of the Mexican Revolution by both the state and the Zapatistas allow for differing responses to state policy on common lands that share an overlapping logic.

The Restructuring of Rural Mexico

The current situation of economic hardship in which many indigenous Mexican families find themselves is linked to Mexican development policy in the 1970s and 1980s, subsequent economic restructuring, and the development of economic conditions conducive to free trade. Decision makers in the Mexican government and business community promoted economic policies that resulted in increasing economic disparities and the availability of fewer resources. The results were economic and environmental impoverishment (Faber 1992, Stephen 1992).

This was the economic backdrop for the 1993 North American Free Trade Agreement. NAFTA attempts to eliminate trade barriers and tariffs among Canada, the US and Mexico, which together have 360 million consumers. More than offer any concrete changes to the Mexican economy NAFTA politically supports the changes created under structural adjustment policies over the past twelve years and cements the condition of extreme differences between a small minority of wealthy Mexicans and a poor majority.

Today, Mexico's agrarian structure is characterized by both pro-letarianization and the continuation of a subsistence-oriented agricultural sector. After 1940 the state's rhetoric made continued references to the legacy of Zapata, but policy shifted to accommodate dependent capitalism (Barry 1995:25). Many have labelled the structure of the Mexican agriculture as bimodal with a large gap existing between large-scale commercial producers and a majority of farmers depending on family labour. As Barry points out, the term 'trimodal' better describes the major categories of Mexican farmers: '1) capitalist producers, 2) medium- and small-scale farmers who are surplus producing but rely primarily on family labor and 3) infra-subsistence or subsistence farmers together with the landless, many of whom work regularly as *jornaleros*, or wage farmworkers' (1995:28).

For those holding land in agrarian reform or *ejido* communities, access to land has not been a guarantee of survival. While in 1950 about 85 per cent of those working on *ejidos* earned more than half their income from farming, in 1985, less than 40 per cent did (Cockcroft 1983:191). By the early 1980s, the expansion of capitalist agriculture in Mexico resulted in the marginalization of a vast portion of the rural subsistence sector. Cockcroft (1983:191) estimated that in 1983, nearly 80 per cent of Mexico's *ejidos* and agrarian communities could no longer support themselves on farming alone.

In November 1992, the government issued reforms to Article 27 of the Constitution that would permit the privatization of previously inalienable community-held *ejido* land. The law also allows foreign firms to buy, rent or lease land for agriculture and forest use, thus ending the government's constitutional obligation to redistribute land. Most significantly, the reforms allow individual *ejidatarios* who have had use rights to land, the possibility of holding an individual title to land once they receive a certificate.

To facilitate the proposed changes in landholdings for more than 28,000 *ejidos* and indigenous communities, a new government office was created, the Procuraduría Agraria or Agrarian Attorney's Office. The certification programme of the Procuraduría is built around protecting the rights of *ejidatarios* through providing them with certificates specifying that particular plots of land belong to them as individuals. The possibility of holding individual title to a piece of land, however small, has motivated some *ejidatarios* to formally enter the government's certification programme. Upon signing up, they receive an onslaught of information, official visits from lawyers and agronomists, advice, teams to measure their community boundaries and individual plots, invitations to participate in programmes to 'help' peasants and a pile of paper to document the entire process. What occurs is massive state intervention, and constant contact with state officials throughout the process and afterwards. Predicted completion dates for the programme are constantly changing as administrators of the Procuraduría continually run into historical land battles between communities, family feuds, and past measuring and mapping errors. The political and bureaucratic procedures of the certification programme are forcing individuals and communities to make explicit decisions about their relationship to land within a short period of time.

Agrarian restructuring comes together with free trade policies at a time when subsistence and small-scale commercial farmers have to compete with highly subsidized US agricultural products in the Mexican market. Due to protests generated by producer organizations during the process of negotiating NAFTA, the Mexican government initiated a programme for peasants in 1993 called PROCAMPO (Support Program for the Mexican Farm Sector). According to government promises, this programme offers a subsidy of about US$65 per hectare for the period from 1993–2008 to Mexican farmers of corn, beans, wheat, rice, soy beans, sorghum and cotton. Meanwhile, guaranteed price supports for these crops were phased out by the autumn and winter seasons of 1994–95, pitting Mexican producers against cheaper US imports and aligning Mexican crop prices to international prices. Maize production has stagnated due to a lack of commercial viability and large debt loads carried by producers (Legler 1995:4, Ovalle Vaquera and López Gámez 1994). In 1995, Mexico imported a record ten million tons of grain, more than 25 per cent of the total annual grain consumption (Reuters 1995). Since price supports were phased out, the small subsidy offered by PROCAMPO clearly did not offset the loss of higher crop prices for small farmers.

By the end of 1993, the future was looking bleak for Mexico's farmers and rural workers. As stated succinctly by Barry (1995:145), Mexican farmers faced six major changes by the end of the governing period of Salinas: '1) the withdrawal of government-subsidized inputs, 2) high interest rates and lack of access to credit, 3) the end of land distribution and the new status of ejidal land, 4) an increased flow of cheaper food imports, 5) inadequate government measures to upgrade productivity and competitiveness, and 6) a widely criticized new subsidy program called Procampo'. A clear signal had been sent out that future policies would weed out the weak from the strong in the countryside. In the remainder of this chapter, I compare the reactions of two groups of indigenous rural farmers and workers to government restructuring policies.

Basta! The Zapatista Army of National Liberation

After the signing of NAFTA in October of 1993, the free trade agreement reappeared in the international media on 1 January 1994. On the same day NAFTA was to take effect, the Zapatista Army of National Liberation started a rebellion. The Zapatista's first communiqué described themselves as the result of 500 years of struggle that began with the fight against slavery and has continued to the present with a struggle against racism, poverty, NAFTA, an authoritarian political system and the end of land redistribution. The Zapatistas immediately linked changes in Mexican land reform to the North American Free Trade Agreement, which they condemned for causing impoverishment for the majority. The Zapatistas found the economic programme of the then-president Salinas unacceptable. Their mestizo spokesperson and military strategist Subcomandante Marcos stated, 'What is at stake in Chiapas is no longer just Chiapas or even Mexico, but perhaps even the free trade agreement or the whole neoliberal project in Latin America' (Golden 1994:3). The self-history of the Zapatistas makes it clear that land conflict, the future of rural production and indigenous rights are all at the heart of the Zapatista movements, a political agenda built on two decades of peasant organizing.

While little is known about their military history, it is important to note the slow but steady growth of the EZLN, particularly in the late 1980s and 1990s. According to their own oral history, Marcos and his compatriots began military training in the mountain caves of the Sierra of Corralchén near Ocosingo and in the jungle above Guadalupe Tepeyac near the Guatemalan border. They arrived in the mid-1980s with links to the National Liberation Forces of Mexico (FLN), a small guerrilla group that suffered casualties in Punto Diamante when the government destroyed a training camp in 1974 (Ortega 1994:54). They engaged in health campaigns promoting vaccinations and encouraged people to engage in military training (Ross 1994:279). Marcos explained that when he and his compatriots arrived in Chiapas, many communities were already engaged in battles over land and had armed themselves in self-defence:

> We could say that for the peasant compañeros, the EZLN began as a group for self defense. There is a very powerful armed group called the 'White Guards' who are gunners for the ranchers. These ranchers have taken away the indigenous peasants' land and mistreated them. The ranchers have also limited the social and political development of the indigenous peoples. So they say that they had to arm themselves to confront them and not remain defenseless. (Petrich and Henriquez 1994:6–7)

In several interviews, Marcos described how indigenous peasants saw that they could not just defend isolated communities and began to establish alliances among communities, forming larger and larger paramilitary contingents, but still with the purpose of self-defence.

Marcos' history of the EZLN underplays two critical factors in the politicization of eastern Chiapas – the growth of regional peasant organizations beginning in the 1970s and the role of the Catholic Church's liberation theology. In the 1970s, grass-roots organizing efforts took off in several directions supported by the Church and leftist activists, although the two groups did not always see eye-to-eye. In 1976, three regional *ejido* unions were formed bringing together two or more communities in the municipalities of Las Margaritas and Ocosingo.[1] Organizers from the Maoist-oriented Proletarian Line were active as advisers in each of these *ejido* unions. In 1980, a different statewide effort to improve the terms of coffee marketing resulted in the unification of the three *ejido* unions as well as other smaller producer groups to form the Union of Ejido Unions and Solidarity Peasant Organizations of Chiapas (UU, often known as Union de Uniones) (Harvey 1994:30, Harvey 1992). UU focused primarily on peasant appropriation of the production process. As described by Harvey, it was 'the first and largest independent campesino organization in Chiapas, representing 12,000 mainly indigenous families from 170 communities in 11 municipalities' (1994:30). In 1983 the organization split. One part of the split plus two other *ejido* unions later formed another organization in March 1988, called ARIC–Unión de Uniones (Rural Collective Interest Association).

As outlined in Harvey (1994), many other sources of independent peasant organizing emerged in the 1970s and 1980s. The Coordinadora Nacional 'Plan de Ayala' (National Coordinator, Plan of Ayala, CNPA) which takes its name from Zapata's 1911 plan to redistribute land, was founded in 1979 with ten regional peasant organizations. Their principlal demands included: 'the legal recognition of longstanding indigenous land rights; the distribution of land exceeding the legal limits for private property; community control over and defence of natural resources; agricultural production, marketing, and consumption subsidies; rural unionization; and the preservation of popular culture' (Paré 1990:85). CNPA participants included indigenous peoples with communal land or no land, minifundia peasants, peasants who were soliciting land and some groups of small producers and agrarian wage workers. The CNPA had 21 member organizations in the early 1980s, many of whom were involved in bloody disputes with ranchers over land.[2]

Another important regional peasant organization that developed in the 1970s was the Independent Central of Agricultural Workers and Peasants (CIOAC) which organized Tzeltal and Tzotzil agricultural workers into unions on coffee and cattle ranches. While the name of the organization did not signal ethnically based demands, its documents reflect an awareness of indigenous identity and politics through the acknoledegment of indigenous claims to lands historically denied, defence of indigenous languages and forms of government and religion, and the need to struggle against efforts to assimilate indigenous peoples.

The period from 1989 to 1994 was marked by both economic and political events that contributed to the politics of land struggles, indigenous autonomy, peasant activism and its linkage to armed struggle in Chiapas. In 1989 after the International Coffee Organization floated the price of coffee on the world market, the impact on coffee-producing communities in Chiapas and elsewhere was devastating. Price drops from US$120–140 per 100 pounds to an average of US$60–70 in combination with the elimination of government coffee subsidies reduced coffee producers' incomes by 65 per cent (Hernández Navarro 1994:58). That same year a ban on logging closed off this income-earning activity to farmers. The dire economic needs of people and the brutal treatment by Chiapas' governors and local police towards legal forms of organizing encouraged some indigenous peasants to consider more radical options. This tendency converged with another movement that had been growing slowly in the Lacandon jungle.

The Zapatistas offered armed training to many young peasants who were already in a range of organizations, particularly those in the ARIC-Union de Uniones. In 1988 the organization split, one side more focused on market and credit mechanisms and skilful negotiations with the government. The other side, affiliated more with the Church, was utterly distrustful of the government. They stuck to demands for land. In 1989, after the collapse of the coffee market, more than half of the communities affiliated with the ARIC began to participate in a semi-clandestine organization, ANCIEZ.

That same year, the Independent Peasant Alliance 'Emiliano Zapata' (ACIEZ) emerged in six municipalities of Chiapas including Altamirano, Ocosingo, San Cristóbal, Sabanillo and Salto de Agua and Las Margaritas. By some accounts, ACIEZ received a high percentage of its recruits (up to 40 per cent by one account) from ARIC-UU (Ross 1994: 280). In 1991, ACIEZ became ANCIEZ, adding the word 'national' to its title after a meeting with delegates from other states in Puebla. The basic document (*documento basico*) of the ANCIEZ foreshadowed demands for land, credit, complaints about lack of inputs and peasant's inability to compete with North American imports (Tello Díaz 1995:132). ANCIEZ's strongest areas of support were in Chiapas in Tzotzil, Tzeltal and Chol communities (Harvey 1994:32). In 1990 and 1991 the organization grew steadily. The announcement in 1992 of an amendment to Article 27 of the Constitution that called for the end of land redistribution and the regularizing of all landholdings was a final straw for some indigenous peasants of Chiapas. Over 25 per cent of Mexico's unresolved land disputes at that time were in Chiapas – news of the end of agrarian reform was not well received. Marcos later stated to the press:

> . . . the government had the brilliant idea of reforming Article 27 of the Constitution and this was a powerful catalyst in the communities. These reforms got rid of any legal possibility for obtaining land . . . This slammed the door shut for indigenous people to survive in a legal and peaceful manner. This is why they picked up arms. (Petrich and Henriquez 1994, author's translation)

As ANCIEZ grew steadily, indigenous and peasant organizing in other areas of Chiapas was also intensifying.

According to Marcos' oral history of the EZLN, at the end of 1992, communities working with ANCIEZ and the social organization of the EZLN voted in assemblies to give the Zapatista military wing one year to prepare for war (Ross 1994:281). By 1993, more than half of the reformists of ARIC (who were previously reluctant to join) signed up for Zapatista military training and had joined ANCIEZ. Peasant leaders and EZLN military commanders also met more and more frequently. Some ARIC members remained steadfastly opposed to the armed option. Following the Zapatista revolt in 1994, however, many ARIC holdouts joined peasant organizations sympathetic to the Zapatistas. Those who remained opposed to the EZLN aligned themselves with the National Peasant Organization (CNC, aligned with the government) and some later supported the army's presence in the region.

Throughout their public life, the EZLN have closely identified with and invoked the symbols of the Mexican Revolution, most explicitly in the figure of Emiliano Zapata. He has appeared as a deity-like figure in many Zapatista communiqués:

> This is the truth, brother and sisters. This is where we come from and where we're going. Being here he comes. Dying, death lives. Vo'tan Zapata , father and mother, brother and sister, son and daughter, old and young, we are coming . . . Receive our truth in your heart dancing. Zapata lives, also and forever in these lands. (CCRI 1994a:16)

Vo'tan Zapata brings together the Tzeltal figure of Vo'tan, the first man, whom God sent to give land to indigenous peoples, with Zapata – the revolutionary hero whose radical proposal was eventually incorporated into the Mexican Constitution. According to historian Antonio García de León, Vo'tan is associated with the third day of the Tzeltal calendar and represents the heart of the people (1994:1). Vo'tan Zapata brings together the mythic past of a warrior-hero with the figure of Zapata who becomes a defender of indigenous peasant rights.

Zapata's face has appeared prominently at EZLN rallies and events and seems to be ever-present in the activities of civilian EZLN supporters, whether in Chiapas or Mexico City. Like other Mexicans who have inaccurately attributed the cry of *tierra y libertad* (land and liberty) to Zapata and the other co-authors of the Plan de Ayala drafted in 1911 (Baitenmann 1995:4), the Zapatistas used this theme as a rallying cry.[3] They have made agrarian politics and land issues a central part of their reform agenda. In 1994 and 1995, the EZLN used the anniversary of Emiliano Zapata's death as a vehicle for celebrating their struggle. The events promoted by the Zapatistas to mark Zapata's death were coordinated with land recuperations or invasions (depending on your perspective) that were taking place in Chiapas. In the first four months of 1994, up to 40,000 hectares of disputed land were taken over by peasant and indigenous communities and organizations (Robberson 1995:21A).

Titled 'The national days of Liberation, Zapata Vive', the EZLN and peasants all over the country marked Zapata's assassination in 1994 with marches, hunger strikes, road blocks and a march in Mexico City. Fifty thousand peasants and Indians marched to the Zócalo reclaiming the ideals of Zapata for peasant and indigenous movements. Marchers opposed what they called the 'neoliberal anti-peasant development plans' imposed by the government and called for an alternative development project (Pérez 1994:5). The Zapatistas carried out their own commemorative ceremony in the Lacandon jungle to which reporters were invited. The principal statements of all these actions included a condemnation of the end of land redistribution and of privatization of *ejido* land and rejection of private landholding corporations in the countryside (Correa et al. 1994:36). The CCRI issued the following communiqué on 10 April, read in the Zócalo in Mexico City:

> Today, April 10th is the 75th anniversary of the assassination of General Emiliano Zapata. His betrayal by Venustiano Carranza was an attempt to drown out his cry of Land and Liberty! Today, the usurper Salinas de Gortari, who claims to be 'President of the Mexican Republic' lies to the people of Mexico, saying that his reforms to Article 27 of the Constitution reflect the spirit of General Zapata. The supreme government lies! Zapata will not die by arrogant decree. The right to land of those who work it cannot be taken away and the warrior cry 'Land and Liberty!' echoes restlessly through these Mexican lands. (CCRI 1994b: 16)

Zapatista Rejection of the Reforms to Article 27: Reclaiming the Commons

When the Zapatistas released their 32-point peace plan at the first round of negotiations with the government in March 1994, agrarian demands were central to their programme. They continued to condemn the modifications to Article 27 of the Constitution and demanded inputs, machinery, credit and price supports. Point Seven of their proposal contains most of their agrarian demands:

> Seventh. Article 27 of the Magna Carta must respect the original spirit of Emiliano Zapata: the land is for the indigenous people and campesinos who work it. Not for the latifundistas. We want, as is established in our revolutionary agricultural law, the great quantities of land, currently in the hands of big ranchers and national and foreign landowners and other people who hold a lot of land but are not campesinos, to pass into the hands of our peoples who suffer from a total lack of land. The land grants shall include farm machinery, fertilizers, pesticides, credits, technical advisory, improved seeds, livestock, and fair prices for products like coffee, corn, and beans. The land that is distributed must be of good quality and include roads, transportation, and irrigation systems. The campesinos who already have land also have the right to all the above mentioned supports in order to facilitate their work and improve production. New ejidos and communities must be formed. The Salinas reform of Article 27 must be annulled and the right to land must be recognized as per the terms of our Magna Carta. (CCRI-GC 1994c: 13)

Many of these demands also reappeared in varied forms at the National Democratic Convention called by the Zapatistas in August 1994 to mobilize civil society towards demanding a transitional government, a new constitution and a specially elected constitutional assembly (Stephen 1995). In 1995 they reappeared in specific proposals from the EZLN during the second round of negotiations with the government in San Andres Larrainzer. In October 1995 the Zapatistas assembled a group of 150–200 advisers and moved to press forward with their demands.

The government's response in 1994 to these demands in the person of Manuel Camacho, named as peace commissioner, was the most explicit to date. An unresolved question that plagued the first round of negotiations as well as the more recent round in 1995 has been how to interpret the revised Article Four of the Mexican Constitution which reads:

> The Mexican nation has a multicultural composition originally founded in its indigenous peoples. The law protects and promotes the development of their languages, uses, customs, resources and specific forms of social organization and guarantees their members effective access to the full range of the state's legal authority

[jurisdiction]. In the agrarian judgments and legal proceedings they are part of, their own legal practices and customs shall be taken into account in establishing the law.

The results of Article Four are recognition of Mexico as a nation having a pluri-cultural composition and the conferring of cultural rights on indigenous peoples. As pointed out by Hindley (1995:11), the fact that Article Four is contained within a chapter titled 'Individual Guarantees', immediately dilutes the concept of indigenous rights as collective. The article does nothing to address collective rights, particularly those regarding participation in economic and political decision making and indigenous claims to resources and territory. The statement – 'in the agrarian judgments and legal proceedings they are part of, their own legal practices and customs shall be taken into account in establishing the law' – provides no specific guarantees for how indigenous peoples will be included in decision making over land use, ownership and allocation. Since land claims and disputes are the most important issues in many indigenous and peasant organizations, this vagueness provided a lot of manoeuvring room for future ruling on indigenous land claims.

While leaving the ambiguity of Article Four unaddressed, the government's responses legitimated the Zapatistas' demands about land and the need for equitable development policies at the state level in Chiapas. As seen below, state negotiator Manuel Camacho did offer proposals for means of furthering land redistribution and for protecting land held in indigenous communities within the state of Chiapas. Many of the solutions offered consisted of massive state aid to meet material and technical needs projected by the Zapatistas. What the document did not do, however, was to address the issues raised by the Zapatistas on a national level. This was ultimately important in the rejection of the document by EZLN supporters. Below, key portions of the government proposal are highlighted in relation to the points raised in the Zapatista document from the 1994 negotiations:

8. Agrarian reform of the Mexican Revolution was never widely carried out in the state of Chiapas. It is necessary to find a solution for the numerous agrarian conflicts while providing guarantees for small property holders. The process to carry this out should be connected to the discussion, approval, and dissemination of the General Law of the Rights of Indigenous Communities . . . whose initiative will be sent to the Congress. This law will provide and establish rules for implementing the first paragraph of Article

Four of the Constitution and the parts that refer to agrarian matters under Article 27 with the goal of strengthening the facilities of the state to reinstate land and to break up latifundios. The law will include:

- the establishment of adequate provisions, reserves and uses of land, water, and forests with the goal of improving population centres.
- procedures for breaking up latifundios in order to promote agriculture, cattle ranching, forestry and other economic activities.
- the determination of cases in which the expropriation and occupation of private property will serve the public interest.
- protection of the property and integrity of communal and *ejido* land of indigenous communities.

[Translated from 'Compromisos para un paz digna en Chiapas', 1994]

The 1994 peace dialogue opened up important political space for future negotiations about land redistribution, indigenous autonomy and the economic rights of rural Mexicans as producers. The proposals of the Zapatistas have remained consistent from the first round of peace negotiations until the present. Discussions continued to centre on the issue of indigenous autonomy which translated into recognition of indigenous territories as well as granting newly-formed autonomous indigenous regions decision-making power to make their own regional development plans. While the government and the EZLN signed a set of accords on indigenous rights and culture in February of 1996, these accords have yet to be implemented. The low-intensity war in Chiapas continues.

Zapatista Development Plans: Retaking the Commons in a Global Market

In terms of their own specific agricultural development plans, the Zapatistas are not longing for a mythical past where indigenous farmers engaged in low-tech subsistence farming. The bulk of the rank and file as well as much of the leadership of the EZLN have years of experience organizing around production and credit issues. Many of their organizations were pushing for better conditions for the commercialization of coffee and other crops. They envision themselves as part of the global marketplace and see commercial crops as central to their well-being. They embrace technology, chemical inputs and sophisticated systems of transport. In conversations I had with Zapatistas in 1994 and 1995, their vision of agricultural development included the use of pesticides, fertilizer and commercial crops, but incorporated into a collective production system. In an interview in August 1994, Mayor Eliseo told me his vision of what the EZLN communities wanted:

> We think that the government should support us with the inputs we need like tractors, seeds, fertilizers, ploughs, and pesticides. We have a way that we organize farming in the communities . . . We feel like we have to change. There are more and more people and less land . . . So now what we are doing is to work collectively. Everything is for everyone. In some places we have planted and harvested this way . . . It's hard to for us to convince people to change from individual forms of farming to a collective model. They would say, 'what's mine is mine.' It was very hard to work with this. We had to struggle among our own people.

The overall model of the Zapatistas calls for a rejection of the reforms to Article 27 of the Mexican Constitution, provision of inputs, credit and access to distribution networks for the marketing of both subsistence and commercial crops, collective forms of production, and a decentralization of political and economic decision making into the hands of indigenous producers. Most of their experiments have been carried out in the context of the *ejidos* formed in the past 30 years in eastern Chiapas in the canyons of Ocosingo, Altamirano and Las Margaritas. Many, not all, of these *ejidos* were formed first by occupation and then by petitioning the government for land (Collier 1994:48). Many who joined the Zapatistas after militating in the ARIC had passed one or two decades either personally or in their families trying to press land claims legally and to get promised government assistance for production.

In sum, the Zapatistas used the radical agrarian legacy of Emiliano Zapata and his Plan de Ayala to build on organizing carried out by peasant and indigenous organizations and the Church. In direct response to the state – which also attempted to invoke the memory of Zapata in its reform of the *ejido* – the Zapatistas refused to legitimate the state's proposed reforms and shouted 'Basta!' ('Enough!') to challenge agrarian reform through support for land reclamations and their insistence that Article 27 be returned to its original intent. The PROCEDE programme to regularize land has met with little success in Chiapas after three years. As of June 1995, only 7 per cent of the *ejidos* and agrarian communities in Chiapas had completed the government programme. In the areas of conflict, only about 3 per cent of *ejidos* and agrarian communities have completed the programme (Moguel Viveros and Parra Vasquez 1995:4–5). In Chiapas, the reform of agrarian reform is not taking place as planned.

Agrarian Reform In Oaxaca: A Mixture Of Resistance and Accommodation

Bordering on Chiapas, the State of Oaxaca shares many characteristics with its neighbour including high levels of poverty, a significant indigenous population and political marginalization from the centre. While reforms to Article 27 were not openly welcomed in Oaxaca, they were not resisted with an armed rebellion. This has to do in part with a recent series of governors who worked to integrate and coopt indigenous and peasant leaders rather than repress them with brutal violence as in Chiapas. Oaxaca also has a different colonial and post-independence land history than the State of Chiapas.

Historical studies of central Oaxaca during the colonial period reveal that unlike other parts of Mexico, indigenous individuals and communities were able to resist Spanish encroachment on their lands. This was partially due to indigenous *caciques* who kept their lands and converted some to private property during the early colonial period (Taylor 1972). This was also due to the fact that indigenous communities held higher numbers of land grants than the Spanish through the sixteenth century (Romero Frizzi 1988:137), and these land grants could be defended in Spanish courts. Often the most bitter land battles in Oaxaca were not between indigenous communities and large latifundias, but between neighbouring indigenous communities. By the time the Mexican Revolution occurred, communities had lost as much land to their neighbours as to hacendados. This fact gave a different twist to the arrival of government officials after the Revolution to help communities formalize their *ejido* petitions and to receive their land endowments. This history, in conjunction with many *ejidatarios'* historical identification of the state with carrying out the plan of Zapata have resulted in a distinct reception of *ejido* reforms in Oaxaca. There the reforms have been met with a mixture of accommodation and resistance. I use the example of one *ejido* I have studied in depth to provide a contrasting case to the response of the Zapatistas. Just like the Zapatistas who used Emiliano Zapata as a central symbolic figure in delivering their message of rebellion, *ejidatarios* in Oaxaca also incorporate Zapata into their receptions of *ejido* reform, but in what initially appears to be a contradictory manner. On the one hand they are sympathetic to the Zapatistas. On the other hand, they decided to enter the government land regularization programme precisely because they believe it will help them preserve their *ejido* land, the land for which Zapata gave his blood.

Like 213 other *ejidos* in the State of Oaxaca, Santa María del Tule has completed the programme known as PROCEDE (or Program for the Certification of Ejidal Rights and Titling of Urban Plots) begun after reformation of Article 27 of the Mexican Constitution in 1992. Santa María is populated by about 10,000 Zapotec indigenous people and pre-dates the arrival of the Spaniards. The economy is a mixture of wage labour, migration, small businesses and small-scale commercial and subsistence farming. In June 1994, each of the 417 *ejidatarios* of Santa María del Tule received a title to their house lot, a certificate that stated the location and size of each of their *ejido* parcels, and an individualized map that showed precisely where their pieces of *ejido* land were located in relation to other local parcels and in relation to the boundaries of neighbouring communities. For many, this visual representation captures not only the present, but is also a map of past community land history.

After receiving their individual certificates and maps, the men and women of the Santa María del Tule *ejido* consciously decided in their assemblies not to move forward with the next possible step of privatizing their parcels with individual titles. Publicly, many expressed pleasure at having completed the government programme and receiving their certificates, but none favoured privatization. In fact, they emphasized more than ever the need for the *ejido* to remain unified. While some officials involved in administering PROCEDE would cite El Tule as an example of an *ejido* enthusiastically embracing the programme, the meaning of their participation and decision upon terminating the programme not to individually title their lands suggests that they do not share the neoliberal agenda behind PROCEDE and the modification to Article 27 of the Constitution. Instead, their participation in PROCEDE and strong decision not to title their holdings as individual parcels is better understood in relation to their interpretations of the past as reflected in their sense of local land relations through history and their specific identification with the figure of Emiliano Zapata and the *ejido* as being responsible for a major improvement in their lives beginning in the 1920s.

While there are important differences between *ejidatarios* – particularly between men and women and the ultimate implication of holding certificates – one of the most interesting processes attached to participating in PROCEDE has been constant discussion, interpretation and reinterpretation of local history. While men and women have different points of entry to the past and identify more strongly with particular types of work and activities in the gendered division of labour, they none the less share the broad outlines of how the community as a whole relates to neighbouring towns and to a large hacienda central to community life for almost 300 years.

While the historical memories of people from El Tule include bitter poverty and exploitation at the hands of the Guendulain family that owned the hacienda on which many toiled, they also recall fear, conflict and violence with the neighbouring community of Tlalixtac. Even after they were granted *ejido* lands, the community of Tlalixtac challenged the ruling in 1918 and succeeded in preventing El Tule from occupying half of their *ejido* for another 17 years. This history must be considered when trying to understand what the current process of cooperating with government officials from the Procuraduría Agraria's office means for the *ejidatarios* of El Tule. Given their historic struggle with Tlalixtac and the fact that a majority of men and women were landless for most of the colonial period until 1917, it is a consistent pattern for them to see agrarian officials as a means to defending their land rights against an ever-encroaching neighbour. Once women and men in the *ejido* secured their certificates, they publicly repeated their commitment to leave their *ejido* intact and not to privatize precisely because they do not want to lose land again to people from Tlalixtac or to outsiders like the Guendulain family for whom they worked for centuries.

Frameworks for Interpreting the Past in Santa María del Tule

In discussing the origins of Santa María del Tule and its relationship to Tlalixtac de Cabrera, six of the most elderly people in the community recited a similar story, reiterating their long-term subordinate status to Tlalixtac, which they call 'the big town' (*el pueblo grande*). Consistent images of precolonial history include a short migration from Tlalixtac to the current site of El Tule, the subservient position of people in El Tule to Tlalixtac, the ceding by Tlalixtac of communal lands to El Tule, and the importance of lime extraction to the local economy. Perhaps the strongest element of historical identity construction that defines the emergence and continuation of Santa María del Tule as a community is continued conflict and confrontation with Tlalixtac and a perpetual defensive position with regard to land.

Documentation of land and labour relations among Tlalixtac, Santa María del Tule and surrounding communities suggest that *terrasguerros*, or landless sharecroppers, who worked for a *cacique* of Tlalixtac, were found around Santa María del Tule by the mid-1600s, hinting at a shortage of community lands (Taylor 1972:43). The amount of communal land El Tule held at the time of the conquest remains fuzzy. In 1917, the community of El Tule presented authorities from the Local Agrarian Commission of the State of Oaxaca with documents dating from 1529 that testify to the existence of communal lands. But these documents do not clearly specify the boundaries of communal land. The presence of landless sharecroppers, their confrontation with a Tlalixtac *cacique* about the legitimacy of his claim to *caciazgo* land, and the accepted history of migration from Tlalixtac to El Tule, suggest that the community's boundaries may have been in dispute as early as 1529.

While a 1573 law declared that all Indian towns were entitled to an *ejido* of one league (a circular area of 2.6 miles) and a later ruling of 1713 reiterated this ideal, in reality few of the Indian communities in the Valley of Oaxaca fit the form prescribed by Spanish law. While some communities possessed only the minimal townsite of the *fundo legal*, others had areas greatly exceeding one square league (Taylor 1972:67–8). The differences were due not only to the variation found before the Spanish conquest, but to active encroachment by some communities onto the lands of others. While the village of El Tule received a royal grant (*merced*) for land to graze sheep and goats in 1615 that incorporated about three square miles of land, by 1700 most residents had lost this land and became sharecroppers on the hacienda of Guendulain (Taylor 1972:104). The Guendulain hacienda is a major institution in descriptions of local land histories.

Local accounts of the history of the hacienda peg its establishment as 'a long time ago', and designate the community's relationship to the hacienda as remaining consistent throughout nearly 300 years. The hacienda is represented in most people's narratives as being a centre of exploitation and power that controlled people's lives and ruled the community. Apparently, the hacienda grew out of the communal lands of surrounding communities. The hacienda's exploitation of people assumes such force in people's narratives that the historical conflict between El Tule and Tlalixtac fades temporarily into the background as both communities assume the same subordinate position as day labourers. The rift between the two communities comes back into focus after the Mexican Revolution.

In 1918, the community of El Tule was awarded 600 hectares of land through a presidential resolution. Most of it was to be expropriated from the Guendulain ranch. On the day before repossession of their land, the authorities of Tlalixtac petitioned the Local Agrarian Commission of the State of Oaxaca to disqualify the land granted to El Tule because part of it included land that belonged to Tlalixtac de Cabrera (SRA 1926b:3). A district judge supported the appeal of the authorities from Tlalixtac. In 1919, the appeal reached the Supreme Court of the State of Oaxaca and the lands that were to be endowed to Santa María del Tule remained under special protection and as a result remained in the possession of Tlalixtac. The community of Tlalixtac had a political protector that gave it a distinct advantage over El Tule in land battles after the Revolution. Tlalixtac had long-standing political ties to General Isaac Ibarra.

In 1924, General Isaac Ibarra – a long-time leader of the Oaxaca sovereignty movement that fought against Constitutionalists for some 15 years in Oaxaca – fashioned a deal which seemed to eliminate all possibilities for the *ejidatarias* from El Tule to lay claim to all the lands they were endowed in 1917. As acting governor, Ibarra arranged an agreement between Tlalixtac and El Tule that granted half of El Tule's *ejido* lands to Tlalixtac (SRA 1926a, 1926b). Many in El Tule state that the general arrived in their community surrounded by heavily armed men and 'suggested' that they accept his proposition for dividing their lands with Tlalixtac. They did. Finally after another eleven years of lobbying the National Agrarian Commission and working with state-level delegates of the Commission, El Tule finally took possession of all of the *ejido* land they were endowed.

The Legacy of Zapata

In oral histories told to me by the remaining original *ejidatarios* of El Tule, Lázaro Cárdenas and Emiliano Zapata are both seen as heroes. In the narrative partially cited below, told to me in the summer of 1993 by 92 year-old Marío González, Cárdenas assumes the role of standard bearer for the ideology of Zapata:

> When Cárdenas came here he said, 'Down with the rich and up with the poor'. He was with Emiliano Zapata. He and Zapata were

for the poor people. Zapata was the one who had the idea about taking land away from the hacendados. Zapata suffered for us. He gave his blood so that the campesinos would have some land to work.

At the end of the story, Zapata assumes a Christ-like image in which his blood is sacrificed for the good of poor campesinos. In a previous part of the narrative, Mario identifies the community as made up of 'pure Indians' who lived in extreme poverty. Cárdenas and by implication Zapata are seen as responsible for lifting the community out of poverty. Cárdenas spent an afternoon in El Tule in 1933 while campaigning for the presidency:

When Cárdenas came here, he fed us. His servants brought us food there below the Tule tree as he spoke to us. We were 'puros indios' then. We didn't speak Spanish, only Zapotec. We were all really poor. We wore white cotton pants and didn't have any shoes. All we had were little cane houses that could just blow over in the wind.

Other historical narratives in Santa María del Tule reflected a similar tone. All of the original *ejidatarios* I spoke with in El Tule repeated that 'Zapata was on the side of the poor. The hacendados were with the rich.' It was cited almost as a mantra as part of each *ejido*'s origin story, even amongst the younger *ejidatarios*. In 1935, the *ejidatarios* of El Tule finally realized their stake in Zapata's legacy. On 28 October 1935, the authorities of Tlalixtac de Cabrera and Santa María del Tule along with the Oaxaca Delegate of the Agrarian Department signed a document witnessed by most of the men and women of El Tule. The document gave them full possession of their *ejido* lands. The Ejido Commissioner of Santa María del Tule promised in the name of all *ejidatarios* to respect the crops which had been planted by people from Tlalixtac until 27 November. After this date, the men and women who were *ejidatarios* of El Tule had permission to tear up anything planted on their lands and proceed with their own planting (SRA 1935).

The farmers of Tlalixtac quietly harvested their crops and turned over their fields to the *ejidatarios* of El Tule at the end of 1935. For the next decade the men and women who were *ejidatarios* in El Tule enjoyed a somewhat peaceful existence after their continued struggle against Tlalixtac and the Guendulain ranch. Then suddenly early in the morning one day in 1945, six people from El Tule were shot to death as they walked up the mountain in front of the community.

The battle for *ejido* lands between the two communities had reached its bloody climax. The shooters were from Tlalixtac. In the 1950s, the community of El Tule quietly ceded about half of its communal land to Tlalixtac – the least valuable mountainous land associated with their origin as a community. Since then, relationships between the communities have been strained, but the violent and legal battles have ended.

Land struggles for the people of El Tule had ceased until the 1990s when the government certification programme served to resurface their troubled past. In April 1994, the Procuraduría Agraria launched a widespread campaign to commemorate the 75th anniversary of Emiliano Zapata's assassination by handing out a record number of *ejido* parcel certificates in Morelos. Pictures of the event were posted in Oaxaca and featured in a variety of publications and national newspapers. President Salinas de Gortari stated that 'Zapata's struggle continues' and has not been set back by the recent reforms made to the Constitution 'in order to help out peasants' (Lomas 1994:3). Pamphlets promoting the programme also featured well-known revolutionary-era peasants and rhetoric (Stephen 1997). The state was not the only actor to use Zapata and the Mexican Revolution in defence of its rural reform programmes. The Zapatista Army of National Liberation (EZLN) also projected the figure of Zapata in its visual culture and written communiqués reaching *ejidatarios* in Oaxaca. During 1994, the Zapatistas were the topic of considerable discussion and speculation in El Tule.

A majority of the people of El Tule whom I interviewed said that they had first heard about the Zapatistas on the radio or on television, and they believed the Zapatistas would be coming to Oaxaca. When discussing the Zapatista rebellion in Chiapas, the *ejidatarios* referred to the fighting that took place during the Mexican Revolution as proof that the Chiapas war could extend into Oaxaca. Some supported both the PRI and the Zapatistas in the same conversation. They supported the PRI government because of the *ejido* land they received. Most people I interviewed compared their struggle after the revolution for *ejido* land with the present struggle in Chiapas. In discussions of their own agrarian struggle, the figure of Zapata assumes a prominent place. But, for the *ejidatarios* in El Tule, the *ejido* is not only tied historically to Zapata, but also to the government and specifically to the PRI as the bearer of original agrarian reform. For them, the material result is the *ejido* land they currently live from. For those I interviewed in Oaxaca, what is going on in Chiapas is a logical outcome of a revolution that never reached the southern part of the country. They identify with the struggle of the Zapatistas and expect the government to facilitate the process of land redistribution in Chiapas, taking it from large landholders and redistributing it to those without land.

The current response of *ejidatarios* from El Tule to the reforms to Article 27 of the Constitution and their decision to enter the land regularization process known as PROCEDE is the result of a complex history of conflict with their Zapotec neighbours and a neighbouring hacienda as well as a discourse laced by the multiple meanings and appropriations of the figure of Zapata. He is the revolutionary responsible for the existence of *ejido* land, but government agrarian officials carrying out his reforms are also seen as responsible for the granting of *ejido* land. From the perspective of those from Santa María del Tule and as reflected in local histories, the community finally came to possess its lands through their own persistence and with the help of agrarian officials over a 20-year period. Throughout this period they were no doubt frustrated with officials from the National Agrarian Reform Commission, but also came to identify with them as defenders of their cause. They probably were not seen as part of 'the state' or 'the nation' because from the vantage point of Oaxaca, the state was a mess. Instead, *ejidatarios* built a special relationship with agrarian officials. In turn they came to identify them both with the state's land redistribution programme and with the revolutionary figure of Zapata.

In the 1990s when the state reappeared and made its presence felt on almost a daily basis in the community through officials from the Agrarian Attorney's Office and an onslaught of information, folders and meetings, the figure of Zapata reappeared in this context – an agrarian revolutionary in the service of the state. The counter-hegemonic discourse surrounding the figure of Zapata as presented by the Zapatista Army of National Liberation was also part of the daily context *ejidatarios* operated in as they relived their land history in the measuring and mapping process of PROCEDE. Because of the specific ways that Zapata had entered local history, they did not necessarily see the state's claim on Zapata and that of the Zapatistas to be contradictory. For them, both discourses focus on the right that farmers, particularly indigenous farmers, have to land and the historical importance of that right.

When we look at the nature of the interaction between the men and women who are *ejidatarios* from El Tule with officials from the Agrarian Attorney's Office who began coming to the community in 1993 to incorporate the *ejido* into PROCEDE, we cannot judge their responses simply from the present. Many talked about entering the programme to secure the boundaries to their land from any possible incursions from their neighbours in Tlalixtac and from the government's oil company (PEMEX) that had already forced expropriation of 30 hectares of *ejido* land and had requested that the community cede more (see Stephen 1997). They were also concerned about keeping out further dangerous industrialization such as a gas plant to be built on the outskirts of town that had been proposed in a recent community assembly. This they saw as consistent with the legacy of Zapata and coincided with the struggle being waged by the Zapatistas of the 1990s. They were therefore capable of being sympathetic to the cause of the EZLN and also entering and completing the state's land regularization programme. Their use of past historical experience to rationalize the importance of securing their *ejido* boundaries should not be confused, however, with an endorsement of the neoliberal agenda behind the PROCEDE programme.

Comparative Conclusions

The reception to counter-reforms to the Mexican Constitution that end the state's obligation to redistribute land and allow for the privatization of common lands have been mixed in southern Mexico. If we measure the impact of the reforms by the rate of incorporation into the government's land regularization programme known as PROCEDE in Oaxaca and Chiapas, then the rate of success in Chiapas is extremely low – 6 per cent of *ejidos* and agrarian communities with communal landholdings had completed the programme as of the summer of 1995 (Moguel Viveros and Parra Vasquez 1995:4). In Oaxaca the rate is also low, but more than double that of Chiapas – 13 per cent of *ejidos* and agrarian communities with communal holdings had completed the programme by the summer of 1995 (Procuraduría Agrasia, Delegación Oaxaca 1995). But merely measuring rates of incorporation into the state's programme not only follows the state's logic, but leaves out the range of responses undertaken by rural women and men such as land recuperations, armed rebellion and grass-roots organizing. It also greatly simplifies the cultural and historical complexity of those *ejidatarios* who did choose to complete the programme.

   To truly understand the dynamics of local responses to the reform of agrarian reform in Mexico, we have to consider carefully the role of the state's historic hegemonic discourse surrounding the Mexican Revolution and the figure of Zapata, local interpretations, revisions and reinterpretations of that history and the counter-hegemonic discourse of the Zapatistas of the 1990s. The ideological package disseminated by the Zapatistas in part also lays claim to and incorporates the hegemonic discourse of the state on the Mexican Revolution. It does not discard it, but builds on it, creating a common element between current state claims to Zapata in carrying out agrarian reforms and the radical rejection of the same reforms by the EZLN.

Thus it is possible to find common elements in the EZLN's proposals and claims for agrarian justice and the logic of *ejidatarios* from places like El Tule for participating in the state's land regularization programme. What both have in common is a historical claim to common lands that is staked through a rejection of outside interest. In El Tule these interests are identified with government industry such as the state oil company PEMEX. In Chiapas among the Zapatistas it is a rejection of the entire neoliberal structural adjustment programme, as symbolized by NAFTA. Both cases offer compelling evidence of a deep belief in Mexican indigenous communities of their right to claim and control common lands, regardless of whether they are operating within a state-controlled regularization programme or have undertaken their own regularization programme through land recuperation. The passion for common lands felt by both the Zapatistas and the *ejidatarios* of El Tule suggests that the ultimate goal of privatizing the 50 per cent of Mexico's territory held in *ejido* and communal status will not be easily realized. Indigenous communities, organizations and guerrilla armies are joining in Mexico's ever-stronger movement for indigenous autonomy, and together they are creating an alternative road for the future of the commons.

Notes

1   These included Ejido Union 'United in Our Strength' (Quiptic Ta Lecubtecel, UEQTL in Oscsingo), Ejido Union 'Land and Liberty' (Tierra y Libertad, UETL in Las Margaritas), and Ejido Union 'Peasant Struggle' (Lucha Campesina, UELC in Las Margaritas) (Harvey 1994:29).

2   For example, the 'Emiliano Zapata' Peasant Organization (OCEZ) formed in 1982 by community members from Venustiano Carranza fought a long battle to recuperate 3,000 hectares of land from local ranchers (Harvey 1992). Dozens of people died between 1982 and 1995 in the struggle to recuperate land (Hernández Navarro 1994:53).

3 The Plan de Ayala was actually signed with a call for *'libertad, justicia, y ley'* (liberty, justice, and law) (Baitenmann 1995:4–5). As pointed by Silva Herzog 1959:230–1) and cited by Baitenmann (1995:5, note 5), the theme 'Land and Liberty' was first used by Pilino Martínez, Zapatista delegate at a banquet for Villa and Zapata on 4 December 1914 in Xochimilco. Baitenmann points out that the framers of the Plan de Ayala were not quite as radical as their reputation, recommending the adoption of nineteenth-century liberal laws that could be used to break up haciendas.

4

In Defence of the Commons: Forest Battles in Southern Cameroon

Samuel-Alain Nguiffo

The notion of the commons has its genesis in Roman law, an inspiration of the French civil code which, in turn, gave birth to the laws in the Francophone and French-colonized countries of Africa. This legal aspect of the commons, however, cannot be found in the legal system of Francophone Africa, a system that has clung to the very classical distinctions on property – private, state and open access or *res nullius*. Here, the commons could be considered as 'private property' belonging to a group of persons with fairly exclusive rights to a pool of natural resources and space. In Africa, debates on the commons have been largely immune to the controversies surrounding Hardin's 'tragedy of the commons'. Up until recently, the intensity of the 'tragedy' debate amongst Anglo-Saxon scholars contrasts with its complete lack of presence amongst African scholars and development practitioners. None the less, today, many externally contrived development practices and professionals – especially those who work for Northern conservation groups and Northern-dominated financial institutions such as the World Bank – are conspicuously playing a lead role in the commons debate in Africa. Through the discursive strategies of foreign developers and conservationists, the Hardin debate has reached our shores (Bromley and Cernea 1989). Indeed, for many development practitioners, rendering the commons 'effective' is viewed as a major step towards 'development' of Africa.

Meanwhile, reconstituting the commons seems to be an arduous task. Its destruction in many countries of the South has been, in fact, one of the priorities of the colonial masters and the newly independent states – to undermine traditional societies so as to better enslave them. In Cameroon, as in other African countries formerly under French rule, the establishment of the postcolonial state and the reinforcement of its social role most often has had a detrimental effect on traditional societies and the management of common property resources. But since the 1960s, development

102

experts have realized the social and ecological 'efficiency' of the commons – albeit through their own cultural lenses – which has seemingly led to the process of reversing the destruction of the commons. Meanwhile, commoners in Cameroon have been trying to resist the cycles of invasions onto their commons, whether they be colonial or postcolonial strategies of enclosure for export commodity production, state-power maintenance, 'development' or 'conservation'.

In Cameroon, the significance and effectiveness of these destructive strategies are proportionate to the economic value of the commons. Although the strategies and mechanisms deployed in the Sahel region are similar to those in the forest zone, the results vary because of the higher economic importance of forest resources. This chapter has a few aims: to explain the common property management techniques in the forest region of southern Cameroon, the dangers faced by both the commons and the commoners, methods of resistance and some alternative strategies being discussed in the forest region today. None of these resistance or alternative-management strategies can be seen, in isolation, as radically changing the power relations on the forest commons. But they do suggest an emerging political recognition of the importance of decentralized control to mitigate the ecological and social crises affecting Cameroon today.

This chapter focuses on two forested regions of southern Cameroon, Campo and Djoum. The forest stretches through the south covering nearly 50 per cent of national territory. The Campo region is situated in southwest Cameroon on the shores of the Atlantic, covering a surface area of 300,000 km, with a population of about 6,000 inhabitants, comprised of the Bakola or Baka communities (also known as Pygmies), native Bantus (Mvae, Yassa, Mabea, Batanga), non-native Bantus working or seeking jobs in logging companies (less than 25 per cent of the population), a few French nationals working for the logging company, La Forestière de Campo and non-Cameroonians in transit to West or Southern Africa (Campo Beach being a meeting point for many illegal aliens).

For those who are not employed by the logging company, the Campo population's main economic activities are fishing and hunting in the reserve. All the actors of the forestry sector in Cameroon are found in this area: the state, a French logging company, some small logging companies working in close collaboration with the French company and marginalized people, amongst whom are some natives of the area. The region has an extraordinary biodiversity, and has been chosen to host a conservation project funded by the World Bank's Global Environmental Facility (GEF). In accordance with the colonial decree of 1932, Campo is a protected area and this status was maintained after Cameroon gained independence. Despite the fact that the law prohibits industrial logging in protected areas, a 25-year concession was granted in 1969 to La Forestière de Campo (Gartlan 1989).

Our second site, Djoum, is situated in south-central Cameroon, south of the Dja Reserve and a few scores of kilometres from the border with neighbouring Gabon. It covers a surface area of about 600,000 square kilometres with a population of about 14,000 inhabitants. The Bantu groups (Fang, Bulu and Zaman) are the majority while the Baka groups are the minority even though they are known to be the first forest inhabitants. There are about 3,000 Bakas, spread over 61 semi-nomad camps, in the Djoum region. The Bantus live mainly on farming; hunting is a secondary activity. The Baka, from the very beginning, were hunters, although a few have converted to agriculture with difficulty. Djoum has five logging companies. All logging titles are granted to Cameroonians with the exception of one, a subcontractor of WTK, the well-known Malaysian company. The presence of these companies has led to an inflow of numerous non-native employees, including Malaysians.

Djoum and Campo regions constitute a striking résumé of the major elements that constitute the forestry problem in Cameroon and, especially, the issues of commons property management. First, there is the local population with multifarious interests and cultural institutions, most of which are relatively unknown to outsiders. Second, there is the presence of the government through the management of a protected area, which restricts the use rights of the local population. Third, there are the logging companies (national and/or foreign) that have instituted the spirit of a commodity market and profit-making in the forest. Finally, the World Bank and other bilateral and multilateral agencies are extremely active in forest conservation practices.

Traditional Management of the Forest Commons

The horizontal social structure of the people of the forest zone of Cameroon leads many observers to believe that they can only have perfunctory forms of organization. Yet in the Bantu and Baka communities, there exist traditional methods of managing common property, although relations between them have always been knotty.

Up to the end of the last century, both groups lived in the heart of the forests. Successive colonial masters encouraged these forest people to settle along the newly constructed roads. The avowed aim was to let these 'backward' people enjoy the advantages of 'civilization', especially education and health. The real objective, however, was to make the population more accessible to the administration for tax collection and to have at its disposal, free workers for forced labour. The Bantus, a sedentary people, were the first to settle along the roads. As farmers, they had little trouble migrating to the new areas, and their proximity to the road benefited their farms. For the Bakas, the situation was different. As nomads, they lived in the forest on hunting and gathering fruits and they were disinterested in permanent settlement. After the state's enforced settlement policy, the two communities developed a new set of working arrangements, one which evolved from that of complementarity to near-feudal dependence.

From the onset, the Bakas and the Bantus bartered much of their goods and services. Bakas exchanged goods (fruits of their hunting and gathering) and services (traditional medicine, labour) for the Bantu's agricultural products, alcohol and iron tools. But many Bakas, attracted by the mirage of sedentary 'modernity', gradually settled along the roads either behind or next to the Bantu villages and they began to work solely as poorly paid labourers for the Bantus.

The Baka (or Bakola) traditional society is characterized by its egalitarian structure and the modest size of its group, with an average of about 50 members. Bantu communities of the forest zone have no leader and live in a socially horizontal structure. Their commons were made up of material resources ('visible' property) and immaterial ones (such as 'traditional' knowledge). An example of institutional mechanisms related to the management of traditional knowledge are the initiation rules into the Djengui rite of the Bakas. In Baka tradition, Djengui is the spirit of the forest sent by god: he comes from a mythical city that is the destination of all Bakas after death. He acts like an intermediary between god and the living, and protects them against the hazards of the forest. This protection, as well as the oracles of Djengui, are not accessible to everyone. Only a very closed circle of initiated persons has knowledge on this subject. Of the material common property, we find numerous examples in Bantu communities. Their typical forest village is divided into distinct zones: the residential area, farms, fallow land and hunting grounds. Hunting grounds, for example, do not belong to any particular individual. They are open to all the villagers under well-known rules governing the hunting of game and the collection of secondary forest products. There are many taboos, for instance, on the consumption of some species (such as duikerbok, crow, gorilla, chimpanzee) that ensure their protection.

The nomadic movements of the Bakas also follow rules that define their living space, and just like the rest of the forest, this space does not belong to any particular individual. Its resources (game and secondary forest products) are possessed by all who manage it collectively. There are also rules that govern the collection of honey from wild beehives. Although the honey is accessible to all, the person who discovered it has the right to first serve him or herself. This also applies to the Moabi species (*Baillonella toxisperma*) whose fruits are used to produce traditional oil and its barks for healing illnesses. As one scholar notes, 'In the forest zone, the type of control exercised on trees varies depending on several criteria, their economic use, their site, and the individual or group who planted or discovered them in the forest' (Karsenty 1996:114).

In nomad or semi-nomad Baka camps, management institutions of common property resources are much less structured – a mirror image of the political institutions of these camps. There is no leader or chief with absolute authority over the other members of the community. The various family heads act like a council and take decisions when the need arises. Quite often, a *de facto* leader emerges and imposes himself by reason of the security he gave to other members. Sometimes, it is either an exceptional hunter, an efficient healer or an oracle of Djengui (the spirit of the forest), but these leaders hardly have exclusive rights. Their authority, therefore, depends more on personal qualities and decisions are taken by family heads and village elders.

The management institutions of the Bantus are quite similar. The chiefs, despite their creation and support by colonialists, never became much more than ancillary administrators in these communities. In the horizontal structure of the society in the forest zone, decisions concerning the whole village are taken collectively by the chief and the representatives of the various families in the community. Deliberations are often public and facilitate the social control of resources or the area managed in common. This transparency enables consensus building around community decisions and, incidentally, the social and ecological sustainability of common property management. Moreover, the role played by elders during a dispute is considered neutral; that is, elders are always acting in the interest of the whole village (de Groot et al. 1995).

Common property and traditional management institutions functioned well during the precolonial period, which partly explains why these resources survived up to the colonial period. The members of the social groups concerned agreed on the functioning of the management systems. As Wouter de Groot points out,

> the breakdown of common property management systems is usually described as having an adverse effect on both social equity and ecological sustainability. Often, the impression is given that common property management has some inherent tendency to be more sustainable than other regimes. (de Groot et al. 1995:212)

These enduring commons institutional relations became an obstacle for aggressive colonial policies in the region. Colonial administrations and, later on, postcolonial independent states, wanted to have extensive control of land and resources so as to be able to redistribute them based on new political alliances.

Outsiders' Attacks on the Commons

Several 'outsider' groups – people who have not historically lived in the forests – are having a profoundly destructive effect on the material, ecological and social aspects of the forest commons. We will focus on the main actors: state agencies (colonial and postcolonial), private companies, poachers and even non-profit and 'philanthropic' organizations. Each set has its own particular rationalizations and objectives for entering the Cameroon forests. Some move in to mine specific resources, such as raw wood materials and cheap labour; others follow in their footsteps to clean up or preserve. Some come as individuals keen on hunting wild animals for urban commercial markets, while others come dressed in the clothing of the state with ambitious legislation to completely restructure social and natural relations in the forest. Whatever the individual enticements may be, these activities combine to create an enormous tide of intervention in the Cameroon forests. Intentionally or not, these actors are in the process of effectively colonizing the forest, marginalizing its diverse inhabitants, and creating the present forest crisis.

Perhaps the first serious threat to common property regimes in the forest came from the French colonial state. In an effort to gain control over valuable forest resources to fuel France's export-based economy, successive colonial administrations have tried to overturn forest communities' management regimes.[1] For example, colonial administrations established 'modern' standards to regulate land and resources that were clear challenges to customary norms governing common property. In the event of any conflict, modern (written) law always prevailed over customary laws and norms. Customary law could only be applied if both parties to the conflict agree, and they choose to bring the lawsuit before a customary court. If only one party so desires, or if the lawsuit is brought before a modern court, written law was always applied. Thus, under French rule, customary law was hardly respected. In the event of a dispute with forest commoners, non-members interfering with the management of common property have always had the right to choose to apply written law which undoubtedly favours the outsider. Thus, the form and content of the commoners' social relations were completely undermined. That is, not only were the particular rules and norms governing forest management de-legitimated, but also the community-based process of decision making, arbitration, negotiation and problem solving were all threatened when outsiders entered the forest for expropriation.

The colonial administration also wiped out most of the existing property regimes by introducing the notion of state property or public domain, granting the state considerable privilege to expropriate the forest for the state. Land that had no official private owner (justified by a land title) became *ipso facto* state property. By the simple stroke of the legislative pen, the state was empowered to take away control of land resources from the commoners, as the first step to transferring forest management to private companies. With the blessing of the colonial administration, large swathes of the forest commons became privatized.

After independence, the state carried on this policy of confiscating commons and granting them to be exploited for profit making. The forest zone was the ideal setting for these practices. The newly independent state, in complete financial crisis from a long epoch of colonialism, used existing forest policy as a vehicle to try to solve the country's economic problems. Consequently, under the postcolonial state, there was a considerable rise in forest resource exports, exploitation and destruction. After decades of successfully expropriating the commons from the commoners, the state now tries to justify these actions through a 'tragedy of the commons' discourse, blaming the 'incapacity of the commoners to sustainably manage the forest'. The official stance by the government is that 'agricultural clearings' are the fundamental cause of deforestation in Cameroon. It is officially claimed that 200,000 hectares of forest are destroyed annually by farmers for agriculture (Ministere du Plan 1991:71). Yet studies such as ours show that farmers' fields are usually of little dimension – less than one hectare per inhabitant. Their cumulative impact pales in comparison to logging enterprises (Nguiffo and Abessolo, forthcoming), as the population density is quite insubstantial, about three inhabitants per square kilometre. The government considers that it's possible to extract five million cubic metres of logs by the century's end without much harm to the environment, thus placing Cameroon as the leading log producer in Africa by the year 2000. This is in total contradiction with conclusions from experts who say such an ambition is totally unrealistic (Dudley et al. 1995).

Perhaps the second serious threat to common property regimes in the forest have come from 'poachers', or outsiders encroaching into the forests for the purpose of commercial hunting. Under traditional customs, hunting grounds are known and generally respected by most forest natives. Poachers are professional hunters who live on selling their catch; they are not natives of the hunting grounds, and have no obligation of respect to the hunting grounds or to the rules for the hunting period or local hunting taboos. They hunt to satisfy the ever-growing demand from urban centres, not the limited demand of forest inhabitants. The poachers generally have important native accomplices that enable them to poach with impunity. Meanwhile, in accordance with the state laws overseeing hunting practices, the local population can only exercise their use right in the hunting grounds, limited by law to killing game for personal consumption.

Hence, there is tremendous competition among poachers in search of short-term profits and locals feeling deprived and excluded from their own hunting grounds, especially since they suspect some civil servants in charge of state-hunting laws of connivance with the poachers. In some villages, frustration has pushed members to become poachers so as to benefit more from their forest resources than these outsiders. This situation results in an incredible scramble for game by well-equipped non-native poachers, locals poaching with traditional equipment and methods, and natives hunting within the purview of use rights.

The poaching problem is symptomatic of the tragedy of the *commoners* in Cameroon. Local populations have no power for fighting against the invasion of non-commoners into their community-managed environments. These non-commoners are usually powerful people benefiting from 'protection' from 'above' and acting as rapacious economic actors with no respects for commoners' traditions. In response, some commoners have rallied together to work with the government to help define the administrative rules and norms governing the exploitation of the forest. Within the context of these endeavours, they have even arrested poachers in their forest and handed them to the appropriate authorities. But, in an audacious display of power and injustice, the administrative authorities immediately freed these poachers and jailed the law-abiding commoners in their place.

A third set of actors feeding the flames of crisis in the Cameroon forests are the logging companies. A number of them arrived during the early years of colonization. In the Campo and Djoum regions, industrial logging began a decade after independence. In Campo, industrial logging is carried out by a French company to whom a 25-year logging title was granted in 1969. In the early 1990s, the average amount of timber exploited was estimated at 100,000 cubic metres per year (Nguiffo and Fosi 1995). By 1994, after the Campo had been considered by the Global Environmental Facility as a likely site for a biodiversity conservation project, La Forestière de Campo failed to obtain a new long-term logging title. Since then, the company has been exploiting a smaller area while it waits for a forest management plan to be established in which there will be areas reserved for logging.

Meanwhile, in Djoum, logging was carried out by Cameroonian companies up to 1995 with extremely high rates of timber production, similar to the non-sustainable rates obtained elsewhere in the country. In 1995, the Malaysian company WTK, with a reputation of non-sustainable logging practices, was granted a short-term logging title as a subcontractor. (For example, although the average number of species felled in Cameroon is about ten, Asian companies fell about 40.) Like other outsiders, logging companies base their activities on the regulations of modern law. After negotiating with the government, they obtain a logging title and operate under the supervision of the Forestry Department. Despite promises to carry out sustainable logging, the main objective of logging companies and the state seems to be only high profits. In its capacity as forest owner, the state lays down management rules that govern logging without taking into account the concerns of the local population. These communities feel excluded from profit-sharing and the management of what they consider to be part of their heritage. The disastrous social impact of logging adds to their frustration and has a tremendous effect on common property management.

For example, there are tree species of cultural, medicinal and food value as well as commercial value to the population. They are generally managed by following acknowledged and accepted rules of local commoners. Logging companies, however, do not recognize these existing rights over such species and exploit them with neither permission nor compensation to the commoners. This is the case with the Moabi and Bubinga species, which are at the origin of numerous conflicts between the logging companies and the local communities. Furthermore, areas that local commoners wish to keep untouched, especially because they are hunting spaces, are generally exploited since they are often rich in rare species. This is the case with the Dipikar peninsula in the Campo region. During a survey carried out in 1994 and 1995 by the author, villagers living in the vicinity of this contested area unanimously agreed that Dipikar is an area to be preserved from industrial logging because it is exceptionally rich in wildlife. Meanwhile, La Forestière de Campo plans to construct buildings, roads and infrastructure for the purpose of logging the area (Nguiffo and Fosi 1995).

Logging is a windfall to poachers who use logging roads to reach the heart of the forest. It also facilitates the transportation of their catch. Finally, it penalizes the population by driving game away from the villages. Furthermore, the arrival of the logging companies has upset the social structure of the villages in many ways. It has led to the emergence of a new social class: wage earners of the logging companies whose incomes are far higher than that of other members of the village and who sometimes defend the interest of the private companies to the detriment of those of the former commoners. The wages they earn sometimes tip the power scales in their favour in the village, and influence decisions to be taken both in their favour, and in that of their employers. Very often, employees serve as brokers between the village and the employer during settlement of disputes and crucial negotiations. In this context, their efficiency is judged in relation to the expectations of their employer and not that of the community. The feeling of exclusion and the negative social and ecological impact of logging have led to numerous disputes between the former commoners and logging companies. The two main causes of these disputes are the population's demand for a fair share of the logging profits, and, sometimes, for an end to logging.

A fourth outsider with tremendous power in the forest is the Washington, DC-based World Bank, through both its structural adjustment and conservation policies. First, the World Bank has played a major role in transforming the Cameroon economy through structural adjustment policies, demanding that the state focus its practices more toward rapid economic growth. Since the forests and their inhabitants represent Cameroon's 'untapped' wealth, the Bank pushes an aggressive forest policy that links forest use and production to the demands and the pace of the global economy. Under Bank-advocated policy, property rights are 'clarified' in such a way that the 'high-value' forested areas are exclusively for logging companies and the 'low-value' areas are exclusively for local communities. Although this new forest policy may appear as a major victory for the commoners who now have 'clarified' property rights, in practice, it henceforth excludes local populations from access to many areas over which they had common property regimes. It also excludes them from accessing logging titles and/or their fair share of logging profits. The requirement by the new forestry law to grant concessions through tenders has resulted in doing away with the usual 'holding of discussions' with the villagers. During such discussions, local populations have requested compensation from the logging companies. This ceremony has been replaced by an ordinary meeting during which the logging companies and government representatives merely inform the local population that the company has a legal right to exploit their forest. The time-efficiency requirements of the World Bank are in direct conflict with these 'customary' practices, the last vestiges of local community involvement in the granting of logging concessions.

Under neoliberal practices instituted by the World Bank, forest communities are now excluded from the discussions over both logging concessions and their rights to use various areas of the forest. Less transparent, but equally detrimental, are the World Bank's new 'conservation' policies. Their main objective is not to ensure decent living conditions for the population in these Bank-declared ecological 'hotspots' – forested sites that are judged in danger of dramatically reducing the world's biodiversity – but rather to enclose species and forested areas that are of interest to non-locals (i.e., the 'global community'). Preserving the Cameroonian ecological hotspots is not without consequences to the local population whose living conditions may be sacrificed on the altar of new global conservation norms. Under the purview of the GEF, Cameroon's conservation projects are created without any consultation with regional NGOs or local populations, thus further compromising the forest commoners and the commons through highly undemocratic decision-making practices.

GEF conservation projects started with a generous idea, that of reducing as much as possible the area of forest being exploited by logging companies. This initiative, though, has shortcomings that make it dangerous for the local community. In Cameroon, the relationship between local people and the conservation projects has always been conflictual. For example, the choice of areas as wildlife sanctuaries never takes into account the people who have always been in charge of conservation. In Campo, the protected area was created in 1932, and overnight all the villages suddenly became part of the reserve and under its land-use rules. It happened in the same way with the well-known Dja Reserve (recognized by UNESCO as a 'common heritage of mankind'). These reflect the fact that the 'global commons' are always constructed through the deconstruction of the local commons. In these projects, local people have no, or very few, alternatives. The interests of 'mankind' are opposed to those of local people, and they are seen as not being a part of 'mankind'. This is similar to what happened during the colonial period, when the 'wild forest people' were not seen as being part of the world's civilized society. Extending 'civilization' to these wild areas of the world was a legitimizing rationality for colonization. Now, the protection of endangered biodiversity is the new tool for the implementation of ecological/social colonialism.

In conservation projects, there are different levels of exclusion of local population from the management of protected areas. Most often, they are physically expelled from their territories, because they are said to be a threat to biodiversity. When they are allowed to stay in the protected area, their use rights are so restricted that they cannot possibly be involved in resource management. But most often, their traditional knowledge of biodiversity is tapped by conservation-project officials and researchers. Hence, exclusion occurs in the use of land and natural resources, but not in the traditional knowledge which must be universally shared, falling under the communitarian rubric of the 'common heritage of mankind'.

Amazingly enough, while hunting is completely forbidden in protected areas in the Campo region, the Forestry Department allows La Société Forestière de Campo to carry out industrial logging there. Thus, in the perception of the Forestry Department, traditional management of the commons may be more dangerous than long-term industrial logging without a prior management plan. These anti-local decisions have infuriated local populations and many conflicts have arisen between the local population and conservation projects. In the Dja area, one of the causes of the conflict was that the European Union-funded ECOFAC project (Écosystemes Forestièrs d'Afrique Centrale) dealt only with the animals and the flora, and acknowledged none of the existing social problems in the area. The local population responded with repeated demonstrations that halted the project for several days.

Forms of Resistance

Foreign influence on common property management has been at the genesis of the resistance movement by the people of southern

Cameroon. Very covert and timid in the past, this movement gained ground in the early 1990s because of an explosion of industrial logging. In 1992, Cameroon became the leading African timber exporter, at the expense of unprecedented pressure exerted on forest ecosystems. The increase in the number of logging companies and in the total area of forest exploited has considerably intensified the socio-ecological problems linked to forest management. Such widespread unsustainable logging upsets the existing social infrastructure and makes the cash economy dominant. It attracts migrants who do not share the values and beliefs of the local population and converts locals into victims of an external invasion. One NGO observer from Nanga-Eboko (where logging has been stopped) describes some of the consequences of logging: 'soils have become infertile, bushmeat is hard to find, the women have now to walk three kilometres to find water' (Verhagen and Enthoven 1993). Some important tree species, such as the Moabi (*Baillonella toxisperma*) are being over-exploited, with about 67,900 cubic metres exported in 1990. Just four years later, Moabi exports dropped by 50 per cent, a sign of the fast depletion of this precious tree.

In the late 1980s, state authority was undermined by an unprecedented financial crisis and by popular protest against authoritarian rule. The increasing influence of multilateral institutions on public life has also contributed to the weakening of the Cameroon state, and has spurred the emergence of new forms of protest. The drop in the prices of raw materials, and the disengagement of the state from social services (such as health and education) led to a deterioration of living conditions in the rural areas. In order to survive, the local communities insistently demanded a share of the profits from forestry exploitation. The forms of resistance varied depending on the communities and the outsiders involved. Due to their peaceful nature, the Bakola and Baka communities preferred withdrawal. Faced with interference from other actors, they suffered various forms of humiliation in silence, and preferred to shift their camps to other areas. Their most common form of resistance has been refusal to collaborate with the Bantus as well as the logging companies that employ them as prospectors. Refusal to collaborate with the Bantus can be generally observed during the hunting season when Bantus need the expertise of Baka hunters. Bakas hide part or all of their catch and Baka guides sometimes abandon their Bantu partners in the heart of the forest.

For their part, the Bantus are more fierce in their resistance. In late 1980s, the Bantus organized a series of protests against the logging companies, not against logging *per se* but their conduct. The population claims its fair share of the excessive logging profits as well as some consideration for their social welfare. Of course, these demands are not revolutionary, as these demands are usually found in written agreements made by the logging companies when they start operating in the villages. These agreements are usually violated by the companies and the protests aim at calling for their implementation. Young, unemployed school graduates who return to the villages after their studies play a significant role in raising awareness. They have a great capacity to mobilize and to protest, and have some basic knowledge of law. They write most of the petitions denouncing the abuses of logging companies, some of which are sent to top state officials. One was even sent to the son of former French President François Mitterrand who was then his father's adviser on African affairs and was suspected of having shares in a logging company in southeast Cameroon. These petitions aim at drawing attention to the poor social and ecological impact of logging, at a moment when the idea of boycotting tropical timber is topical amongst Western NGOs. Scared by the possibility of being blacklisted, some logging companies have yielded to the demands of the villagers.

In some cases, villages were forced to erect roadblocks so as to prevent the transportation of timber. This strategy was sometimes dangerous because it is illegal and gives the government the opportunity to intervene on the side of the logging companies to 'prevent disturbances on the highway'. Sometimes, the villages are amateurish in organizing their protests and are very often trapped in carrying out violent acts to claim their rights. By doing this, the logging companies have had the opportunity of getting them punished for violence, and their initial claims remain completely ignored.

Since the early 1990s, some villages or groups have engaged in eco-guerrilla warfare by setting fire to trucks transporting timber to the Douala seaport for export. It is interesting to note that the upsurge in calls for democracy in Cameroon was preceded by the clamour that had its genesis in the forest region. Its effectiveness, however, has been considerably limited because it benefits neither from the same media coverage nor from the same support from urban and international communities.

The Long Road to Democratizing the Commons

Destructive processes brought by outsiders to the forest commons have forced the Cameroon state to make some attempts to reverse these trends and revive traditional and endogenous commons management institutions. Two initiatives will be presented here: government-supported community forestry and timber certification. This section ends with a succinct description of the fundamental conditions necessary for the revival of common property management in Cameroon.

The political space for forest communities to regain rights to their forests has recently opened up. Until 1994, forests belonged to the state and the local people had no rights whatsoever on these lands. Interestingly, by the late 1980s, as discussed above, the World Bank promoted a forest policy that included the recognition of local people's rights on some portions of the forest. Coupled with local and international political protest, the state agreed to incorporate the concept of community-managed forests in the 1994 forestry law and its implementation decrees. These changes, however, are problematic for the following reasons. First, community forests are still part of state property, and people have no ownership right over them. They have only exclusive use rights. Second, a community forest may not exceed 5,000 hectares, which, in some areas, is far below the size of what is considered a village forest. Third, management has to be supervised by the Forestry Department, which is notorious for its repressive activities. Fourth, not every community can obtain a community forest; the requests of those close to either protected areas or protected forests cannot be considered. Fifth, community forests can only be owned in a non-permanent forest estate, which, according to the land-use plan, are greatly reduced in size. Furthermore, there is rivalry between community forests and small logging titles on these forest portions and the latter is favoured because of their expected contributions to the state budget. Sixth, the state administration maintains a strong influence on the implementation of community forestry. The impression one has is that the administration considers the communities as being unable to carry out the management of their forests themselves. In fact, the law itself promotes community failure as various notions of community are not well-defined. Also, the procedure to be followed by 'the community' is incompatible with the horizontal structure of the population of the forest region. Finally, one wonders whether or not the government wishes to see community forests succeeding as none has been granted since this law was enacted despite numerous community requests. Nothing indicates that the trend will be reversed in the near future.

The second new strategy for revitalizing the commons is the certification process for tropical timber, a response to the ecological and social impacts of timber exploitation. Certification is an attempt to promote socially and ecologically sustainable timber and is being promoted by international green NGOs. Among the different initiatives sharing this same aim, the Forest Stewardship Council (FSC) is most appropriate for the Cameroon case, as it focuses on the social aspect of timber production. The first criterion attempts to ensure local population rights to land security in the immediate vicinity of logging concessions. The second criterion emphasizes local populations' rights to natural resources, preservation of religious and cultural sites, fair financial compensation for the use of indigenous people's traditional knowledge and more. These two criteria, as described by the FSC, could actually be a key instrument in the defence of the forest commons.

But for Cameroon, the international FSC initiative misunderstands the realities of the state and of forest struggles in areas outside the purview of logging companies. That is, certification under FSC principles wrongly assumes, first, that national laws are balanced with regards to local populations' rights and interests, and second, that the disastrous social impact of timber exploitation is solely a consequence of non-compliance of logging companies with national laws. Certification advocates believe that international consumer pressure on logging companies will force them to respect national laws that protect local populations. In addition, certification advocates believe the major lever for social change in the world's tropical forests will come from enlightened Northern consumers that will force big timber producers to change their exploitative practices.

As this chapter shows, the logging companies are just one of many actors in the forest, and they work in only some parts of the forest. The state and its old and new forest laws, policies and implementing agencies are major culprits in the historical disempowerment of forest communities and destruction of the commons. Simple consumer pressure on logging companies addresses only small fragments of the total story. None the less, certification *may* increase the political pressure that could reverberate into the realm of state activities, which in turn could allow for greater liberty for the people in the management of the forests. In this way, the move toward certification may unleash unintended powerful forces that reconfigure the political terrain in Cameroon's forests. It is certainly clear that certification, coupled with the creation of community forests, can regenerate the political space for local populations to regain control over more of their forests.

A third alternative is being discussed in Cameroon today, emanating from an international organization with a very uneven track record in issues concerning social power in forested areas. After decades of dealing with forest problems strictly through the narrow lens of 'conservation', hence alienating forest commoners in the process, the International Union for the Conservation of Nature and its Resources (IUCN) is now changing its approach by trying to involve local peoples as so-called partners in conservation. The aim of their 'social sustainability' approach is to create viable alternatives for local population living in the protected areas, and to involve them in protected area management. This involvement of local peoples should gradually lead to a withdrawal of the conservation project from the protected areas, and to leave the conservation under the exclusive authority of local populations. This is not actually a new idea: such attempts have been made, with more or less success, in India and in other African countries. These approaches are actually very logical, since they assume that local people are able to manage the forest and to organize conservation by themselves. For centuries, they have had the most sustainable forest management, without the help of any conservation programme or Northern NGO, and problems arose only when they started facing the interference of these actors in the forest management.

When all is said and done, one has the impression that, while observing development projects and other similar initiatives in Cameroon, the commons are of negligible interest for development agencies and the state. Political action is urgently needed that hands back the management of commons to local communities.

Conclusion: Reviving Commons Management in Cameroon

The fact that the forest commons still thrive in southern Cameroon is a testament to the sustainable institutional practices of the forest people. Despite all the described threats and encroachments, the common property regimes are still well integrated in local people's lives, albeit in greatly diminished and weakened forms. The commons in Cameroon therefore have to be considered in terms of defence of what is still remaining, and of revival. The strength and financial interest of external actors have led to the exclusion of commoners from the management of natural resources. Threats to the commons come in two forms: first, the marginalization of the commoners by the efficient and destructive power of various state agencies, private firms, non-native poachers, biodiversity prospectors, some conservation projects, and development agencies. Due to these overwhelming pressures, commoners are less able to manage the forests and sometimes are forced to adapt to the destructive tendencies in ways that undermine the commons. Second, local struggles to control the commons are at the centre of most expropriation strategies in the forest. It is therefore a double tragedy, both of the marginalized commoners and of the disputed commons.

What, then, should be done to revive and defend the commons in Cameroon? The recognition of local peoples' ownership rights over the land is an unavoidable prerequisite, without which the local population cannot regain their power and security over the forest, without which they cannot maintain and expand their own non-exploitable production and reproduction practices. It is also necessary to help support the reinforcement of the capacities of commoners, so as to rejuvenate solidarity among them as well as strengthen their effective methods of organization, decision making and social control. Emphasis should be placed on the respectful empowerment of local cultures and values and should not in any way serve as a pretext to introduce 'modern' values and norms. Empowerment should not be a tool for the perpetuation of acculturation. It will also be indispensable to reduce competition with external actors in the management of forest resources. Every step should be taken with the view to attaining the highest decentralization of management, both in terms of state laws and agreements, as well as in the everyday practices of state officials and local, regional and international actors in the forests of Cameroon. What we find today is a pivotal moment in which the forests can be revived ecologically and socially or they can die a swift and devastating death. How we all act to create the secure political space for the defence of sustainable commons practices will determine the fate of the Cameroon forest, the forest commoners and the nation.

Note

1   de Groot et al. (1995:211) point out that 'commons property management is based on two necessary conditions: 1) that internal regime arrangements work successfully, and 2) externally, that the common property is indeed property, defended against access by outsiders'.

5

Nature as Community: The Convergence of Environment and Social Justice

Giovanna DiChiro

'Sheila, I think they're trying to kill us!' This was the only logical conclusion that Robin Cannon, a resident of South Central Los Angeles, could imagine, as she attempted to convey to her sister in a late-night phone call the ominous contents of the environmental impact report (EIR) she had just spent the entire evening poring over. Earlier that day Cannon had attended a public hearing sponsored by the Los Angeles City Council, where she first learned of the proposed 1,600-ton-per-day solid-waste incinerator known as LANCER (Los Angeles City Energy Recovery Project), which was planned to be sited in the centre of her neighbourhood. City officials who advocated the waste incinerator facility intended to allay 'unfounded' fears and misconceptions about what an incinerator would mean for the community. The residents who attended the meeting were treated to splendid images of the waste incinerator site encircled by beautifully landscaped picnic areas that, according to LANCER's proponents, would offer an attractive place to host wedding receptions and outdoor parties. These city officials could not have suspected that this ordinary woman who was asking so many questions about the health effects of burning tons of waste in her community would actually read the entire three-inch-thick EIR that documented the project's scientifically based standards of safety. As Cannon's phone call to her sister suggests, the layers of information embedded in the technical document actually conveyed a very different message. Highly toxic dioxins and fluorons were only some of the chemicals that would most likely contaminate the air, water and land of the people who lived in South Central Los Angeles.

Cannon, her sister Sheila, and her friend Charlotte Bullock, all residents of this predominantly African American, low income community, formed Concerned Citizens of South Central Los Angeles in response to the distressing implications of the EIR. These three women's immediate actions toward building an organized response to the perceived threat to the welfare of their community dispelled the stereotypes of low income and poor neighbourhoods as 'unaware', 'unconcerned' and 'compliant'.[1] Through Concerned Citizens they mobilized a citywide network of community organizations and local political and business leaders, which successfully blocked the construction of LANCER by defeating the city-sponsored $535 million bond issue. Not only did this grass-roots organization thwart the city's plans to build the incinerator; it forced the city to re-evaluate the long prioritization of incineration in its waste management policy and to pursue instead a commitment to recycling. The fight against the LANCER facility also initiated a host of other community actions on issues such as housing, schools, drugs and neighbourhood security. These issues were seen by the activists to be as 'environmental' as those of hazardous waste, air quality and land use.

I met Robin Cannon in 1993 and was surprised to learn that these issues were *not* deemed adequately 'environmental' by local environmental groups such as the Sierra Club or the Environmental Defense Fund. When members of Concerned Citizens first approached these organizations in the mid 1980s for support to fight LANCER, they were informed that the poisoning of an urban community by an incineration facility was a 'community health issue', not an environmental one.[2] Addressing this question of the discrepancy between what does and does not count as 'environmental' is, I believe, crucial to the effort to produce a broadly based environmental movement that really works. Part of this effort requires a close analysis and historical reading of how different groups of people have understood their relationship to 'nature' and the environments in which they live. What, for example, are the diverse and sometimes contradictory meanings and metaphors that different people deal with when negotiating the multiple environments they encounter in their everyday lives? What does it mean to talk about nature as a 'benevolent mother', as 'wild places unspoiled by human hands', or as the 'place where family and community convene and share life experiences'? We can also learn a lot about how people understand, live in and change their environments, not only by studying diverse *ideas* about 'nature' or human/environment interconnections, but by examining social practice. What are the complex forms and structures of social and cultural organization that emerge in diverse locales to resist the destruction of particular human/environment relationships and to support specific ways of life? In other words, how do people mobilize through action in order to sustain or transform certain relationships with 'nature' and their 'environment'? In this chapter, I examine the emergence of the US environmental justice movement, a social movement strongest in low-income communities of colour that, like Concerned Citizens of South Central Los Angeles, conceive of 'nature' and 'environment' as those places and sets of relationships that sustain a local community's way of life. The grass-roots organizations that make up the movement identify such issues as social justice, local economic sustainability, health and community governance as falling under the purview of 'environment'. They see their community's physical living, working and playing space in US inner cities – suffering under state disinvestment policies for decades – as degraded social commons that are neither exclusive nor undifferentiated. Like those defending and revitalizing the Brazilian and Mexican commons, these people-of-colour ecoactivists are redefining what constitutes a healthy and socially just urban commons, based on their actions in the flowering US environmental justice movement. In our discussions on reinventing the commons, we should better appreciate the city – home to much of the world's human population – as a robust site for political contestation and change in efforts to create more sustainable forms of ecological-social relations.

Redefining Environmentalism: The Struggle for a 'Green' Justice

The extensive national and international network of community/environmental organizations referred to as the environmental justice movement challenges dominant meanings of environmentalism and produces new forms of environmental theory and action. The term 'environmental justice', which appeared in the United States sometime in the mid 1980s, questions popular notions of 'environment' and 'nature' and attempts to produce something different. In this chapter, I explore some of those differences as they are articulated through the voices of activists in the movement. The vast majority of activists in the environmental justice movement are low-income women and predominantly women of colour, including Dana Alston, Pam Tau Lee, Penny Newman, Esperanza Maya, Juana Guttierrez, Vernice Miller, Marta Salinas, Valerie Taliman, Marina Ortega, Lois Gibbs, Rose Augustine and Janice Dickerson.[3] From the start, the gender, race and class composition of the movement distinguishes it from that of the mainstream environmental movement, whose constituents have historically been white and middle class and whose leadership has been predominantly male.[4]

The history of mainstream environmentalism locates its adherents in an ideological position that constructs a separation between humans and the 'natural' world. Environmentalists are therefore often said to be obsessed with preserving and protecting those 'wild and natural' areas defined as places where humans are not and *should* not be in large numbers. Social movement historians have occasionally referred to environmental justice activists as the 'new environmentalists', a term that I find misleading (Gottlieb and Ingram 1988). Many of the grass-roots activists with whom I have spoken are reluctant to call themselves environmentalists at all, much less newly converted ones. In part, this is due to the dominance of the mainly white, middle class, and uncritically 'preservationist' political culture from which much mainstream environmental thinking has developed.[5] Again, in these mainstream terms what counts as environment is limited to issues such as wildland preservation and endangered species protection. Issues pertaining to human health and survival, community and workplace poisoning, and economic sustainability are generally not considered to be part of the environmental agenda. Additionally, many activists perceive much of mainstream environmentalism to be either fixated on anti-urban development campaigns (read as 'no jobs for city-dwelling people') or utterly indifferent to the concerns of urban communities. Many of the community organizations that make up the environmental justice movement are located in low-income and working-class communities in and around industrialized urban centres throughout the country. Crucial issues in these communities, as we saw in the case of Robin Cannon and Concerned Citizens, include lead and asbestos poisoning in substandard housing, toxic waste incineration and dumping, and widespread unemployment. Until relatively recently, these were problems that the mainstream organizations located outside the domain of the 'environment'.[6]

Environmental justice activists define the environment as 'the place you work, the place you live, the place you play', a definition that resonates with many non-urban commons activists around the world. Many mainstream US environmentalists, however, would find this formulation incomprehensible, even ethically indefensible, because of its apparent anthropocentrism. Putting humans at the centre of environmental discourse is a grave error, they argue, because humans are the perpetrators of environmental problems in the first place. Environmental justice activists maintain that some humans, especially the poor, are also the victims of environmental destruction and pollution and that, furthermore, some human cultures live in ways that are relatively sound ecologically. They therefore contend that the mainstream environmentalists' invention of a universal division between humans and nature is deceptive, theoretically incoherent and strategically ineffective in its political aim to promote widespread environmental awareness. Pam Tau Lee, the labour coordinator for the Labor and Occupational Health Program at the University of California at Berkeley and a board member of the National Toxics Campaign Fund and the Southwest Organizing Network, describes environmental justice as being

> . . . able to bring together different issues that used to be separate. If you're talking about lead and where people live, it used to be a housing struggle; if you're talking about poisoning on the job, it used to be a labor struggle; people being sick from TB or occupational exposures used to be separate health issues, so environmental justice is able to bring together all of these different issues to create one movement that can really address what actually causes all of these phenomena to happen and gets to the root of the problems.[7]

The merging of social justice and environmental interests therefore assumes that people are an integral part of what should be understood as the environment. The daily realities and conditions of people's lives have not been at the centre of mainstream environmental discourse. Traditional environmental arguments have commonly constructed 'society' and 'nature', and urban versus wild/natural, as hostile dichotomies. As William Cronon (Cronon 1996) and Candace Slater argue persuasively (Slater 1996), traditional Euro-American conceptions of 'the natural' as 'Edenic' or 'sublime' posit nature as a place or state of original purity, uncontaminated by human intervention and avarice. As these authors have demonstrated in their writing on the history of ideas of wilderness and on Western imaginings of Amazonia, this type of Edenic thinking, which locates nature outside of human culture, separates humans from nature while constructing nature as in need of human control and domination. Cronon and Slater describe how the human populations that Euro-American colonists considered to be closer to nature and part of the 'wilderness' landscape (for example, the native Indians in the Americas or the enslaved Africans brought to the New World, who were both classified as savages and likened to animals) are people who were also seen to be a part of a wild, untamed nature that had to be exploited and controlled.

How can these historical analyses inform us about the contemporary environmental conditions of human groups situated differently in the society, and about their different responses to the environmental problems that confront them? Numerous studies have demonstrated that it is primarily low-income communities of colour that are often targeted for industrial and toxic waste disposal sites (Bullard and Wright 1987:21–37, Bullard 1990, Anderson and Greening, 1982:204–18, US General Accounting Office 1983, Pollack and Grozuczak 1984). Many environmental justice activists argue that this reality is nothing less than history repeating itself, this time in relation to who suffers the consequences of modern-day environmental pollution. Dana Alston, a longtime activist, discusses how the environmental justice movement's redefinition of 'environment' to account for the presence of people reflects one of the primary differences between it and the mainstream movement:

The Nature Conservancy defines itself as the 'real estate' arm of the environmental movement and as being about saving nature, pristine areas, sensitive ecosystems, endangered species, and rain forests. But the reality of the situation is that there is hardly anywhere in the world where there aren't people living, no matter how remote you get, and the most vulnerable cultures are in the areas that are most remote, whether you are talking about here in the U. S. or in Latin America or wherever, so immediately it puts us in confrontation with the Nature Conservancy. We continue to raise these issues not only in the international arena but here as the Nature Conservancy goes to buy large tracts of land in New Mexico or out west where indigenous and Chicano people have lived for decades and have sovereignty or land-grant rights . . . with total disregard for how these real estate dealings affect the social, political, and economic life of our communities. We feel that many of these communities are just as much endangered species as any animal species.[8]

Consequently, activists in the environmental justice movement are unlikely to identify themselves as the 'new environmentalists', because they do not view themselves as an outgrowth of the 'old' environmental movement, with its 'Save the whales and rain forests' slogans. It would be more accurate to regard environmental justice activists as the 'new' civil rights or 'new' social justice activists, since many of the prominent organizers affirm their roots in and political continuities with the social justice movements of the 1960s, including the civil rights, welfare rights and labour and

farmworker movements. Moreover, the term 'new environmentalists' suggests that the members of these emerging grass-roots
organizations, who come from predominantly African American,
Latino, Native American, and Asian American communities, have
only recently become aware of the importance of 'environmental'
concerns. Numerous histories of activism by people of colour on
environmental issues exist but often are not classified by mainstream
groups as authentic 'environmental history', because of these crucial
questions of definition (Pena 1992:1–25, Bullard 1990, Pulido 1991,
Churchill 1993).

What is new about the environmental justice movement is not the
'elevated environmental consciousness' of its members but the ways
it is transforming the possibilities for fundamental social and
environmental change through processes of redefinition, reinvention
and construction of innovative political and cultural discourses and
practices. This includes, among other things, the articulation of the
concepts of environmental justice and environmental racism and the
forging of new forms of grass-roots political organization. I will
illustrate some of these conceptual inventions by examining a few
key historical moments that have defined the environmental justice
movement.

Re-visioning Environmental History: Whose Stories are Told?

Some movement historians identify the large-scale civil disobedience
that occurred in Warren County, North Carolina in 1982 as the
first active demonstration of an emerging environmental justice
movement (Bullard 1993). At this demonstration, hundreds of
predominantly African American women and children, but also
local white residents, used their bodies to block trucks from dumping
poisonous PCB-laced dirt into a landfill near their community. The
mainly African American, working-class, rural communities of Warren
County had been targeted as the dumping site for a toxic waste
landfill that would serve industries throughout North Carolina. This
demonstration of nonviolent civil disobedience opened the gates for
a series of subsequent actions by people of colour and poor people
throughout the country. Unlike social activism against toxic
contamination that pre-dated this event, such as the struggle against
Hooker Chemical Company at Love Canal, New York, in the late
1970s, this action began to forge the connections between race,

poverty and the environmental consequences of the production of industrial waste (Gibbs 1982).

The Warren County episode succeeded in racializing the anti-toxics agenda and provoked a number of studies that would document the historical pattern of disproportionately targeting racial minority communities for toxic waste contamination. One such study, which represents another key moment in the history of the environmental justice movement, was a report sponsored by the United Church of Christ Commission for Racial Justice (UCC-CRJ) and published in 1987. Although people living near toxic waste facilities have known for many years about industrial pollution's detrimental effects on their health and their environments, it was not until this report that an awareness of widespread environmental racism entered mainstream political consciousness.

The UCC-CRJ report, 'Toxic Waste and Race in the United States: A National Report on the Racial and Socioeconomic Characteristics of Communities with Hazardous Waste Sites', compiled the results of a national study that found race to be the leading factor in the location of commercial hazardous waste facilities. The study, presented to the National Press Club in Washington, DC that same year, determined that people of colour suffered a 'disproportionate risk' to the health of their families and their environments, with 60 per cent of African American and Latino communities and over 50 per cent of Asian/Pacific Islanders and Native Americans living in areas with one or more uncontrolled toxic waste sites. The report also disclosed that 40 per cent of the nation's toxic landfill capacity is concentrated in three communities: Emelle, Alabama, with a 78.9 per cent African American population; Scotlandville, Louisiana, with 93 per cent African Americans; and Kettleman City, California, which is 78.4 per cent Latino (Commission for Racial Justice 1987).

The term 'environmental racism' entered into political discussion on the environment in 1987 when the Reverend Benjamin Chavis, the Commission's executive director who was most recently the head of the NAACP, coined it. According to Chavis, environmental racism is

. . . racial discrimination in environmental policy-making and the enforcement of regulations and laws, the deliberate targeting of people of color communities for toxic waste facilities, the official sanctioning of the life-threatening presence of poisons and pollutants in our communities, and history of excluding people of color from leadership in the environmental movement. (Grossman 1992)

In the mid to late 1980s, this process of naming and researching the material realities of environmental racism made possible a significant transformation in what would count as properly environmental concerns. This new political concept also provided an organizing tool for galvanizing into action the multiple and diverse communities and constituencies for whom environmental racism was a painful reality.

How did the appearance of the UCC-CRJ report on toxics and race and the public naming of environmental racism affect the national environmental agenda? By 1990 a variety of coalitions of people-of-colour environmental justice organizations had emerged, including the extremely dynamic Southwest Network for Economic and Environmental Justice (SNEEJ). In January and March of that year, representatives from many of these grass-roots coalitions sent two recriminating letters to the Group of Ten national environmental organisations, 'calling on them to dialogue on the environmental crisis impacting communities of color, and to hire people of color on their staffs and boards of directors' (Moore 1992:7). The letters presented an analysis of environmental racism and defined the ways that the primarily white, mainstream organizations have complicitly supported it:

> There is a clear lack of accountability by the Group of Ten environmental organizations towards Third World communities in the Southwest, in the U.S. as a whole and internationally. Your organizations continue to support and promote policies which emphasize the clean-up and preservation of the environment on the backs of working people in general and people of color in particular. In the name of eliminating environmental hazards at any cost, across the country industrial and other economic activities which employ us are being shut down, curtailed or prevented while our survival needs and cultures are ignored. We suffer from the results of these actions, but are never full participants in the decision making which leads to them. (Moore 1992:8)

According to the activists with whom I have spoken, responses to these challenges have varied. At worst, some of the Group of Ten have expressed outrage and denial and all but ignored the invitation to 'come to the table as equals'. On the other hand, some have begun to enter into discussions about building 'multicultural and multi-racial organizations', to share resources such as technical expertise, legal assistance and funding, and to seriously modify their organizations' structure and mission. The Earth Island Institute, Greenpeace and the now defunct National Toxics Campaign are often cited as the environmental groups that have responded to these challenges by expanding the scope of their projects to include environmental justice issues and by diversifying their staff and leadership.

In October 1991, the First National People of Color Environmental Leadership Summit convened in Washington, DC, signifying a watershed moment in the history of the movement. According to conference participants, this event foregrounded the importance of people-of-colour environmental groups' insistence on self representation and speaking for themselves (Alston 1990). It also marked an unequivocal rejection of a 'partnership based on paternalism' with the mainstream environmental movement.

The summit brought together 300 African, Native, Latino, and Asian American delegates from the United States and a number from Canada, Central and South America, Puerto Rico and the Marshall Islands to shape the contours of a 'multi-racial movement for change' founded on the political ideology of working from the grass-roots. Conference participants heard testimonies and reports on the local effects of environmental racism, including the extensive poisoning of air, water and land that disproportionately devastates their environments and health. These discussions also provided a supportive context for people of colour to 'reaffirm their traditional connection to and respect for the natural world', which was collectively understood as 'including all aspects of daily life'. Environment so defined expands the definition of environmental problems and so includes issues such as 'militarism and defense, religious freedom and cultural survival, energy and sustainable development, transportation and housing, land and sovereignty rights, self-determination and employment' (Moore 1992:8). Dana Alston describes how the leadership summit helped to bring people of colour together in a spirit of political solidarity:

> The most important thing that came out of the summit was the bonding. Many people might think that because they're nonwhite that they're going to come together, but the society is built on keeping people divided, and we all know about the tensions between African Americans and Asian Americans and Latinos and Native Americans, but it's the history, the culture, the society that's keeping us divided . . . because that's how the power structure stays in power, by keeping us separate, so we had to from the very beginning put together a set of principles from which we were going to relate to each other.[9]

The composition and programme of the second day of the leadership summit shifted with the arrival of another 250 participants from a variety of environmental and social change organizations, together with a sampling of 'professionals' like lawyers, academics and policy makers. Engaging in critical discussions and debates, the conferees articulated key issues of the building of the environmental justice movement, including the definition of environment and environmental problems, leadership and organizational strategy, and the formation of coalitions and partnerships. Working by consensus, the leadership summit drew up a set of 17 organizational principles that would guide the emergent political process. These 'Principles of Environmental Justice' profile a broad and deep political project to pursue environmental justice in order to 'secure our political, economic and cultural liberation that has been denied for over 500 years of colonization and oppression, resulting in the poisoning of our communities and land and the genocide of our peoples' (Environmental Health Coalition 1993).

All of the activists with whom I have spoken maintain that the most promising achievement of the leadership summit was its commitment to the construction of diverse, egalitarian and non-hierarchical leadership and organizational processes and structures. The participants wanted something different from the technocratic rationality and top-down managerialism that the mainstream environmental organizations have adopted by mimicking the decision making approaches of the very corporations they are opposing. As grass-roots activists working in direct response to the threats of pollution, resource exploitation and land-use decisions in their communities, they contend that the decision making process is itself a primary issue in the debate over environmental problems. They reject the top-down approach as disempowering, paternalistic and exclusive and instead are committed to developing a more democratic, locally and regionally based, decentralized organizational culture. A commitment to such values, they argue, will build an environmental movement that truly works.

Reinventing Nature through Community Action

To forge a vigorous, effective environmental movement, the emergent grass-roots coalition of environmental justice organizations in the United States is producing a coherent analysis of the causes and consequences of environmental problems and a political culture based on community-governed and network-oriented social organization. In large part, these analyses and social practices are based on diverse interpretations of, and experiences with, nature and social injustice. In response to different cultural histories and to different experiences of environmental injustice, these low-income communities construct distinct meanings and definitions of 'nature' and of what constitutes proper human/environment interrelations and practices. These divergent definitions and practices, and their implications in the world, indicate the core discrepancies between the environmental justice and the mainstream environmental movements. They also represent approaches to understanding nature, and to *reinventing* it, that are very different from those that appear in many discussions on the environment and the commons, including some of the chapters in this book.

In the final section of this chapter, I want to focus on aspects of environmental justice that illustrate the ways that activists in the movement are 'reinventing nature'. As I mentioned earlier, environmental justice activists explicitly undertake a critique of modernist and colonial philosophies of unlimited progress, unchecked development, the privileging of Western scientific notions of objective truth and control of nature, and the hierarchical separation between nature and human culture. This antimodernist analysis is also implicitly a critique of the mainstream environmental movement, which, activists argue, upholds the same underlying colonial philosophy of nature as 'other' to human culture.

The activists' approach to reinventing nature, I suggest, contains both deconstructive and constructive elements. Their critiques of conventional or dominant ideas of nature and environment demonstrate how these constructs and their policy implications are detrimental to certain *human* communities, primarily the poor and people of colour. Exposing the historical and ecological effects on humans *and* the non-human world of these dominant ideologies reveals their limitations as theoretical foundations for a just environmentalism. Environmental justice groups, while strongly criticizing mainstream conceptions of nature, also *produce* a distinct theoretical and material connection between human/nature, human/environment relations through their notions of 'community'. Community becomes at once the idea the place, and the relations and practices that generate what these activists consider more socially just and ecologically sound human/environment configurations. These processes of critique and construct both engage the project of reinventing nature. In the paragraphs that follow I will briefly discuss some of their key points.

Communities of colour involved in environmental justice organizations develop a critique of what I call the colonial discourse of Euro-American forms of 'nature talk'. Colonial discourses of nature, they argue, constitute one of the historical progenitors of contemporary environmental racism. Although 'nature talk' separates humans from nature and posits them as superior to nature, it specifies that some humans are in fact part of nature. In other words, particular Euro-American romantic constructions of nature have been and continue to be problematic and even genocidal for people who have been characterized as being more like nature and thus less than human. The discourse that opposes an Edenic or sublime nature to a fallen culture (Cronon 1996) either categorizes people of colour as identical *with* nature, as in the case of indigenous peoples or Third World natives (thereby entitling Western colonizers and slave traders to exploit and have dominion over some humans in similar ways in which they would feel entitled to exploit non-human nature), *or* classifies them as people who are anti-nature, impure and even toxic, as in the case of poor communities of colour living in contaminated and blighted inner cities or in the surrounding rural wastelands (Haraway 1989, Gould 1981, Merchant 1980 and 1989). Images of people of colour in the mainstream environmental literature not infrequently depict throngs of overbreeding, slashing-and-burning, border-overflowing and ecologically incorrect Third Worlders or illegal immigrants. Such images encode these groups as anti nature or out of touch with the natural world. Wilderness or Eden must be located where these 'toxic' or 'fallen' peoples are not.

The Edenic notion of nature becomes, for many communities of colour, a tool of oppression that operates to obscure their own 'endangered' predicaments. Such a conception of nature is also seen by many activists to be the moral authority on which white, bourgeois culture bases its often genocidal environmental policy decisions. So the trademark slogans of mainstream environmentalism, such as 'Save the whales' or 'Extinction is forever', are seen to reflect concerns of white people who are blind to the problems of people of colour. The obsession with saving the rainforest and preserving biodiversity at the expense of local cultures is seen as a decision to trade them off. As a consequence, many white environmentalists claim that people of colour aren't interested in saving nature or the environment – even though US Congress' Black Congressional Caucus has registered the strongest voting record on Capitol Hill on issues of the environment. Clearly, activists of colour have substantial interests in the conceptual project of 'reinventing' the dominant idea of nature in mainstream environmentalism.

How a particular community of colour perceives its relationship with nature or reinvents it is based on specific experiential and historical realities. One of the central premises of this book is the argument that what we understand as nature is historically dynamic and culturally specific. What counts as nature is therefore different among various people-of-colour groups that have very different cultural histories. In fact, for many environmental justice activists from different ethnic backgrounds, the 1991 leadership summit revealed that there is no 'natural' bond among people-of-colour groups. They had to tackle the hard work of recognizing one another's specific cultural understandings of nature and the environment, as well as one another's specific experiences of environmental racism. Paul Ruffins, an African American journalist who attended the summit, explains that for various human groups in North America the different definitions of and relationships to nature that they espouse depend on how they got there. Obviously, the experience of dislocation and relocation in relation to the land and to 'place', was very different for Native Americans, European settlers, enslaved Africans, indentured Chinese labourers and Mexican inhabitants of the Southwest. Ruffins argues that, as an urbanized African American, he was forced to consider that a Native American's thinking about 'mother nature' and 'whales as brothers' – terms that sounded suspicious to him at first – may be different from the colonial nature talk embedded in a mainstream environmentalist's insistence on saving an endangered species at the expense of human cultures. He writes:

Many African American environmentalists define ourselves by our concern for the urban environment. We have vigorously attacked white environmentalists for their concern with saving birds and forests and whales while urban children were suffering from lead paint poisoning. For me personally, the most spiritually uplifting part of the Summit was the opportunity it gave me to temper that thinking, and spend more time considering the need to protect the land for its own sake. This came about partly from meeting black ecologists from the south who are fighting to save black farmers from losing their land and to preserve traditional black communities such as the Georgia Sea Islands, which are threatened by resort development.

But the most unique experience was the opportunity to interact with so many Native American and Hawaiian brothers and sisters and experience cultures that can only be understood in relationship to a piece of land or a body of water. Hearing Native Americans who`have been oppressed since 1492 explain the need to protect 'our brothers the whales,' helped me to truly experience the moral imperative of protecting animals and trees and land. (Ruffins 1992:11)

The multi-racial dialogue afforded by the summit provided the opportunity for people-of-colour groups to understand their historical and cultural differences, to see how they are similarly or differently positioned within colonial discourses of nature, and to begin to build a common environmental justice discourse that may embrace ideas as seemingly polarized as 'whales as our brothers' and cities as ecologically sound environments.

Ruffins's testimony speaks to the point that cultural and historical differences in perceptions of nature and environment among people-of-colour groups may be productive of, or militate against the formation of, environmental justice coalitions. He cited the summit as a moment when these multiple histories and cultures were able to unite in a collective conversation. This process of community and coalition building for environmental justice may be similarly inspired when people-of-colour groups share their different experiences of environmental oppression in everyday life. These may include experiences of racism, economic hardships, toxic poisoning affecting one's health or the health of one's children and feelings of alienation from one's surroundings and sense of place. Colonial discourse of nature often emphasizes the problem of increased alienation from nature as a consequence of capitalist advancement. The construction of wilderness as Eden was necessary to ameliorate the problems of alienation, spiritual depletion and corruption brought about by unrestrained capitalist greed.

Carl Anthony, director of the Urban Habitat Program of the Earth Island Institute, in San Francisco, writes about the forms of alienation that people of colour, especially African Americans, have been made to suffer (Anthony 1995). This alienation, he argues, is a result of a profound sense of loss suffered by many people who have been forced off their land and detached from their sense of place (such as the Native Americans and Mexicans who were dispossessed of their land, or the Africans who were shipped to America on slave ships) or by those who, because of class and racial oppression, must live in the forsaken, highly polluted inner cities with 'no functional relationship to nonhuman nature'. He and others are interested in examining the nature of the psychological damage being done to inner-city youth when they compare their environment with the resplendent images normally associated with the American landscape

(Lee 1993:41). For Anthony, reinventing human relationships with nature depends upon the production of what he calls a culturally and historically sensitive form of 'ecopsychology' – an analytical method to understand how different groups' specific views of nature are central to human identity formation. The histories of racial and class oppression that underlie an inner-city-dwelling person's 'non-functional' relationship to nature, and the reality of living in an impoverished environment, would result in a form of alienation and notion of self that, according to Anthony, must be addressed in order for the ecological health of the local community and natural environment to be transformed.

Experiences of alienation from nature, from one's environment and sense of place, and the forms of identity that ensue, differ among various people-of-colour communities. As numerous scholars of the environmental justice movement have shown, however, the framing of a collective experience of alienation and oppression often works to mobilize community activism (Edelstein 1988, Hofrichter 1993, Bullard 1994, Szasz 1994). Many activist members of the Western Shoshone, for example, invoke their cultural heritage in relation to their intergenerational connections to the land as the political motivation behind their decades-long struggle against the US government's annexation of their ancestral ground for the Nevada Nuclear Weapons Test Site (Churchill 1993). The experience of alienation and dispossession, in the case of the Western Shoshone's land-rights claims, constructs activist political identities. African Americans have different ties to the North American landscape. As a result of historical and demographic patterns of industrial development and post-Reconstruction labour migration, they live in predominantly urban communities. As Anthony has argued, the 'non-functional' relationship with nature that results from living in an impoverished, polluted environment may produce a disabling alienation that breeds hopelessness in local communities.

This is not, however, the only possible response to experiences of environmental injustice. Often the only *functional* relationship with nature for many city-dwelling people or those living near toxic waste sites becomes the core of their political strategy. In other words, their knowledge of the destruction of nature and natural systems in their local communities may function to mobilize them to act on these negative experiences. This knowledge often pits them against health department experts who would claim that there is nothing wrong with the environments in which they are living. But the community activists know otherwise – they often pay close attention to the changes they are living through as a result of toxic contamination of their environments. Many describe in great detail the profusion of respiratory illnesses, skin disorders and cancers that they and their neighbours suffer. They talk about the increased miscarriages, stillbirths, deformities, pet deaths, deformities in animal births, plants that won't grow or that come up out of the earth in strange contortions, bad-smelling air and foul-tasting water (Brown and Mikkelsen 1990, Newman 1994). Such direct knowledge about changes in the environment, obtained through experience, is essential for the environmental justice movement's argument that people of colour are often the ones who suffer the most from the effects of environmentally unsound industrial development.

Experiential knowledge of environmental degradation and toxic poisoning, and the community mobilization focusing on public health concerns that follows, is often, though not exclusively, an urban phenomenon. Industrial activity and its labour forces are concentrated in and around urban centres, as are most community organizations struggling for environmental justice. Because the overwhelming majority of African American, Latino, and Asian American communities in the United States are urbanized, the predicament of the 'sustainable' city becomes one of the primary concerns of environmental justice activists (Lee 1993, Gottlieb 1993). Consequently, another one of the essential reinventions of nature that environmental justice activists highlight is the relationship of nature to the city – the constructed or built urban environment. Mainstream environmentalism generally describes the city as being in opposition to nature. As Michael Pollan has put it, the city is 'written off as fallen, lost to nature, irredeemable' (Pollan 1991:188). In fact, many organizations, such as the Wilderness Society, the Nature Conservancy, and Not Yet New York, portray the large, modern, industrial city as a menacing, noxious sprawl of humanity representing the major threat to the survival of the natural world. The colonial discourse of nature has positioned cities as the repositories of waste, garbage, vermin, disease and depravity – all features that, in colonial nature talk, are also associated with the people who must live there. Activists in the movement argue that attention to the social and ecological sustainability of cities is the key environmental issue of the late twentieth century, a sobering proposition considering that most mainstream environmental organizations and environmental studies programmes in US universities pay scant attention to the problems and potentials of the urban environment (Lee 1993, Bullard 1994). The Urban Habitat Program, a project of the San Francisco Bay Area environmental justice group Earth Island Institute, warns:

In the next decade, important decisions about the future of cities and surrounding agricultural land will have consequences for millions of people. The deteriorated infrastructure of urban areas must be rebuilt. There are hidden rewards for undertaking a program of rebuilding our urban cores in tune with nature. The investment of the billions of dollars that will be required offers a multitude of opportunities for fresh approaches to affordable housing, public services, resources and waste. There is room for small projects and for bringing wilderness back into the city. (Anthony 1990:43–4)

For those who live, work and play in industrialized urban settings, largely populated by people of colour, the current rhetoric of 'cities in crisis' is much more than empty words. Environmental justice organizations enumerate the many ways that US inner cities and their poor and low-income inhabitants are in peril, often using the language of 'endangerment'. The question of what (and who) counts as an endangered species is therefore another crucial aspect of the environmental justice movement's reconceptualization of the relationships between non-human and human nature and the emergence of new ideas of nature and new forms of environmentalism. Activists use the highly potent and provocative signifier 'endangered species' in strategic ways. For example, the brochure published by San Francisco's Citizens for a Better Environment sets up a counter-intuitive use of a mainstream, yet very controversial, environmental slogan. On the front cover of the brochure, underneath the bold appeal 'Save an Endangered Species . . . ,' we see depicted a cheerful scene of mixed gender, multi-racial community members busily working in a very fruitful community garden that appears to encircle the city where they live. The slogan continues inside and, surprisingly, identifies as its object of concern not an endangered 'warm and fuzzy' animal or a spotted owl but '. . . YOU!'. The text asserts, 'When California's water, land or air is poisoned, it's not just fish and wildlife that are threatened. So are we. Our families, our neighborhoods, and our cities are all at risk from irresponsible toxic polluters and unenforced laws.' The accompanying image portrays an army of concerned citizens forming an angry and determined barrier between the encroaching toxic polluters and their beloved, clean and sustainable city. In this organizational brochure, Citizens for a Better Environment claims possession of the term 'endangered species' in order to reinvent its limited use by mainstream environmentalists. The group shows that by focusing on a single issue, such as the federal listing of an endangered species, mainstream environmentalists miss or obscure the many other related problems that contribute to environmental deterioration for all species, including people.

The anthropologist Stephen Feld critiques the notion of endangered species effectively in the liner notes for his CD *Voices of the Rainforest,* a recording of a day in the life of a Bosavi rainforest community in Papua New Guinea. Feld (1991:139) writes:

> When I read that we lose 15–20,000 species of plants and animals a year through the logging, ranching and mining that escalates rainforest destruction, my mind immediately begins to ponder how to possibly calculate the number of songs, myths, words, ideas, artifacts, techniques – all the cultural knowledge and practices lost per year in these mega-diversity zones. Massive wisdom, variations on human being in the form of knowledge in and of place: these are co-casualties in the eco-catastrophe. Eco-thinout may proceed at a rate much slower than cultural rubout, but accomplishment of the latter is a particularly effective way to accelerate the former. The politics of ecological and aesthetic co-evolution and co-devolution are one.

His argument suggests that it is neither logical nor socially just for environmentalists to focus their efforts on decontextualized 'endangered species' because of the profound historical interconnections among human and non-human species. Moreover, his analysis implies that an environmentalism that conceives of the notion of endangered as also encompassing human cultural systems would be significantly more vigorous and effective. The reconceptualization of the idea of endangered species to include specific human cultures, developed by Feld and Citizens for a Better Environment, implies the reinvention of the definition of a critical environmental issue and how it should be addressed by a more socially just environmental movement.

All of the preceding reinventions advocated by environmental justice activists have in common their rejection of the philosophical tenet that I have labelled 'colonial nature talk', separating nature and culture, separating a non-human natural world and non-natural human communities. The environmental justice movement, in challenging mainstream environmentalism, argues that an effective movement must integrate, not dichotomize, the histories and relationships of people and their natural environments. Most environmental justice activists' discussions of nature are balanced with an analysis of the impossibility of separating it from 'life', from cultural histories, and from socially and ecologically destructive colonial and neocolonial experiences. Many activists point to the importance of thinking 'ecosystemically', and not just focusing on single-issue environmentalism. They offer a framework that insists on making linkages among the multiple aspects of the ecosystem, including the biophysical environment, the built environment and the social environment (Gottlieb 1993). For these activists it is incomprehensible and inaccurate, as well as immoral, to separate them.

Conclusion: Struggling for a Multicultural Commons

Ideas of nature, for environmental justice groups, are therefore tied closely to ideas of community, history, ethnic identity and cultural survival, which include relationships to the land that express particular ways of life. The place – geographic, cultural and emotional – where humans and environment converge is embodied in the ideas and practices of 'community'. One concept of community advances group identification with common histories, experiences and endurances of oppression, whether racial, ethnic, gender-based or socio-economic. This view of community is often said, in the language of social science, to represent a 'unity of sameness'. In other words, those whom we identify as members of our community we recognize as having similar or identical features. Other, less anthropocentric and, some would argue, less conservative[10] conceptions of community exist, however, and emphasize the notion of 'unity in difference' (Fowler 1991, Anderson 1983, Hummon 1990). This idea of community presupposes connection to and interconnectedness with other groups, other species, and the natural environment through everyday experiences with family, comradeship and work. The cultural theorists Laurie Anne Whitt and Jennifer Daryl Slack (1994:21) argue that communities should be understood as 'sites where the human and other than human are drawn together in multiple articulations'. They propose the term 'mixed communities' to signify the relations of interdependence that inhere in geographically diverse 'mixed species' (human and non-human) assemblages. An environment contextualizes a particular mixed community, 'situating it within and bonding it to both the natural world and the larger "containing society"' (Whitt and Slack 1994:21). Communities and environments are therefore conjoined and must be understood as being mutually constitutive. Whitt and Slack (1994:22) continue:

Communities, then, are as much results as they are causes of their own environments. One practical political consequence of this is that discussions of development cannot proceed reductively, by divorcing communities from their material contexts. Mixed communities and their constitutive environments are inseparable; they are the unit of development and of change. All development is, for better or for worse, co-development of communities and environments. And the relation between a particular community and its environment 'is not simply one of interaction of internal and external factors, but of a dialectical development' . . . of community and environment in response to one another.

Environmental justice activists express their involvement with their natural environments as 'community' or 'mixed community' in the terms of living, working and playing. This may include the diverse urban community projects organized by the San Francisco Bay Area 'People of Color Greening Network'. The Greening Network sponsors various urban environmental initiatives, such as creek restoration, farmers' markets and gardening projects in the local prisons. One venture of this sort is led by Trevor Burrowes and the East Palo Alto Historical Agricultural Society, which reintroduces African American communities to their 'agricultural heritage' through the cultivation of healthy, organic food in an urban setting. According to Burrowes, this is a direct way to confront and transform the 'non-functional' relationship to nature suffered by inner-city African American communities. The community/environment 'unity in difference' concept is also demonstrated in a community revitalization project, 'The Great Los Angeles Gutter Clean-Up and Graffiti Paint-Out', subheaded 'Healing Ourselves, Our Community, Our Earth', sponsored, in part, by Concerned Citizens of South Central Los Angeles and reaching out to the entire city of Los Angeles as an 'imagined' community writ large. Community members work together to 'paint out graffiti and toss trash and toxins out of gutters, streets and alleys to clean up neighborhoods and prevent pollution from reaching our beaches'. Transforming the environment in which one lives, according to these activists, extends a sense of alliance and connection far beyond the boundaries of one's local habitat. This sentiment is reflected in remarks made by Robin Cannon during the battle against LANCER, when Concerned Citizens was joined by other women activists from different racial and class backgrounds all across Los Angeles: 'I didn't know we all had so many things in common . . . millions of people in the city had something in common with us . . . the environment' (Bullard 1994:213).

Barbara Lynch (1993) has argued, in an article examining ideas of nature, community and environmentalism shared by Latinos living in the United States, that the relationship with nature for these cultural groups has always been associated with an understanding of community. She writes of Dominican Astin Jacobo's Crotona Community Coalition, which reclaims redlined housing and empty lots in the South Bronx of New York City, transforming them into community gardens to plant corn, tomatoes, beans and garlic, thereby re-creating a small inner-city Cibao (the Dominican Republic's agricultural heartland). She also tells of Puerto Ricans living in New York, such as Dona Licha, who speak of their relationship with the sea and fishing as central to life itself and who feel that their lives are endangered because of declining fish populations and the increasing pollution of New York's coastal waters. Fishing, for New York Puerto Ricans, also represents a relationship to community, one they feel is jeopardized by recent New York State restrictions on the recreational fish catch. According to Lynch (1993:109), although these Latino communities support conservation efforts, they are concerned that state restrictions on activities such as fishing 'will deprive them of an opportunity for contact with nature by restricting their ability to use the catch as an occasion for generosity to family, friends, and neighbors'. Lynch argues that both ideas and experiences of nature, inherent in 'the garden and the sea' for US Latinos, are manifest through and firmly rooted in community, and not only an expression of community as 'sameness'. Specific cultural groups, be they Puerto Ricans in New York, Chicanas in East Los Angeles, or Salvadorans in the San Francisco Bay Area, have built environmental coalitions, such as the Mothers of East LA, El Pueblo pare el Aire y Agua Limpio in Kettleman City, and the El Puente Toxic Avengers in Pennsylvania, both in the United States and across the border with Mexico. Once again, we see relationships with nature and the environment converging with social justice considerations, and activated through ideas and practices of 'community', as the essential feature of environmental justice organizations in the United States.

How could knowledge of these specific 'inventions' of nature, which intimately associate it with everyday social and cultural life, inform a more inclusive and effective environmental movement? Moreover, in what ways can the environmental justice activists' reconceptualizations of the social and ecological connections between communities and environments help bridge the conceptual gap that splits humans from nature and likewise separates environmental from social justice concerns? Scholars of environmental justice make the argument that for people of colour in the United States, nature is located in many cultural histories, including painful histories of colonialism, and is tightly linked to alienating experiences of oppression, yet also to the experiences of affinity and partnership building that materialize in community. Their scholarship, together with the extensive political organization and insights of grass-roots environmental justice organizations such as Concerned Citizens, the Center for Community Action and Environmental Justice, and El Pueblo pare el Aire y Agua Limpio, offer clues about ways of unearthing existing inventions of nature that emerge not from mainstream nature talk but from other cultural histories. These ideas, experiences and practices can offer a rich source for grounding our debates on reinventing the commons in new multicultural environmentalisms.

Notes

1   These are stereotypes of low-income communities that have been 'scientifically' established by research and consulting firms, such as the Los Angeles-based Cerrell Associates, Inc., in its document 'Political Difficulties Facing Waste-to-Energy Conversion Plant Siting' (320 North Larchmont Blvd., Los Angeles, CA 90004, California Waste Management Board, 1984). This research provides corporations with information about the level of resistance they can expect from local residents to the proposed siting of a hazardous facility.

2   Eventually, environmental and social justice organizations such as Greenpeace, the National Health Law programme, the Center for Law in the Public Interest, and Citizens for a Better Environment would join Concerned Citizen's campaign to stop LANCER.

3   The phenomenon of the predominance of women, specifically 'marginalized' women, in environmental justice organizations has been documented by various sources. See, for example, Celene Krauss, 'Women of Color on the Front Line', in Robert Bullard (1994); Lin Nelson, 'The Place of Women in Polluted Places', in Diamond and Orenstein (1989); Jane Kay (1991); and Barbara Ruben (1992).

4   I am using the term 'mainstream' in the sense of the commonly understood meanings and social organizations that constitute environmentalism in the United States. This would include ideas that embrace nature as a threatened wilderness separate

from polluted, overpopulated cities and the preservation of wild animal species and the non-human world in general. 'Mainstream' also refers to organizations that invoke a historical legacy that includes the writings and philosophies of figures such as John Muir, Aldo Leopold and Gifford Pinchot. Such organizations include the Sierra Club, the National Wildlife Federation and the Nature Conservancy.

5   Discourses of environmental preservation, protection and the conservation of the 'aesthetics of nature' dominate the environmentalism of mainstream groups, especially the 'Group of Ten', also called the 'Big Ten', including Friends of the Earth, the Wilderness Society, the Sierra Club, the National Audubon Society, the Environmental Defense Fund, the Natural Resources Defense Council, the National Wildlife Federation, the Izaak Walton League, the National Parks and Conservation Association and the Nature Conservancy.

6   In recent years and in response to the exhortations of many people-of-colour organizations in the United States, the importance of addressing the complexities of 'urban environments' and 'urban ecologies' has appeared in some mainstream environmental discourse. Organizations such as Greenpeace, the Sierra Club and the Earth Island Institute's Urban Habitat Program have begun to link inner-city needs with environmental concerns. These projects construct the awareness of urban areas as 'multicultural ecosystems' that require specific environmental knowledge to ensure sustainable and socially and ecologically sound development (Stren et al. 1991, Platt et al. 1994, Cronon 1991).

7   Author's interview with Pam Tau Lee at the University of California's Labor and Occupational Health Program, Berkeley, California, 25 January 1993.

8   Author's interview with Dana Alston at the Public Welfare Foundation, Washington, DC, 22 December 1992.

9   Alston interview, 1992.

10   A notion of community that focuses exclusively on 'unity in sameness' is conservative, according to some analysts, because of its nativist or nationalist overtones. In other words, community as 'sameness' seeks to repress or eliminate the threat of difference, to resist change and to shore up the existing power and authority structure. Raymond Plant argues that this notion of community likens itself to an 'organic unity within which each individual has an allotted place and a part to play' (Plant 1978:95).

6

Biodiversity: Of Local Commons and Global Commodities

Michael Flitner

Biodiversity is a hot topic in the 1990s. Few other environmental issues have drawn comparable public attention over the past few years and everyone agrees today that the world's biodiversity is under imminent threat. In the first place this high degree of attention may be due to the increase in startling facts about ecosystem destruction in general and species extinction in particular. Only a small fraction of existing life-forms on earth are known to science today, and according to different estimates between 50 and 100 of them are lost every single day. A quarter of all species could become extinct in the next two decades (UNEP 1992).

A second reason for the growing interest in biodiversity is linked to the technological developments that have taken place during the last two decades. Biotechnology and especially recombinant DNA technology are creating new incentives to inventorize and screen the whole range of known and unknown organisms. The first products of genetic engineering have just reached the market and the future of the bio-tech industry looks very promising, even if some of today's bright forecasts may turn out to be exaggerated. Biodiversity is the raw material for a growing industry, and, side by side, managers of pharmaceutical companies and Third World policy makers are hoping for a profitable 'gene rush'.

This double interest has brought biodiversity into a global focus. Efforts to protect and analyse biodiversity have multiplied and new rules are presently being negotiated on many different levels. Is there another 'global commons' emerging, as has been suggested for the oceans and atmosphere? What would be the physical and institutional boundaries of this commons, and who would be its 'appropriators' (Plott and Meyer 1975)? If it is not a new commons, then what would be the relation of this new global object to the countless existing local commons all over the world, nearly all of which have to do with biodiversity? To deal with these questions it is necessary, first of all, to see what the concept of biodiversity implies. No doubt, biodiversity includes the grass on Mongolian pastures, the wildlife on Yek'uana lands and the insects in Costa Rican forests. But, as I will argue, the discursive construction of 'biodiversity' itself suggests a global perspective and it tends to favour top-down approaches in dealing with nature and natural resources. This perspective is reflected, and partly due to, new 'decision making arrangements' (Oakerson 1992), in particular an international political and legal framework shaped over the last years to regulate what is called biodiversity today. In a second step, I will highlight the gradual expansion of capitalist markets into this realm of nature over the past decades which has prepared the ground for some of today's central conflicts. Local institutions and practices are not being nested in a larger set of supportive political arrangements but, as I will argue, are rather forced into a new 'disabling framework'.

Finally, I will introduce the main actors on the global biodiversity stage: transnational chemical companies active in the business of 'biodiversity prospecting' and the World Bank-led Global Environment Facility (GEF), whose mandate is based on biodiversity problem solving. The chapter will conclude with some thoughts on the overall relationship between the construction of biodiversity as a global issue and the revived interest in the commons.

Elements of the Biodiversity Discourse

To understand the concept of biological diversity or biodiversity it is worthwhile having a closer look at its origins. The term has been used now and then since the beginning of the 1980s. But only following the National Forum on BioDiversity held in Washington, DC in 1986 did it turn into a catchword for environmentalists and policy makers. In just a few years the terms biological diversity and biodiversity have spread like wildfire. Today we find thousands of publications using this expression, political programmes, legal instruments, and even private companies bearing it in their proper name. Biodiversity has turned into 'the metaphorical magnet that currently galvanizes the conservation, scientific, and funding communities' (Zerner 1996:72). The publication resulting from the National Forum was edited by Edward O. Wilson (1988) and it can be seen as the 'bible' of biodiversity. As Harvard evolutionary scientist Stephen Jay Gould describes this timely publication, it is 'the most comprehensive book, by the most distinguished group of scholars, ever published on one of the most important subjects of our (and all) times'.

With contributions by more than 50 authors, the 500-page volume *Biodiversity* is certainly far too heterogeneous to be reduced to one single message. There are articles on technical and ethical aspects of conservation, development aid and economics, indigenous people and botanic gardens, embryon transfer and the University of Wisconsin's arboretum, climate change and the Christian view of the biosphere. Besides an impressive range of topics, there are differing and sometimes contradictory statements on closely related issues. Thus, the book itself is very diverse and, at a first glance, this diversity may seem quite well suited to deal with the subject. Still, it is one book, *one* book on *one* subject, and that may already be the first and most important message: there is this new something out there which has a lot to do with rainforests and economics, and a little less with development aid, technology and ethics, and this something can or should be treated as one coherent thing from now on.

Some reference points shared by many authors can be tracked down comparing the book with another work on a closely related topic that has been very influential, too, about 20 years earlier. *Genetic resources in plants – their exploration and conservation* was edited by Otto H. Frankel and Erna Bennett in 1970, presumably the first major work systematically linking plant (gene) conservation and utilization. By contrasting the two books, we find at least two new elements that have emerged in the 1980s. In the first place, there is an astonishing increase in neo-Malthusian arguments. Whereas the early work – although arising from the debate on the 'green revolution' – hardly mentions population growth at all, in *Biodiversity* it is probably the most often cited cause for the destruction of nature. In the book's introduction, Edward O. Wilson – who has proven his good sense of social moods a few years earlier in forwarding the neo-Malthusian notion of 'sociobiology' – brings 'explosive population growth' as the main factor in diversity's decline. His words are immediately followed by Paul Ehrlich, the father of the 'population bomb', who reiterates this argument *in extenso* in the first chapter. The argument is certainly not shared by all authors, yet it is repeated so often throughout the volume that it finally must be looked upon as an integral part of the 'biodiversity discourse'. More than 20 chapters in the book make the alleged connection, even while these authors do not even attempt to employ analytical tools to explain the complex terrain of social factors and processes related to the proposition that increasing population rates *cause* biodiversity declines.[1] For these budding biodiversity specialists, the connection is quite natural, such that it neither requires scientific substantiation nor debate. Eschewing long-standing social-scientific arguments to the contrary, they maintain a very simple and attractive belief: more people equals less 'biodiversity'.

The second new element in the biodiversity discourse is the increased importance of economics in discussions on conservation, and the primacy accorded to the market and the supposed monetary value of biodiverse 'objects'. To be sure, Frankel and Bennett's 1970 book leaves little doubt about the economic interest in the diversity of life-forms. The term 'genetic resources' illustrates this aspect even more frankly than the term 'biodiversity'. But in the 1970 book, no one explicitly deals with economic aspects. There is an underlying assumption that the loss of 'genetic resources' is an unavoidable by-product of agricultural modernization and that it is up to public, national and international institutions to deal with this problem. At the time, discussions on the free market as solution to ecological problems were almost completely absent. The new importance attributed to market forces in *Biodiversity* reflects both the general ideological shift in the 1980s and its material-scientific realization – the new technical possibilities through genetic engineering. Whereas it often took decades to make use of genetic resources with classical breeding techniques, recombinant DNA technology can drastically speed up the transformation of a wild organism into a marketable good. Biotechnology has brought life closer to the market.

If we sum up these elements in a first attempt to outline the biodiversity discourse, we get a somewhat contradictory result. Biodiversity obviously brings very different aspects of nature and social relations into one 'holistic' concept with the prefix 'bio-'. Even though this concept has global reach it gives scope to deal with 'indigenous people' and their so-called local or traditional knowledge. Karen villagers collecting their herbal medicine and Andean farmers classifying their potatoes are obviously included in the new concept. At the same time, people are seen as a major problem, being too numerous and hence a threat to biodiversity. Furthermore, biodiversity seems to have an enormous value – market value, that is – and this value is said to be the key to save it. Here is where bio-technology enters the scene, facilitating its conservation as well as opening up the possibilities to realize its potential market value. 'The terms biotechnology and biodiversity already sound as if they were made for each other' (von Weizsäcker 1993:122).

We can find the mentioned elements in many other important publications on biodiversity, in *Conserving the World's Biodiversity* for example, issued by leading environmental agencies in collaboration with the World Bank (IUCN et al. 1990).[2] If Wilson's book is the founding document of the biodiversity discourse, this is the basic policy paper of the 'Global Resource Managers' (see Chapter 1). It is remarkable how little is said in the whole book about the underlying causes of environmental degradation; instead, it 'averts the gaze from the biodiversity-destroying aspects of elite rule' (Lohmann 1991:98). The main actors in the conservation of biological diversity seem to be industry, commerce, the World Bank and international conservation organizations. Consequently, diversity can best be protected through an expanded role for these actors, who will effectively assign 'appropriate prices' to biological diversity and design market-based incentives for their trade on capitalist markets. 'The major requirement from government policymakers', then, is that they 'recognize the many values of biological resources, and take advantage of opportunities to invest in the continued productivity that such resources require' (IUCN et al. 1990:15). Larry Lohmann (1991:98) remarks on this concept:

> . . . [I]t advocates . . . scattered, top-down projects, . . . corporate-funded programmes, schemes to siphon a bit of funding out of large diversity-depleting development projects for 'mitigation' or watershed protection, foreign ecotourism, debt swaps, capital investment in biological resources, set-asides, and projects which give 'total management control' to the 'private or NGO sector'.

Indeed, most of what can be found in this document is traditional World Bank policy trimmed up with some remarks on the 'value of traditional knowledge' and how this can be integrated into 'existing expertise' which is 'primarily located in industrialized countries' (IUCN et al. 1990:52). Many of the projects resulting from this view have been criticized in detail – Nepal's Arun Dam and Brazil's Planafloro project are the latest famous failures of this approach (Hagemann 1995). Even more disturbing, when it comes to 'new partners' that shall be enlisted for the conservation of biodiversity, the single actor getting most attention is the military, premised on the view that 'in short, the various national military establishments operate for the benefit of their respective nations'. The military might thus 'reasonably be expected to have a serious interest in resource management issues', it may help to 'enforce international legislation', and it includes a 'large number of post-adolescent males as recruits, who are put through intensive training programs' (IUCN et al. 1990:131). Accordingly, to demonstrate the military's 'positive influence on conservation of biological resources', a series of case studies is suggested, proposing Madagascar and Burma, two murderous military regimes, as good examples.

The rhetorical greenwash of a traditional development approach thus ends up with 'coercing conservation' (Peluso 1993). At the same time, comparably little attention is directed in this policy document to the substantial shifts that occurred over the last years in the legal framework surrounding biological resources. These changes correspond to some of the main developments in the biodiversity discourse and they set the conditions for access to biological resources and the sharing of benefits derived from their use for years to come.

The New Legal Framework

Today, the Convention on Biological Diversity (CBD) is the most important legal instrument dealing with biodiversity. In effect since December 1993, the CBD's objectives are threefold: the conservation of biological diversity, the sustainable use of its components, and the fair and equitable sharing of the benefits arising out of the utilization of genetic resources (Article 1). If we look to earlier legislation, this combination of objectives is rather surprising. First, with the notable exception of hunting and trade in endangered species, international agreements rarely made the links between the conservation and the use of species or ecosystems.[3] Second, the whole area of access to genetic resources as well as sharing of benefits arising from their use is brought into a legally binding arrangement for the first time in history. Both aspects are of outstanding importance to our topic and for a better understanding of their role in the construction of the global issue of biodiversity, we must have a closer look at the process that finally led to the CBD.

In international relations, plants and seeds had ceased to be in an 'open access' regime long before they were named 'genetic resources' or even 'biodiversity'. The interest in the control over life-forms dates back to ancient times and has been a strategic economic issue since at least colonial times (Brockway 1979, Juma 1989). Attempts to restrict the export or the use of certain organisms or seeds multiplied in the eighteenth and nineteenth centuries, but in most if not all cases it turned out to be impossible in the long run to physically prevent the removal of these organisms from the territories of monopoly holders.[4] Thus, the most important utilized species spread all over the globe until the beginnings of the twentieth century, when a slow but steady change in the focus of interest began to take shape. The new science of genetics helped to systematize cross-breeding in Northern countries, and henceforth it was the variability within species, varietal diversity, that became more and more interesting. What geneticists saw and needed was not the organism as an entity anymore, but rather as an accumulation of properties each of which could be treated separately as a building-block for novel varieties.

In the 1920s, Russian scientist Nicolai I. Vavilov came up with the 'theory of gene centers' or centres of diversity. Evaluating the results from his numerous collecting expeditions, he noticed that the diversity of utilized species was far from being equally distributed in space. Most of the varietal biological wealth of the world was concentrated in only seven or eight regions. These centres of diversity were mostly in subtropical, mountainous regions, largely situated in what are now called developing countries. By 1927, Vavilov saw quite clearly that this unequal distribution of genetic variability among countries might lead to future political tensions. In his pathbreaking speech to the Berlin International Congress on Heredity, he warned that 'a lot of interlaced interests are centered' in the regions of diversity, and he urged for an internationally organized scientific effort to investigate and make use of this potential (Vavilov 1992:157). The following decades, however, saw a rise mainly in nationalistic efforts to secure genetic resources. While the Soviet Union's programmes were paralysed by ideological turmoil, the United States, the United Kingdom and Germany multiplied their collecting efforts in the 1930s and 1940s.[5]

It was only after World War II that the newly founded UN's Food and Agriculture Organization came up with the first multilateral programme on 'genetic stocks', as they were named then, and it took another 20 years until this programme gained momentum. With the launching of large-scale agricultural development schemes in the 1960s and 1970s, the link between plant production and the use of genetic diversity had been fundamentally changed around the world. Following the industrial paradigm, agricultural modernization was perhaps the most important building-block of the US-led global development project. The Rockefeller Foundation's project in Mexico, the Ford Foundation's efforts in India and Cold War programmes like 'Point-4' in Iran were the starting points of what was later called the 'Green Revolution' – a term most likely invented by USAID expert William S. Gaud in 1968 while 'red revolutions' were seemingly threatening Western interests in Southeast Asia and elsewhere (Grall and Lévy 1985).

In 1970, when CIMMYT (Centro Internacional de Mejoramiento del Maíz y del trigo) plant breeder Norman Borlaug was awarded the Nobel Peace Prize, trade with seeds and other agricultural inputs had turned into a global business, with multinational chemical companies such as Hoechst, ICI, Sandoz and Shell selling high-value, external-input agriculture all over the globe. The World Bank took the lead in establishing the Consultative Group on International Agricultural Research (CGIAR) and, a little later, the International Board for Plant Genetic Resources (IBPGR), two closely related coordinating institutions that were empowered to ensure that this Northern-based vision, and new profit base, would be the road most likely taken globally in the future (Grall and Lévy 1985, Mooney 1979 and 1988).

The emerging seed business in the North was faced with a fundamental dilemma resulting from the 'dual character' of its product. Although more and more farmers purchased high-yielding seeds from Northern companies to produce everything from corn, straw and green manure, they could also use these seeds to reproduce the next season's seeds. Hence, once purchased, the manufactured seeds could be used as a means of production for the farmer/consumer, thus rendering it unnecessary to return to the breeder for next year's seed supply. As US sociologist Jack Kloppenburg points out, 'The reproducibility of the seed furnishes conditions in which the reproduction of capital is highly problematic' (1988:38). The natural ability of organisms to reproduce themselves has been the main problem posed by nature to commercial interest. Different attempts have been made during the last decades to deal with this difficulty of commodification, but, as we will see, it continues to be a major issue for today's volatile bio-tech industry.

Historically, seed companies and other industries concerned with the production of self-reproducing organisms have pursued two different routes to solve this problem: a biological-technical one, and a legal one. The bio-technical route aimed at the development of plants that lose the ability to reproduce with stable qualities. This can be reached, for example, through the production of hybrids: two inbred lines are crossed so that they reproduce good-quality seed in the first generation, but in the following generations the specific combination of qualitites will get lost as they are genetically redistributed among the offspring. As a result, farmers will have to return to the factory to buy seed every year if they want to keep up production. This commodification strategy has been tremendously successful for companies producing seed for certain plants such as corn or sugarbeet where the acreage planted to hybrids exceeds 90 per cent in Northern countries. Yet for other important species, this technique could not be easily applied successfully, and this is why other ways of securing the commodification of organisms are still of great interest.

Plant Breeders' Rights and Farmers' Rights

The second strategy for retaining economic control over organisms is the legal option, where commodification is made possible by an intellectual property right (IPR). From the beginning of the century, several attempts have been made to extend the industrial patent system to cover micro-organisms, plants and even animals. Plant breeders and seed companies have urged for a specifically tailored right for plants which for legal, technical, and political reasons seemed better suited for the subject matter concerned. In several Northern countries, their political pressure led to the development of so-called plant breeders' rights (PBR), a kind of exclusive right like a patent, but with a reduced scope of protection due to two important restrictions. First, farmers were allowed to plant back saved seed on their own farm and to hand it to others 'over the fence' (the so-called farmers' exemption). Second, the protected varieties could be used for further breeding by anyone, without consent and free of charge ('breeders' exemption'). Thus, the exclusive right of the breeder extended only to commercial acts regarding the propagating material of the protected variety.

The first international agreement on PBR was the UPOV (Union internationale pour la Protection des Obtentions Végétales) Convention in 1961, drawing its membership exclusively from industrialized countries. This convention has drawn a lot of criticism since the 1970s when its impact on the development of plant breeding became visible. This PBR system has been a key factor in both the concentration of ownership in the global seed industry and the acceleration of genetic diversity loss world-wide (Fowler and Mooney 1990). The system concretizes fundamentally inequitable relations between those providing genetic 'raw material' and those selling 'modern varieties'.[6] Thousands of so-called land races or primitive varieties were brought from Southern fields to Northern genebanks without any compensation, whereas the final products of 'scientific breeding' returned to Southern markets as commodities that had to be paid for in hard (i.e., US dollars) currency.

Once these inequitable rights became apparent, the 'seed wars' started in the UN's Food and Agriculture Organization (FAO). In 1981, with the support of other Southern countries, Mexico called for a convention on plant genetic resources – a demand that was met with opposition from Northern countries. By 1983, a large majority of countries decided to establish an FAO Commission on Plant Genetic Resources and adopted the 'International Undertaking on Plant Genetic Resources'. The most controversial message of this legally non-binding FAO Undertaking was the questioning of intellectual property rights for plant varieties. All plant genetic resources were defined as a 'heritage of mankind', including 'special genetic stocks' and 'breeders' lines'. Predictably, this definition was fiercely opposed by UPOV member states seeing it as a 'strike at the heart of free enterprise' (Kloppenburg and Kleinman 1988:188). Still, and this is less frequently mentioned in historical accounts, there were also reservations from Southern countries concerning the concept of 'heritage of mankind'.[7] This concept seemed to challenge the widely accepted principle of national sovereignty over natural resources, obliging countries to grant unrestricted access to their genetic diversity. Southern countries particularly rich in diversity joined major industrialized countries in declining to accept the Undertaking.

In the following years, the FAO Undertaking has been qualified through several resolutions, and it is being revised at present to be brought in line with the Convention on Biological Diversity (FAO CPGR 1995). Yet in a changing environment, the Undertaking already has considerably changed its character. The principle of national sovereignty was explicitly confirmed to calm down Southern fears of a further loss of control over their biological riches. Even more important, plant breeders' rights as provided for under UPOV were declared compatible with the objectives of the Undertaking. To counterbalance the effects of plant breeders' rights, however, the concept of 'Farmers' Rights' was established:

> Farmers' Rights mean rights arising from the past, present and future contributions of farmers in conserving, improving, and making available plant genetic resources, particularly those in the centres of origin/diversity. These rights are vested in the International Community, as trustee for present and future generations of farmers, for the purpose of ensuring full benefits to farmers, and supporting the continuation of their contributions, as well as the attainment of the overall purposes of the International Undertaking. (FAO CPGR 1989)

This concept has hardly materialized by now for several reasons. First, FAO failed to raise substantial contributions from its main donor countries to replenish the International Fund established to make the

Undertaking work. Unwillingness of Northern countries to agree to a mandatory fund was made easy by the fact that nobody really seemed to know what it should be used for. Should it be given to national governments according to their nation's 'genetic contribution' to world-wide agriculture? Should it be put into existing international programmes, as Farmers' Rights are 'vested in the International Community'? How could farmers effectively benefit from the fund? And, last but not least, what about compensation for and access to truly *wild* species in a system that has its rationale in 'past, present and future contributions of farmers'?

Meanwhile, other international debates forestalled resolution of these problems. Instead, both the TRIPS Agreement and the Convention on Biological Diversity have completely transformed the global discursive strategy on biodiversity rights and wrongs.

The TRIPS Agreement and the Convention on Biological Diversity

Although Southern countries had opposed any negotiations on intellectual property in the GATT framework in 1986, the conclusion of the Uruguay Round in 1993 included an agreement on Trade-Related Aspects of Intellectual Property Rights, Including Trade in Counterfeit Goods (TRIPS). This agreement aims at an international harmonization of the standards of a whole array of intellectual property rights, such as copyrights, trademarks and patents – all topics that were once treated exclusively in the UN-affiliated World Intellectual Property Organization (WIPO). Within the context of WIPO, however, the majority of Southern countries had shown reluctance to indiscriminately extend IPR protection, as Northern countries demanded (Bifani 1989).

Thus, from the mid-1980s on, the US (and to a lesser extent the EU) had followed what administration officials called a 'carrot-and-stick approach' to make the newly industrializing countries accept higher standards of IPR protection. The stick is the specifically tailored set of trade sanctions ('Super 301' of the US Trade Act) and the carrot is better access to Northern markets. Heavy bilateral pressure made countries such as Mexico, Brazil and Thailand give in before the GATT round was concluded (van Wijk 1991). Although the agreement on TRIPS received much less attention in the Northern media than the trade settlement for agricultural products between the United States and the European Union, the results of the TRIPS negotiations will have a much more substantial impact on international economic relations in the medium and long term. Moreover, the fate of 'biodiversity' may rest on it.

The agreement obliges all GATT/WTO member states to provide patent protection for any invention, whether products or processes, in all fields of technology, within a few years. To be sure, members may exclude from patentability 'plants and animals other than microorganisms as well as essentially biological processes for the production of plants or animals other than non-biological and microbiological processes' (Article 27 TRIPS). This limited exception, however, will be reviewed in 1999. Meanwhile, members are required 'to provide for the protection of plant varieties either by patents or by an effective *sui generis* system or by any combination thereof'.

These provisions tie down most countries of the world to essentially follow the road taken in Northern countries during the last decade, that is, to allow for IPRs to enter the realm of nature, agriculture and food production, and of biodiversity in all its forms. The consequences of this development are manifold, but they include two dominant tendencies: the increased expropriation of the essential means of production from millions of farmers and the accelerated expansion of the commodification process of nature. With patents on genes and micro-organisms and what is called an 'effective *sui generis* system', the grip of multinational chemical and pharmaceutical companies on everyday livelihood will tighten considerably on a world scale.

The concept of a *'sui generis* system' is, of course, quite ambiguous. Yet, in introducing this term the drafters of the TRIPS agreement certainly had the rights of corporate plant breeders in mind. Meanwhile, the UPOV Convention was revised again in 1991 and it reads like a patent protection document. The farmers' privilege is now left at the discretion of the contracting states, and thus has become an exception from the rule. Equally important, the UPOV 1991 Act prohibits unauthorized use for further breeding purposes of any variety that is 'essentially derived' from a protected variety. It boldly extends breeders' rights to harvested material. Finally, it lifts the ban on 'double protection', which traditionally prevented member states from offering patents and plant breeders' rights for varieties of the same species.[8]

All these changes represent a profound restructuring of the utilization of biodiversity. To be sure, patenting of genetic material does not directly prevent people all over the world from continuing with their so-called traditional practices of, for example, using plants for herbal medicine. Patent monopolies come via the market and restrictions on research and development options. It is commercial activities and not subsistence activities that will be most seriously affected by new patent laws, although of course the distinction between subsistence and commercial can be quite blurred, especially when multinational companies start marketing their own 'herbal cures' and demanding proprietary rights. Threats to biodiversity will come primarily from increased commodification of biological use-values, which will be fuelled by new incentives for chemical and pharmaceutical companies to get involved in the business of 'biodiversity prospecting'. Increased profits from biodiversity prospecting only intensifies current trends of market concentration and dominance by a handful of Northern-based large corporations. With concentrated corporate control of international research and development on the 'science' of biological diversity comes even greater uniformity in public and elite discursive strategies regarding the biological commons and the social relations embedded in the management and reproduction of the commons.

The notion that the carrying of life's diversity is most efficiently managed on a globalized 'free' market is emblematic of the broader biodiversity discourse and is dominant in debates on how the Convention on Biological Diversity (CBD) and international governing bodies will operate in the future. The CBD has already established the principle of reciprocity concerning access to and benefits from biological resources, leaving the question of IPRs on these resources open (Glowka et al. 1994). Access, where granted, shall be 'on mutually agreed terms' and be subject to prior informed consent of the state providing the resources. Similarly, developing countries' access to products and technologies that make use of those resources will have to be on terms mutually agreed upon. Thus, although some phrases in the convention seem to oppose extensive IPR protection on 'living material', the CBD favours this approach as it balances IPRs on the one hand and rights to biodiversity on the other. The very functioning of the CBD depends on the restriction of both access to 'raw biodiversity' and access to technologies and organisms derived therefrom. Bio-technology, itself largely protectable according to the TRIPS provisions, will be the key element in this relationship.

To sum up, the new legal framework can be seen as a materialization of some of the central elements of the biodiversity discourse. It pretends a positive correlation among the conservation of biodiversity, the growth of the bio-tech industry, and the acceleration of capitalization and integration into the world market of 'traditional societies' with their 'undervalued resources'. According to this scheme, the main actors to safeguard the future of biodiversity have been voted upon: the multinational companies with bilateral 'biodiversity prospecting' agreements and the World Bank-dominated Global Environmental Facility (GEF).

Win–Win Scenarios?

Over the past few years, 'biodiversity prospecting' is the new catchword and nearly all major transnational corporations are into the new business (Reid et al. 1993). Glaxo Inc. is collecting in Ghana and Latin America; the British Technology Group in Cameroon; Novo Industries in Nigeria; Merck, Sharp & Dohme in Costa Rica; SmithKline Beechham in Malaysia; Bristol Myers Squibb in Surinam and Hoechst Company in India – to name just a few examples (Hermitte 1991, Cunningham 1993, Reid 1993, Flitner 1995). Most, if not all of these companies have made bilateral contracts with the respective country, contracts which in general are not made accessible to the public.

One of the rare examples where some details are known is the contract between US-based pharmaceutical company Merck, Sharp & Dohme and Costa Rica or, more precisely, the semi-public Costa Rican Instituto Nacional de Biodiversidad (INBio). The main features of the contract are the following (Aldhous 1991, Blum 1993):

- INBio supplies Merck & Co. with several thousand samples of plant, animal and microbial extracts from all over Costa Rica, including from protected areas. Products developed from this material can be patented and marketed exclusively by Merck & Co.
- Merck & Co. pays US$1.1 million to INBio to boost its research and collecting capacities. Additionally, INBio will receive an unrevealed proportion of licence fees from future Merck patents based on the material handed over.
- One-tenth of the actual budget and half of possible future gains will be handed over by INBio to the public National Park Fund. The rest of the budget is used for the further inventorization of Costa Rican biodiversity.

Concluded in 1991, the contract was certainly intended to promote a whole new model for business. Although it has been denied by leading actors on several occasions, it is clear that this contract was not just between anybody at any random moment. It was between one of the world's largest pharmaceutical companies and Costa Rica, one of the global 'biodiversity hotspots'. Precisely when the main features of the contract were presented to the public, member states were fighting over the CBD's final draft. 'We are prepared to pay for access to biodiversity' was the strategic message from the much-suspected chemical industry. But this bold concession was modified by the fine print: 'as long as it is not too much and we get exclusive rights'. The general message circulating in the press: 'multinationals agree to save the rainforest'. Still, today, the Merck deal reverberates throughout the biodiversity literature as a resounding victory for rationality and sustainability. A public relations coup for all actors involved.

Another message, less visible but equally important, was the unquestioned positive role of science in the deal. The scientific inventories were declared necessary to make money and to strengthen conservation. Hence, if the money went back to science this would lead to a closed circuit: more science means more conservation and money, which again means more science. In the enthusiastic words of plant scientist David Marsh, it is a 'win–win scenario' (Marsh 1993). In the *Global Biodiversity Strategy*, this logic reappears in what is called a 'triple mechanism of saving it, studying it and using it – all components of which are mutually reinforcing . . . ' (Holdgate and Giovannini 1994:4).

Many aspects of the Merck-INBio deal have been criticized: the modest amount of money for access to a 'biodiversity hotspot' of global importance, the doubtful legal status of INBio selling public (?) resources, the exclusiveness granted to the Merck company, the secrecy kept on some important details and finally the role of local people in the deal (Rodriguez Cervantez 1993, Chauvet and Olivier 1993, Gettkant 1995). It is the latter aspect that merits our attention. What about the fate of the 'local commons'? How are the people living in the concerned areas represented in the contract? What about ensuring their access to biodiversity? There is nothing said about sustaining 'traditional resource rights' or 'indigenous knowledge'. Where are the famous 'local people' who are standard references in most environment and development rhetoric?

The INBio deal does refer to locals in the context of Costa Ricans employed as collectors or 'parataxonomistas'. About 30 men and women were taught basics in collecting and systematics so that they could become responsible for the collection and the (pre-)screening of organisms from the protected areas. According to promoters, 'INBio decided to tap an abundant underutilized resource – Costa Rica's rural populace – . . . to get the job done within a decade at a reasonable cost' (Janzen 1993:223). In the construction of a new global discourse on biodiversity, the only space for local people is where they are most familiar: cheap labour.

The same year of the signing of the Merck-INBio contract, the World Bank-led Global Environment Facility (GEF) launched its three-year pilot programme with biodiversity high on the agenda. The conceptual framework of the World Bank's work on biodiversity was developed in the Bank Conservation Community Task Force, together with representatives of World Resources Institute (WRI), World Wide Fund for Nature (WWF) and the International Union for the Conservation of Nature and Natural Resources (IUCN). Right in time for the UN Conference on Environment and Development in Rio, the World Bank saw a good opportunity to redefine its position and function in the global environmental arena, and it found France and Germany to willingly provide the seed funds (Unmüssig 1995).

In just a few months, some 20 countries joined the project, and with UN Environment (UNEP) and Development Programmes (UNDP) as junior partners the World Bank administered US$1.3 billion for a GEF pilot phase, thus bringing the young project in a very strong position to take the financial lead in the post-Rio process. Despite ongoing criticism, the GEF still is the 'interim financing mechanism' of the CBD five years after the Rio summit. With US$300 million and 40 projects in its three-year pilot programme, GEF has had a strong focus on biodiversity. There are projects on tropical forests and protected areas in Africa, Asia and Latin America which include 'forest concession management' in Indonesia, 'identification of biodiversity hotspots' in Malawi and 'zoological inventories' in Cameroon.[9] Although still in the early stages of implementation, already problematic patterns of traditional World Bank policy are becoming visible. Wrong or missing priorities, a top-down approach with little participation and lots of external expertise, and large-style intervention in a short timespan were among the points that conservation agencies found worrisome in these biodiversity projects (McNeely 1994).

A good example is the project in the World Bank-led Kenyan Tana River National Primate Reserve. To protect two endangered primate species, the Red Colobus and Crested Mangabey monkeys, the Bank's experts considered it necessary to resettle one of the largest Pokomo villages in the area and to restrict access of many other people to their fields and forests. Neither local people nor NGOs working in the area for 20 years were asked their views in the planning phase. The project, now being redesigned as a result of considerable public pressure, is not the first experience with the World Bank for the Pokomo people. The water problems in the

Tana River region are largely due to two earlier Bank projects in the same area: a dam for which 6,000 Pokomo people had to be resettled and an irrigation project downstream which has never kept its promises (Unmüssig 1995).

Charles Zerner (1996) has analysed the 'coercive narrative' in GEF's documents for the project. He finds that the story is comprised of three main elements: non-human biodiversity which is constantly valorized as 'rich' and 'most unique', romanticized human activities as performed by 'traditional' Pokomo agriculturalists (as long as they were not too many), and finally 'outsiders' that have intruded as bandits, poachers and encroachers. He concludes:

> The Tana River reserve is conceptualized as a beleaguered citadel of nature, set in opposition to and beset by human practices and presences. Within the boundaries of this special precinct, a reserved state of nature, the only fully enfranchised citizens are the Red Colobus and Crested Mangabey primates. Within the boundaries of the reserve, Pokomo people are tolerated as second-rate, albeit primate, citizens, while other social groups, the Somali agricul-turalists and the nonlocal hunters, are classed, respectively, as illegal aliens or criminals. (Zerner 1996:86)

The 'global good biodiversity' thus can be claimed by national governments to coerce and evict communities with support of the international donors.

But the projects' problems are even more deeply rooted in GEF's conceptual framework and its criteria for project eligibility. The general strategy of GEF can be found in the problematic concepts of 'global benefits' and 'incremental costs'. Global and local benefits and costs are not so easily isolated or measurable. None the less, GEF leaves no doubt in its criteria on what comes first: specific attention shall be paid 'to those projects and measures which primarily result in global *rather than* domestic benefit' (GEF STAP 1991:7). The Tana River Primate Reserve project shows how this can be translated into practical terms. As Wolfgang Sachs (1993:19) observes, the global vantage point in general,

> . . . requires ironing out all the differences and disregarding all circumstances; rarely has the gulf between observers and the observed been greater than between satellite based forestry and the *seringueiro* in the Brazilian jungle. It is inevitable that the claims of global management are in conflict with the aspirations for cultural rights, democracy and self-determination.

The second conceptual pillar, 'incremental costs', is no less troublesome. There is no agreed definition on what 'incremental' really means. The term is intended to separate the domestic from the global costs and benefits, as only the latter shall be relevant for GEF funding. On a first glance, it may seem acceptable that international funding should at least partially be tied to international benefits. Still, to make this concept operational in the field of biodiversity, it would be necessary to assign exact monetary values to the different components and functions of ecosystems (Unmüssig 1995). Even though many economists have tried their best, the value of the Tana River monkeys still cannot be expressed in special drawing rights or US dollars. 'With experience', the GEF remains optimistic that 'the monetary cost-benefit effect will become more apparent and measurable' (GEF 1991:2). It could be concluded then, that in the meantime – until the specialists can measure nature's value – the GEF will be forced to stick to the kind of reliable data the Bank has utilized in the past: the dubious calculations of value in terms of cumulative numbers of agricultural exports, cubic metres of wood and the like.

The shortcomings of GEF's conceptual framework further lead to a technological fix, which can best be illustrated in the proposed research priorities relating to the protection of biodiversity. Six out of eight priorities named in the initial implementation draft prepared by the GEF advisory panel are purely (bio-)technical, ranging from *in vitro* propagation and embryo transplant to plot experiments and reproductive biology. Social dimensions figure in the last-mentioned point exclusively as 'economic, ethical and cultural value estimation of an area's biodiversity' (GEF STAP 1991:7).

Conclusion: Local Commons and Global Commodities

With the discursive construction of biodiversity and the development of a corresponding legal framework, with countless programmes of international governmental and non-governmental organizations and the creation of new supranational institutions, the social relations on the interface between nature and humankind are being restructured on a global scale. The attribute 'common' is used extensively in the current debate. FAO's Undertaking on Plant Genetic Resources contains the notion of 'common heritage', at the same time confirming national sovereignty over plant genetic resources. The Convention on Biological Diversity talks about biodiversity as a 'common concern' but again strengthens the member states' control over biological resources. Thus, it can be argued that on the international level biodiversity is presently being made 'subtractable' (Oakerson 1992), at least in terms of potential monetary benefits. On the other hand, it is not merely new entry and exit rules, and questions of ownership and access that undergo fundamental changes. All aspects of resource management and its socio-economic surrounding are concerned. The debates on traditional resource rights and farmers' rights illustrate this dimension.[10] They highlight at the same time the new representations of nature and human practices. The 'master story' about indigenous communities is not only the story of a natural world in which local communities are conceptualized as separate from the natural world and as impediments to its conservation (Zerner 1996:71). It is also the story of their 'valuable knowledge' and their potential 'contributions' to ends such as 'sustainable development' and biodiversity conservation, ends they rarely have the opportunity to set for themselves. Thus, it would be too simple to see only the mechanism of exclusion of local communities in the construction of biodiversity. In many cases the local commons and their custodians may be very interesting for development experts and global resource managers; they may be included as long as they contribute to 'global benefits' or can be mobilized for economic growth.

But certainly, the new global regime as a whole will not work 'decentralized' or 'community based'. What we see currently is not the construction of a global regime made up of local commons, neither in the sense of an addition, nor in the sense of a synthesis on a higher level. Essentially it is through the dissolution and destruction of local commons that the global regime gets its substance. The global market for genes is not based on local markets for natural products and their respective rules and mechanisms are rarely joined together in an 'enabling framework'. On the contrary, private (intellectual) property created through new legal regulations built over the last years is based on the negation of existing *de facto* access rights and entitlements. The inclusion of genes, whole organisms and related indigenous knowledge into the market is coming via *exclusive* biodiversity prospecting agreements and *exclusive* rights on patented genes.

Hence, the scarcity of resources (Yapa 1993) becomes socially constructed and based on bio-technologies or on economic and legal measures, and not necessarily on the *physical* control or destruction of the natural resource on which the local commons are based. Only in a few cases is the modernization process logically tied to the destruction of the natural base itself, such as with genetic resources for plant breeding, where the successful spread of 'modern' varieties directly leads to a loss of genetic diversity. As industrialized agriculture needs the genetic diversity which it is itself destroying, there is also an interest in preserving pre-capitalist sectors that can guarantee continuing supply of genetic diversity. For the whole range of wild or semi-wild biodiversity, however, this contradiction seems less important. Biodiversity in general is not (yet) scarce for bio-technologists. In most cases, biodiversity is not yet physically a subtractable good, and thus the link between continued existence of certain commons and the mid-term possibilities for accumulation is not clearly visible. It may be mainly a theoretical question in how far such a linkage exists at all; in practical terms the process of exclusion is certainly not dependent on the physical destruction of natural resources. As pointed out above, exclusion comes much more via social developments and new institutions, that is, the destruction of local commons by economic, administrative and legal developments that accompany bio-prospecting activities.

To date, the legal framework of this construction-by-exclusion is not yet fully operational to stabilize the newly created sphere of biodiversity. In many countries the Convention on Biological Diversity has not yet been transformed into national law. Few states have laws governing access to genetic resources on their territories. Material Transfer Agreements (MTAs) and Genetic Acquisition Agreements (GAAs) are currently being debated to deal with some of the open questions around genebanks and future collections (Barton and Siebeck 1994). The *sui generis* right necessary to comply with WTO standards still has to be developed in most countries (Leskien and Flitner 1997). In the FAO, attempts are underway to exempt some plant genetic resources for food and agriculture (PGRFA) from the general trend towards privatization (FAO CPGR 1995). But these open questions and uncertainties are leaving the main developments and their underlying assumptions unchallenged. The question raised is not whether biological resources should be collected, inventorized and monetarized or not, but how this should happen. For the global resources managers it goes unquestioned that more science, more market and more development are the right answer to the ecological crisis. To many of their opponents – the 'human ecologists' according to Michael Goldman (see Chapter 1) – the contrary seems true: the defence of traditional commons, less development and less market should entice conservation and sustainable living. But it is neither static preservation nor unhindered market forces that will bring 'the' ecological crisis to a solution.

It is the very idea of 'the' crisis, the global 'we' in the biodiversity discourse that has to be questioned. If 'we' lose Andean folk taxonomy for potato varieties, to use a famous example, this can be defined as very different losses of 'value': the loss of knowledge vital for a certain village economy, the loss of a cultural good for a certain community, and maybe also the loss of power for certain people within this community. The loss may also entail a loss of knowledge that facilitates screening of potato germplasm at the Sturgeon Bay or Brunswick collections, or the loss of a source of extra profit for a leading potato breeder in France, the loss of work for ethnobotanists, the loss of a source of income for Andean market women, the loss of a cultural heritage of humankind, and – not to forget! – a loss for scientists writing articles about development issues. There are obviously different subjects concerned in different ways by all these losses and there is neither a scientific nor a global 'we' perspective to easily resolve these differences. Yet it is easy to see that only some of the mentioned 'values' are relevant to vested corporate interest or qualify for bargains on 'benefit sharing' between North and South.

Biodiversity – as seen as a construction to integrate much larger parts of nature and its relations with societies into the project of global development – is rejected in many places by social movements with diverse interests and backgrounds. In this context, the 'common concern' biodiversity is rather seen as a 'globalitarian' tool of Northern dominance, or simply a specific mode of rescheduling Southern debts. Still most people's livelihood in most parts of the world is inseparably linked to 'biodiversity' (now seen as the culture-nature surrounding them, including a multitude of local commons), and most of the social struggles in the world are closely related to questions of access, of ownership and 'management' of biological resources. Social struggles may primarily focus on land titles, or on cultural autonomy, or on farmers' rights to plant back last year's saved seed. The Seed Satyagraha movement in India rejecting the TRIPS provisions, the struggle for community-controlled forests in northeastern Thailand, or the Venezuelan Yek'uana fighting for land titles, are just a few highlights from the flip-side of hegemonic constructions of biodiversity.

Thus we find many competing claims to the hegemonic biodiversity discourse. On the one hand, biodiversity conservation is constructed as an act of coercion and redemption: it justifies all kinds of measures to protect 'wild nature' from human intervention and at the same time aims to bring larger parts of this nature into a globalized economy. On the other hand, biodiversity remains physically tied to local livelihoods and, in the political sphere, creates new spaces for the participation of local and indigenous communities. As a participant in a Costa Rica workshop for forest communities put it (Rodriguez and Camacho 1995:12): 'I am understanding that the word "biodiversity" – too much used in these days—is made out of two words.' By unpacking this highly politicized discourse – breaking it down into its composite parts – perhaps we can make the political processes surrounding 'biodiversity' much more transparent.

Notes

1 The argument is represented in articles coming from very different backgrounds, including the following authors: N. Myers, G. C. Ray, H. H. Iltis, D. Ehrenfeld, R. E. Jenkins, J. Spears, F. W. Burley, N. C. Brady, T. E. Lovejoy, R. J. A. Goodland, L. R. Brown, R. L. Peters (all in Wilson 1988). See in particular, the epilogue by D. Chalimor.
2 See also IUCN et al. (1991); WRI et al. (1992).
3 See the Convention concerning the Protection of the World Cultural and Natural Heritage ('World Heritage Convention', Paris 1972), the Convention on the Conservation of Migratory Species of Wild Animals ('Bonn Convention', 1979) and the Convention on Wetlands of International Importance especially as Waterfowl Habitat ('Ramsar Convention', 1971), none of which puts major emphasis on the relation of conservation and use (Kiss 1989).
4 France, for example, lost its control over indigo production and the Dutch lost their monopoly on many spices; an English adventurer in the employ of Kew Gardens crashed Brazilian rubber production by smuggling out of the country several thousand Hevea seeds that little later gave rise to plantations in Southeast Asia (Brockway 1979).
5 For the development in the US during the 1930s and 1940s, see Kloppenburg (1988:91–135); for the development in Nazi Germany, see Flitner (1995: 51–121).
6 For a critical assessment of the concept of modern varieties, see Yapa (1993).
7 The notion of 'common heritage' was developed basically in the context of the preparation of the UN Convention on the Law of the Sea (UNCLOS) which already had been signed in 1983 by most developing countries. It is thus certainly not by accident

that the attribute 'common' was not used in the 1983 version of the FAO Undertaking. Ironically, it was introduced in 1989 with the acceptance of Farmers' Rights and PBR according to UPOV (see below).

8　For a more detailed analysis, see Leskien and Flitner (1997).

9　See UNDP et al. and *GEF Work Program* FY 92 and FY 93, Annexes; The World Bank (1995: Annex).

10　For the current discussion, see Swaminathan (1995); Posey and Dutfield (1996); Brush and Stabinsky (1996).

7

Fairness, Social Capital and the Commons: The Societal Foundations of Collective Action in the Himalaya

Sanjeev Prakash

Often the community is an expression of hope, rather than a description of reality. Twelve countries north of Africa call themselves the European Community – and who would say, after recent events, that the word was well-chosen? . . . Perhaps the most pernicious community of all is the international one. Regularly invoked, constantly cried, endlessly expected to sort out every mess in every country, you might think that such a thing as the international community actually existed. It doesn't. There is something called the United Nations Organisation and numberless bodies that try, for better or the worse, to promote economic development, settle refugees, heal the sick, feed the hungry and count the dead. But a community? You might as well put more trust in Snow White.

Article in *The Economist*, 13 August 1993

Introduction: The Commons as Property or Society?

This chapter examines some issues of management and distributional allocation in commons institutions. The principal discussion centres around the complex social dynamics and relationships that support real-life commons, including the interplay of divergent notions of fairness and the accumulation of networks of trust and reciprocity within the execution of everyday tasks of management, allocation and decision making which have received relatively little attention from conceptual analysts. These processes are explored through an analysis of rule-setting and distributive allocation in a village forest commons institution in Tehri District of the Garhwal Himalaya, Northern India. I suggest that the social and normative processes discussed in this chapter are a principal foundation of successful commóns regimes. Their great variation across social and cultural contexts is significant, for commons institutions reflect the form of the society in which they are embedded.

For the most part the conceptual analysis of the commons (also described as common property resources, common pool resources and CPRs) has concentrated on the universal principles, conditions or rules that characterize successful regimes and institutions (Ostrom 1990, Bromley 1992, Wade 1987, McGinnis and Ostrom 1993). In the process the analysis has largely circumvented the implications of internal differentiation or asymmetry including the plurality of beliefs, norms and interests involved in interactions between resource users, the effects of complex variations in culture and society, as well as wider aspects of social, political and economic conflict relating to the commons. Although the policy analyst's quest implies abstraction from the complexities of field settings in order to consider theoretical variables in schematic models (Ostrom 1990), these are significant omissions and have led to a reification of concepts, models and strategies. This is particularly so when simplified institutional models are incorporated into centralized development and foreign assistance policies.

As other authors in this volume have documented, the zeal to universalize across political contexts, cultural spaces and institutional modes evident in the contemporary discourse on the commons originates within a notion of development that is uncontextual-ized, unlocalized and value-free. At its most extreme this usage represents development as something akin to an evolutionary process that is applicable to whole cultures, institutions and populations. Perhaps not surprisingly, the historical beginnings of the modern commons discourse lie in an economic analysis of property rights defined along a binary axis between public and private goods. This analysis, based on culturally conditioned, Western notions of the social meaning of property has now given way to more socially contextualized and nuanced explanations,[1] but clearly some founding assumptions remain pervasive and influential.

The issue of voluntary coordination has long interested analysts. The interest arises essentially because individual strategies based on rational self-interest can lead to disastrous collective consequences. Attempts have been made to use rational choice theory to explain both the success and failure of collective action. The tragedy scenarios of the Garrett Hardin school (Hardin 1968, Gordon 1954), in suggesting that the commons *must* therefore have disastrous consequences given continued exploitation and population growth, are symptomatic of one general trend among explanations based on rational motives.

The other trend is summed up by Jon Elster who, while commenting on the efforts of analysts to explain successful collective action using no more than the mechanism of rational prudence, remarks that such efforts are heroic but fail to provide any clarity (Elster 1989a). Elster further argues that attempts to explain collective action simply 'by assuming that the participants must be moved by a norm of cooperation or by a propensity to behave irrationally' are trivial and soporific unless the specific norm or type of irrationality can be defined in terms that are independently meaningful (Elster 1989a:186).

Mancur Olson, in *The Logic of Collective Action* (1965), questioned the common belief that a group of rational individuals can be expected to cooperate with each other if such cooperation is in their collective interest. This argument has frequently been applied to the commons in order to support one or the other of two broad prescriptions: *privatize* the commons, or *nationalize* the commons. Both prescriptions arise within the simplistic model of institutions in neoclassical economics and in the belief that the distinction between markets and hierarchies exhausts the range of plausible institutional possibilities. Both imply that when actually existing commons institutions are successful, they are an aberration that cannot endure. Both justify centralized policy interventions that, by undermining existing commons, serve to reinforce and reify these simplistic models in a reductionist and vicious circle, ignoring the demonstrable abilities of real people to create collaborative institutions for the protection, management and use of natural resources and other local assets.

In *Governing the Commons*, Elinor Ostrom suggests that the design of sound policies requires a far more thorough and contextualized analysis of the role and functioning of institutions:

> Instead of presuming that the individuals sharing a commons are inevitably caught in a trap from which they cannot escape, I argue that the capacity of individuals to extricate themselves from various types of dilemma situations *varies* from situation to situation. (Ostrom 1990:14)

Empirical studies reveal that each commons institution is different in its management practices and assumptions, its allocation of rights and responsibilities, its relationship with state agencies. This plurality derives from the fact that each institution is largely an outcome of interactions between a specific set of users with respect to a local resource. These variations present obvious difficulties for those who want to study such institutions as a system. How do local commons institutions originate? How are preferences for managing or conserving resource stocks negotiated? At what times will specific violators be identified and punished? What effect will new policies, laws and larger institutional frameworks have on local commons regimes? In most cases, the analytical literature provides few satisfactory answers to these and related questions. While it is possible through patient and rigorous sifting of empirical material to discover the principles that distinguish successful regimes and institutions, such principles do not explain the regimes nor are they sufficient conditions for their success.

Clearly, the sources of the commons are deep and complex. Since the unregulated self-interest of users with respect to a natural resource may lead them collectively to disaster, their actions require regulation. Such regulation can be enforced by the state through laws, policies, taxes and other formal rules and instruments. Users can also agree to cooperate through decentralized and uncoercive means. Because these means and the institutions through which they are accomplished are largely an outcome of interactions between the users themselves, they do not possess the standardized features associated with state or market institutions. Instead the largely informal and self-governing nature of commons arrangements reflect the relationships, experiences, interests and beliefs of their members.

One possible analytical approach is to consider how these social attributes structure levels of interaction among members, and how within such interaction the problems of coordination and trust arise and are overcome. Inherent in this approach is the view that such institutional arrangements originate in the form of local society, not merely as an aspect of property arrangements, and that the pattern of interaction within the commons forms part of the larger social process in which these interactions are rooted. If such interactions are central to the process of joint consumption involving different levels of capabilities, preferences, trust and reciprocity, then their analysis is important for the study of commons institutions. This is the approach I take here.

I differ with analysts such as Keohane (1993) who argue that these issues are inherently intractable because they involve interdependent utility functions. Social interaction within the commons, as Elster (1989b and 1989a) argues for the social sciences in general, is an area more suited to the specification of plausible, frequently occurring patterns or mechanisms instead of universal, strongly predictive theories. In such areas which involve the wide range of normative variation in human functioning, Martha Nussbaum's admonition that it is better to be imprecisely or vaguely right rather than precisely wrong (Nussbaum 1992: 215) is an apposite reminder of priorities.[2]

Before proceeding further let me clarify some terms subject to further definitions. As will be evident, I use *commons* and *CPRs* almost interchangeably though the two have origins in widely different literatures and perspectives. *Institutions* I take to mean both the general rules – legal or customary – for assigning resources as well as the organizations defending particular interests, in the sense used by various authors (Lipton 1994, North 1990).

I am not using *fairness* in the formal sense in which it appears for instance in philosophical and legal discussions, but in the more amorphous sense in which it is used by people in everyday contexts of transaction and allocation between themselves or with institutions. Ideas of what is 'fair' in this sense can vary tremendously among different individuals, institutional contexts and allocative sectors. However, there is also in every society a vague but lively sense of the value of the goods and services that are the subject of exchange or allocation, and a range beyond which these cannot go without seeming unfair or abnormal.[3]

The concept of *social capital* refers to features of social organization such as trust, norms and networks that improve the efficiency of social institutions by facilitating coordinated actions. While a fuller discussion follows later in this chapter in 'Fairness and Social Capital in the Commons', let us note that social capital contributes to institutional success by overcoming dilemmas of collective action and the self-defeating opportunism they produce. In the absence of trust, it becomes very difficult for commons institutions to address the problem of defections and 'free-riding'[4] that can undermine any effort at collective endeavour (Coleman 1990, Putnam 1992).

The next section discusses aspects of praxis and advocacy of the local commons in India and describes the evolution of a village forest commons over more than a decade, followed by a development of the main conceptual themes and their implications, and, finally, some general conclusions.

The Commons in Praxis and Advocacy

Institutional arrangements around the commons in India are marked by a diversity of historical, political and environmental conditions. The steady and widespread erosion of traditional resource regimes under British rule has been extensively documented by historians of the Subaltern School (Ranajit Guha 1981–88). The implications of this for the subsistence of poor communities and the continuing hiatus between formal and customary law have been analysed by Chhatrapati Singh (1986) and others.

One result of the gradual appropriation and erosion of the commons has been a continuing pattern of agitations by local communities in various parts of India. Ramachandra Guha (1989) describes the history of conflict over forest rights in the hill regions of the state of Uttar Pradesh in Northern India. Whereas in the Kumaon Region the consolidation of direct British rule after the Anglo-Gurkha War in 1815 was followed by a pattern of local protests over British administered forest management policies that ultimately resulted in the establishment of *van panchayats* (local village forest councils) in the early decades of this century, west of the Ganges River in Tehri-Garhwal the situation was markedly different. Here the Tehri kings, aided and abetted by British forest contractors and consultants, embarked over the same period on centralization of state control over forests. Traditional forms of protest and successive representations were unheeded and culminated in the massacre of protesters at Tilari in 1930. The momentum of this appropriation process and its associated institutions continued over the early decades of Indian independence.

In many parts of Garhwal the well-documented Chipko Movement has played a leading role in organizing and linking protests in favour of local control over hill forests. The northern branch of this movement located in Chamoli District has protested against the commercial working of forests by lumber contractors from the plains, and lobbied with success for a policy of development in which local cooperatives are given primary responsibility for the sustainable working of local forests (Guha 1989). On the other hand, the southern branch of the movement located in Tehri District, while rooted in a similar pattern of local protests over the 1970s, has explicitly opposed any working of forests except for purposes of subsistence. None the less, it has lobbied successfully for a ban on commercial felling above 1,000 metres in 1983, consistently arguing against mainstream market-based development in favour of a Gandhian model of sustainable self-reliance and local empowerment (Shiva and Bandyopadhyay 1987, Weber 1989).

Both areas are characterized by a partial and incomplete development of markets for reasons including the physical and social characteristics of mountains such as inaccessibility and marginality (Jodha 1992).[5] The subsistence of local communities requires collective regimes for the management of forest, pasture and irrigation. These resources are usually managed as commons, not so much because the nature of the natural resource demands it but because a system of joint supply of inputs and joint consumption allows individual households to 'pool' risks within the settlement or village (Prakash 1997). Such risks may arise due to the possibility of local crop failure, illness and bereavement, inadequate labour or other factors. Although observers argue that the Chipko movements are now literally defunct, their 'energies sapped by excessive adulation' (Aryal 1994), these early local protests were essentially concerned with social and economic policies that affect communities largely dependent on local resource regimes and commons. At various times these protests opposed centralized state policies for natural resource management, regional investment and tourism development. (Shiva and Bandyopadhyay 1987, Guha 1989).

The moral economy and social capital

There is considerable moral passion evident in such spontaneous protests and demonstrations, often held at considerable risk to life and limb from police action. Moreover, such protests are not limited to agitations and demonstrations alone but extend to innumerable acts of pilfering, petty arson and sabotage. Is this an expression of mere anarchic lawlessness as it often appears to the official, or does it require another explanation? The answer lies in understanding the way peasant societies view the appropriation of their subsistence, which in turn involves issues of the 'moral economy', social capital and fairness.

In *Weapons of the Weak*, James Scott suggests that peasant resistance to the appropriation of local resources should not be considered as limited to agitations, rebellions and other acts of confrontation. It should include those subtler yet no less effective 'everyday' forms of resistance: dissimulation, pilfering, false compliance, feigned ignorance, slander, arson, sabotage, evasion and deception (Scott 1985:29–31). In *The Moral Economy of the Peasant*, Scott suggests that two recurring principles in the patterns and injunctions of a wide variety of a peasant societies are the norm of reciprocity and the right to subsistence (Scott 1976). Reciprocity serves as the central moral principle for interpersonal conduct while the right to subsistence defines the minimal needs that must be met for members of the community within the context of reciprocity. It is by guaranteeing a minimal standard of subsistence (or at least not interfering with its realization) that the elite draws from less well-endowed members of the village an acknowledgement of its status and position in the community. Scott cites Karl Polanyi's survey of historical and anthropological evidence to show that the modest yet intricate redistributive mechanisms arising from these two principles have been a nearly universal feature in all traditional subsistence societies. Such forms of solidarity may explain the virtual absence of *individual* starvation in subsistence societies throughout history (Scott 1976:5, Polanyi 1944).

One must be careful not to romanticize such societies or consider them a form of radical egalitarianism. Redistribution is not without cost. When circumstances dictate that one must draw upon the resources of the community in order to survive, then status and autonomy are thereby lost, and obligation is incurred that must be fulfilled in the future. Similarly, when the right to subsistence is violated even the pretence of reciprocity is dropped and the offender retains no claim to obligation, status or recognition. Scott claims that these essentially moral principles apply as strongly to relationships between unequals as between equals. In some measure they also apply to relations with larger entities such as the state. The presence, frequency and form of protest against the state is often a matter of context. In many cases there is no option available to the peasant other than a sullen acceptance.[6]

In general, norms of reciprocity are an essential feature of social capital necessary for any successful collective endeavour. In his study of civic traditions in modern Italy, Putnam (1992) describes how communities that follow the norm of generalized reciprocity – 'I'll do this for you now, in the expectation that somewhere down the road you'll return the favour' – can more effectively restrain opportunism and resolve problems of collective action. A continuing pattern of reciprocity results in dense networks of social exchange and engagement that facilitate communication about the trustworthiness of individuals, increase the potential costs to individual defectors, embody past success in building institutions which informs future efforts, and result in more robust patterns of reciprocity (Putnam 1993:137–8).

If elements of social capital are important in maintaining the pattern of social relationships necessary for collective action, fairness (as we shall see) is involved in ascribing relative value to the goods and duties that are involved. As Durkheim remarked, 'In every society and every age, there exists a vague but lively sense of the value of the various services used in society and of the value of things that are the subject of exchange.' Such value 'very rarely coincides with the real price, but these cannot go beyond a certain range in either direction without seeming abnormal' (Durkheim 1957:209–10).

Such notions of equal exchange are a universal moral principle found in nearly all cultures.[7]

Poverty and the commons

Jodha (1986 and 1995) provides empirical evidence of the relative dependence on the commons among various economic strata in rural India. In a study of 82 villages in 7 states, he found that 84–100 per cent of the rural poor[8] depend on the commons for the majority of their biomass needs as well as a substantial proportion of their employment. In contrast, less than 20 per cent of the rural rich depend on such resources. Goods typically obtained from the commons include products such as fuel, fodder, roots, leaves, skin of plants, honey, fish, small game, silt and clay, as well as grazing for livestock (Jodha 1995).[9] These resources can be used by the poor themselves, or sold or exchanged with others.

Jodha argues that within the prevailing social structure of rural India the commons remain an important survival resource for the poor. Under official policies of land reform and redistribution,

> . . . the transfer of marginal commons lands to individual private crop cultivation represents a step towards long-term unsustainability in dry areas, as it ensures only a meagre grain output while imposing a huge cost in terms of more ecologically appropriate products (i.e., biomass) which would help sustain diversified farming . . . The poor suffer the most severe consequences.

He concludes that the reason for this situation is that the commons have 'been degraded and their productivity is much lower today than in the past' so that the rural rich do not find it worthwhile to use them (Jodha 1995:23–6).

While this is true, a fuller explanation might lie in relating the poor's access to the commons to an implicit acknowledgement of their right to subsistence within rural social tradition. With the increasing penetration of the modern market economy in rural India and the new forms of socio-economic relationships this engenders, these traditions have become blurred and diffused. The result is that the poor must largely fend for themselves within new social structures and private property regimes that, despite the occasional success of land reform policies, give them a marginal status and fewer options to accumulate social capital.

This situation leads to numerous acts of 'everyday' resistance, of which pilfering from public lands and state forests is a common example. Such lands are in the vast majority of cases neither well protected nor fenced, and nor are their boundaries well marked on the ground. Moreover, since in most parts of India biomass collection is mainly done by poor peasant women, forest officials (who are mostly men) often report that the main problem is the large number of 'women offenders'.

The official agency responsible for India's forests, the Forest Department, is grossly understaffed and underpaid and finds it difficult to monitor effectively the enormous area under its charge.[10] Cases of illegal deforestation, corruption and the collusion of politicians with timber smugglers are frequently reported in the Indian press. Industrial requirements for raw materials derived from timber have also steadily contributed to pressure on forest cover since the 1970s. Given these circumstances, it is hardly surprising that conflicting data on the actual extent of national forest cover led in the late 1980s to a prolonged debate among technical experts, a burgeoning number of environmental groups, and official agencies on the credibility of different estimates of forest cover.[11]

A number of studies published over the same period described how local institutions in a variety of physical and social conditions had created stable regimes of sustainable forest management. Agarwal and Narain (1989) presented a series of cases of local natural-resource management and argued for a strategy of 'participatory and sustainable' rural development. Meanwhile, research in the hills of Uttar Pradesh yielded some intriguing statistics: Forest Department lands in the region had an average forest cover of 50 per cent, Department of Revenue lands an average of 10 per cent, while lands managed by local village institutions had 70 per cent average forest cover (Saxena 1988).

By the late 1980s demands for replacing the forest hierarchy with co-management methods involving local communities had begun to originate not only from NGOs and grass-roots movements but from elite groups and constituencies, though the justifications offered were different in each case. This fact probably played a significant role in the political evolution of co-management policies in India, for the ultimate test of a policy lies not only in meeting the needs of the communities most directly affected, but also in reassuring other constituencies and groups of the policy's efficiency, sustainability and expediency. It was in this broader contextual set of circumstances, pressures and politics that the joint forest management policy (JFM) was initiated in India in 1990. The policy was intended to provide for co-management of selected forests by local communities and the Forest Department, with voluntary agencies and NGOs acting as catalysts and facilitators. The forests would continue to belong to the state.

So far we have discussed issues and trends concerning some general aspects of the commons in India. The 'mixed' character of both those institutions induced by modern policies of co-management as well as of many 'traditional' institutional arrangements should be evident. While neither resembles markets nor state they are not entirely self-governing or autonomous either.[12]

We now turn to an example of an informal village commons institution in the Himalaya. Studying the formation and functioning of a specific institution will enable us to consider the complex patterns of social interaction as well as the embedded processes of fairness and social capital that are involved in such institutions. It will also allow us some insights into a specific forerunner of JFM, one of those many scattered experiments across India that created the experiential basis and contextual legitimacy of this policy.

Social interaction in an informal commons institution

This account relates to a hamlet in a relatively isolated valley, Saklana, at the southern end of the Himalayan district of Tehri in Uttar Pradesh State. Much of the following description is drawn from my own notes and memory based on conversations, observations and interactions with the people of this hamlet as well as with officials of Tehri District over the period 1986–93.

The altitude of Saklana ranges from about 1,200 metres to 3,000 metres. In marked contrast to most of Tehri District much of Saklana, especially in its upper reaches, is covered with coniferous and mixed oak forests. Human habitation in the upper part of the valley consists of nine villages further divided into numerous hamlets, the basic unit of settlement. The main economic activity of the local people is mountain farming and rearing livestock – mainly cattle, buffalo and goats. Of late, one or two vegetable crops are being grown for the market. These help supplement subsistence farming on the valley floor and terraced hill slopes. Saklana's inhabitants derive most of their fuel and fodder requirements from local forests. These are divided into many categories but chiefly comprise three types of state forest: reserved forests protected for ecological purposes, forests worked under contract from the state authorities and revenue or civil/*soyam* forests, which are highly degraded and open access. In addition there are community or village forests and private fields, both of which support mainly broad-leaved trees.

Villagers have access and withdrawal rights to certain state forests under various 'concessions' and traditional rights conceded them in the past. The precise details of these concessions are extremely intricate and confusing. In practice the Forest Department, represented by one forest guard for the some 200 square km of state forests in Saklana, will prosecute major offences such as agriculture, tree felling and construction in state forests but not withdrawals for subsistence. Commercial felling has been successfully opposed by the local people in the past and this, combined with the fragility of the steep valley slopes, led to a ban on commercial felling in 1988–89. Forest management, including decisions on which areas to close for regeneration, are achieved through informal, collective arrangements in each settlement. Such decisions may mean that women and children, who do most of the collection of biomass, have to walk long distances to fetch their family's daily needs. While high rainfall (over 200 cm per year) and alluvial soils aid regeneration, the forests located closer to settlements are generally thinner due to lopping and forest fires. Because of their high fuel and fodder content, oak trees are under particular pressure. They have been lopped to bush height in places to make collection easier.

The hamlet we are concerned with lies roughly halfway along the valley at an altitude of about 1,600 metres. It has 32 households belonging to two extended families of upper (brahmin) caste. Kinship bonds are strong and in general the two groups are well integrated. The occasional disputes within the village do not tend to follow caste or family alliances. Recent instances of commons institutions are few since the traditional irrigation system collapsed in the mid-1980s.[13]

In 1988, after intense lobbying by villagers, the subdivisional magistrate decided to transfer control of civil forests to village councils provided they instituted suitable rules and procedures and elected office-bearers. Although the order did not include rights of resale, virtually every other aspect of management (including access, withdrawal and exclusion) was transferred to the local councils. The villagers of our hamlet chose a degraded piece of land near their village to initiate the experiment. This land, a windswept hillock measuring some 10 hectares, was being used as an open grazing area.

Literally overnight, the villagers organized their council. A meeting of the entire population of the hamlet was called the next day in order to discuss details of the management regime. At this meeting some families who lived close to the hillock protested its closure for grazing and argued that alternate grazing would entail many additional hours of work for them. After the matter was thoroughly discussed, however, the following rules were unanimously accepted:

1. The office-bearers, consisting of a president, secretary and watchman, were elected. They were authorized to call meetings and make suggestions about policy. Executive decisions could only be made by the general body consisting of every adult in the hamlet, either through consensus or simple majority. No office-bearer would be paid except for a watchman, whose job would be to guard the plantation until maturity.
2. All grazing was closed for five years till 1993, and withdrawals of grass allowed only in the lean fodder (winter) season. Violations of this rule after warnings by the watchman would be fined by the contribution of twice the amount of usual labour. (This rule had an exception as discussed below.)
3. One able-bodied person from each household would plant oak saplings and high-yielding grass on the hillock for four hours every Sunday during the season July–September 1988.
4. At the end of five years a regime for distribution of forest products from the plantation would be evolved through collective discussion.

The work of plantation began the next Sunday. As well as oak saplings provided by one of the villagers, a high-yielding perennial grass was planted to provide fodder until the oaks attained maturity.

By consensus, the second rule was suspended in the case of the only widow in the village, who was permitted to gather her biomass requirements freely throughout the year. In the first year of operation, this regime worked well. Of a total of three violations of Rule 2 over 1988–89, two were punished. In the third case, punishment could not be enforced due to the continued recalcitrance of the offender.

Events over the following years can be briefly recounted. After 1989, the only major violations of the regime were occasional cases of grazing by villagers living near the plantation. The watchman's interventions were to no avail. In one case he was attacked and beaten up. Despite repeated warnings and threats this problem was never entirely resolved. The situation led to some harsh words between the offenders and the other villagers. The office-bearers determined that tempers might run high and the situation would worsen if fines were enforced. Thus no fine was ever levied.

In late 1992, during discussions about the distribution of products from the plantation at the end of the agreed closure period, a major disagreement occurred. It began with the question of the watchman's salary. The salary had been paid for the first three years by an NGO from Delhi on condition that the remaining amount would be raised by the villagers. It now emerged no one had remembered to organize the collection. The watchman demanded that his contract be observed and threatened to prevent access to the plantation until he was fully paid.

Bisu, the watchman, was old and rather stubborn and though his threat was not entirely serious, the consensus was that he should be paid the agreed salary. At the next meeting, instead of discussing details of how benefits were to be allocated, the council had to address this problem. The meeting was attended by representatives from 14 of the 32 households. Jagdish, a villager who has become relatively wealthy by transporting vegetables to market on mules, offered to pay the outstanding salary in exchange for exclusive rights to use the plantation for five years. This private bid over the common resource was agreed to by those present and a written agreement was drafted and signed on the spot. Jagdish paid Bisu the remaining salary at once. Yet matters did not end here.

Upon learning what had transpired, many people who had been absent at the meeting protested that the agreement reached was illegitimate and unfair. They argued that the meeting had constituted a minority that could not change rules formulated by the consensus, nor could the benefits of a regime involving collective burden become the property of a single individual. Many commented that this agreement in fact permitted Jagdish to degrade and destroy the forest without being accountable to the village council's management and supervision.

The disagreement led to violent arguments between the two factions within the village over the next days. On one occasion Jagdish and the president of the council, Rajendra, traded abusive words and some fisticuffs. Although Jagdish remained adamant, a consensus emerged that a regime of benefits shared according to some commonly agreed principle was the only acceptable outcome; such an outcome could not be undermined by the decision of a minority.

Murari, one of the people who had been absent at the earlier meeting, went personally to each household (except Jagdish's) and obtained equal amounts of money for providing Bisu's salary. A second meeting of the village council had to be called, at which representatives of 17 households signed a fresh agreement for the joint use of the plantation. The watchman was given his salary again and asked to return Jagdish's money.

Now the dispute became whether or not this second agreement superseded the first one. Jagdish and some others held that the first agreement had come into force with the payment to Bisu and could not be challenged except in a court of law, while Murari and others claimed the first one was void since the second represented a true majority. A number of people had signed both agreements. They now became the source of some merriment. In the end virtually everyone concurred with Murari that despite the legalistic wrangling of Jagdish, the welfare of the community took precedence over the benefit of an individual.

Jagdish consistently refused to accept the money he had paid Bisu, a situation that nobody (except Bisu) was very happy with. On a later occasion Jagdish became violent and abusive, vowing that succeeding generations of his family would extract retribution for the injustice done to him. The village council then decided that Jagdish should pay a fine equal to the sum he had paid Bisu, which would be used for the maintenance of the forest all had planted.

Fairness and Social Capital in the Commons

Published accounts of empirical commons institutions are most often edited and organized to suit some particular analytical methodology. If I have described this account at length it is because it is in the details, in the interstices of interaction and argument, that the principal sources of interest lie.

The alacrity with which this commons institution came into being suggests that it was in some way already present in the form of the local society. As we have seen, the transfer of land (or rather, officialdom's expression of intention to transfer it) under certain conditions acted as a signal prompting institutional articulation. Where information about, and trust in, other members has accumulated through repeated face-to-face interaction, sufficient social capital can exist to overcome the costs of negotiation, monitoring and enforcement that an institution entails.

Information about the responses and preferences of others, however, is always incomplete in real-life social settings, and the pattern of relationships, reciprocity and trust on which informal institutions are founded is continually reinforced and reinvented through social interaction. The discussion and framing of rules evolved out of everyday interaction and did not have to be complete initially for the creation of the institution. Indeed, one could argue that this is the case with most institutions, but particularly so with informal institutions. We see here a social consensus from within which layers of rules emerge through a continual, dynamic pattern of social interaction and engagement. Incomplete information may also relate to the response of the local ecosystem, or to uncertainty about other events that the institution must confront. This process of continual interaction and adaptation in institutions has been counter-intuitively termed 'clumsy' (Thompson 1993, Schapiro 1988) but in a good sense, implying flexibility and resilience in the face of surprise and disequilibrium. We have also seen that certain violations of the rules were not punished. Even the most robust commons regimes will have occasional offenders, for there are always 'times when and places where those who are basically committed to following a set of rules succumb to strong temptations to break them' (Ostrom 1994:8). As long as these offences remain minor and isolated, and given the delicate balance of relations within the institution, their remaining unpunished does not necessarily weaken the regime or lead to more offences. Instead, as Mauss suggested, they may form part of a 'running balance' in transactions that binds actors to further interaction, reciprocity and solidarity (Mauss 1989, Rayner 1994).

Another notable feature is the degree of heterogeneity within the institution as seen in the divergent principles, arguments and preferences forwarded by members as well as in the often violent disputes between them at various times. One way to evaluate the beliefs and values in commons institutions is to study the normative principles that underlie the allocation of benefit and burden. Certainly, such allocative issues seem to be a central feature of commons institutions. By studying how members of such institutions interact, how they invoke various beliefs and arguments in the process of interaction and decision making, we may learn something about the way perceptions and interests interact in the context of allocative decision making.

In the commons institution outlined above, many contending allocatory principles are advanced by different parties at different times. Although the initial set of rules is apparently based on equal contribution, the closure of grazing on the plantation area involves differential burdens, since those who lived closer to the plantation used it more. We have also seen how in the case of the widow, the principle of need is applied to grant priority of access. As a single householder, this woman had to perform strenuous daily chores to survive. Acknowledgement of her greater need and vulnerability makes her the exception to the general closure rule.

In the allocation of benefits, Jagdish and later Bisu both represent their bargaining strategy as a proportional one in which benefit is allocated in some relation to contribution or input. Over time it becomes apparent to other members that Jagdish, by bidding for his innovative five-year contract in exchange for the unpaid salary, intends to appropriate virtually all the benefits of a process that has involved collective burden over several years. Jagdish's strategy is seen essentially as a form of opportunism, defined as 'seeking self-interest with guile' by Williamson (1985:30).

The watchman Bisu's position suggests a proportional principle mixed with hierarchy. The former is apparent in that he negotiates a salary at all – there are many forest commons in Garhwal and elsewhere that are guarded by conventions other than a paid watchman – and in the way he negotiates fulfilment of his contract. His bargain and threat strategy ultimately yields a dual salary, which unfortunately he cannot keep. The threat of preventing access to the plantation is based on hierarchy. Although his powers as watchman derive from the common consent of the other members, he is also a respected elder of the village. Thus Bisu's threat is intended both to emphasize his status and to bind the community into honouring its agreement with him.

Contributing the watchman's salary in equal shares presents coordination problems that are familiar to students of commons regimes. These are overcome when another agent, Murari, decides to lend a hand. It is his intervention combined with Jagdish's reluctance to modify his stance that transforms the outlook of other members from one of passive avoidance of the coordination problem to strong egalitarianism in the enforcement of the parity rule in contribution, though the process takes some time. One of the enduring traits of egalitarianism is a continual assertion of the unity of the group, manifest here in Murari's energetic efforts at consensus building. In fact, this is vitally necessary because individualist strategies represent a fatal threat to the delicate balance of parity in social bonds and relations that maintain egalitarian groups (Schwarz and Thompson 1990).

As Oran Young (1995) noted, most existing commons are not isolated, self-contained entities but are increasingly affected by exogenous factors and policies. Even in the case of an isolated Himalayan valley, a variety of state interventions were behind both the failure and success of regimes administered largely by local, informal institutions. A traditional irrigation institution collapsed when the state decided to line the earthen channels with concrete. Yet, the transfer of a degraded tract of land from state to community property prompted institutional articulation and investments in the land's rehabilitation. While such external interventions can be disabling or enabling of local institutions, it is useful to consider them in the context of fairness. When policies are perceived to be fair, it is possible for local actions to be nested in larger regimes and enterprises (as in the case of joint forest management). When policies are perceived to be unfair by the majority, disruptive tactics will likely ensue.

In viewing events within this small Himalayan village commons we are confronted by a set of strikingly diverse and fluid interactions between agents and groups employing plural interpretations of fairness and unfairness. Dynamic transactions and relations embedded in contextualized notions of fairness result in a consolidation of information about the positions, beliefs and interests of others (though the possibility of surprises is always present). The accumulation of trust and social capital within complex bonds of solidarity generates continual entitlements and expectations of reciprocity, networks of interaction and institutional instruments for collective endeavour. Even in the case of perceived unfairness a 'balance of fairness' continues to operate by generating obligations and entitlements to future reciprocity.

These interactions reveal a plurality of beliefs, preferences and contributions maintained and supported by interlocking webs of social solidarity and engagement. Despite the divergent beliefs and strategies employed by different individuals, the community negotiates, monitors and enforces its collective decisions and rules internally. Indeed, it might be remarked that rather than the degree of homogeneity or heterogeneity it is the *process* by which agreements among divergent positions are coordinated that is of central interest. In order to examine this process further we now turn to a conceptual and empirical analysis of issues relating to fairness.

Fairness: principles, perceptions and process

In this section I will, first, outline some general principles of fairness identified in the literature and distinguish between procedural and outcome fairness. Then I argue that what is important in the context of the commons institution is the various perceptions of fairness adopted in specific contexts by different actors. Although empirical work on fairness in the commons is sparse and uneven, we may draw on some studies describing allocative decision making in the broadly similar context of quasi-autonomous local institutions. Finally, utilizing empirical studies by Jon Elster and others, I consider the working of fairness as a pluralist process influencing allocative decisions within a single institution.

As mentioned earlier, I am discussing fairness in an everyday sense as it applies to the allocation of benefits and burdens or goods and duties and not in any legal sense nor – as has been done in some studies of collective action – as a 'social norm' of cooperation that applies only to contribution, not to outcomes or benefits.[14]

Three enduring principles of distributive justice provide us with distinct notions of fairness (Young 1993, Deutsch 1975):

- *Equality, or parity* (impartial justice) requires that all parties receive equal shares or make equal sacrifices, irrespective of their contributions or needs. This direct, unambiguous principle resonates with common intuitive ideas of impartiality and is frequently applied in a diverse variety of contexts despite the fact that there are problems when (a) goods are indivisible or heterogeneous, (b) the parties involved are very unequal in some sense and (c) it becomes difficult to answer the classic question 'equality of what?' (Albin 1993).

- *Equity, or proportionality* (balanced or proportional justice) implies that benefits and burdens are distributed in proportion to contribution. Although it is often confused with equality, it can produce very different allocative decisions. The equity principle is seen, for instance, in contexts of wage distribution and economic investment, where fair returns are those that are in proportion to contribution. Equity is a cardinal principle, so that for it to operate the contributions of different parties must be measurable on some common scale or metric (Young 1993).

- *Need*, sometimes referred to as *priority* (compensatory justice) requires that resources be allocated based on a consideration of the parties' needs, that is, relatively more to those who are judged to have less. According to this principle those who have the least deserve the most; it is related to common or intuitive perceptions in favour of redistribution so as to achieve greater equality. In contrast to equity this principle is essentially ordinal in that it says one party is more deserving than another, but not how much more. Problems in applying this principle include the misrepresentations of needs, measuring and comparing relative wants, and motivating those who have more to share what they have (Albin 1993). The application of this principle in allocative contexts should be viewed flexibly, not only as a redistributive one aimed at greater equality but also as encompassing other kinds of socially determined priorities, for example, age, seniority, status. Such a broad meaning will be in accordance with the 'priority' principle of fairness, in which some external factor determines allocation.

While the above classification is not exhaustive and only lists the major principles supporting different ideas of fairness, its advantages are that the classifications are mutually exclusive.[15] Whatever be the sources to which the principles are attributed, they are pervasive in nearly all contemporary societies. Moreover, some or other combination of these three principles seems to underlie notions of fairness used in the broad majority of distributional and allocative contexts.

So far we have discussed allocative fairness essentially in relation to outcomes. Zartman (1993) provides an *interactive* perspective arguing that what is 'fair' can only emerge in the context of negotiation. Since negotiating strengths and bargaining positions are not the same for all parties, fairness may also be involved in the adoption of appropriate procedures and rules for negotiation. As such, fairness can act as a guide to negotiations and procedures though it may not itself be negotiated (Albin 1993). In cases where negotiating parties are inherently unequal, equality can sometimes emerge as the focal point for resolution even though there is no consensus that it is 'fair' (Schelling 1960).

Rayner points out that common responses to combinations of procedural and outcome fairness vary significantly because

For many actors procedural equity is, in theory and practice, a higher moral and psychic good than a preferred distribution. We are all familiar with the satisfaction of a preferred result fairly obtained, our capacity for stoicism in the face of an undesired result that we nevertheless consider to be fairly obtained, our lingering sense of guilt about a preferred result unfairly obtained and our outrage against an undesired result unfairly inflicted upon us. (Rayner 1994:59)

Rayner's argument relates perceptions about fairness to contextual, socially embedded responses. Individual reactions like guilt and satisfaction occur within complex constraints imposed by social associations and relationships, the influence of social norms and interactive networks of obligation and entitlement. While most current understanding of procedural fairness is dominated by an ethnocentric principle derived from Anglo-Saxon law, that is, similar cases are to be treated similarly, other cultures possess entirely different notions of procedural fairness. For instance, Comaroff and Roberts describe the contextualist focus of African traditional law which seeks to discover the unique features of cases and claimants and their place in the community, rather than attempting any standardization of procedures (Comaroff and Roberts 1981).

What this essentially means is that the structure and relationships inherent in each cultural system result in a particular organizational style that legitimates and is linked to certain recurring patterns of negotiating fairness. It does *not* mean to say that each idea of fairness is always accompanied by its corresponding negotiation or decision process – for in practice principles, interest groups and negotiating styles will be mixed as they are affected by the positions of other parties and contextual factors.

It is precisely such a complex, heterogeneous process, rather than any 'commonality' of norms, beliefs or interests, that can explain how commons institutions decide what principles constitute fairness in the distribution of benefits and burdens. Simple equality may indeed sometimes be a salient principle, though very often it is not. Much of the empirical literature on CPRs reflects this variegated social complexity suggesting that related theory lags behind in remaining attached to the constricting view that 'commonality' or homogeneity in beliefs and values is necessary for coordination among members of a commons institution or 'community' (Keohane and Ostrom 1995, Taylor and Singleton 1993).

For an illustrative example, let us return to the Himalayan commons institution. The initial regime adopted was a mixed one including strong aspects of *parity* (in the form of equal participation in voting and rule-making) as well as *priority* (in the differential burdens on some members and the use of the need principle for the lone widow). The later regime was at first one of rough *proportionality*, or rather opportunism represented as proportional fairness (in the bidding for exclusive rights to benefits by Jagdish in exchange for the watchman's salary) and *fatalism*. This regime was subsequently contested by other members who, by constructing a coalition, were ultimately able to create the near-unanimous consensus around the parity principle.

A feature of considerable interest in this account is that the various allocatory issues are not determined in advance so that the process of collective decision making unfolds and evolves as parties relentlessly invoke different principles and strategies in order to arrive at some favourable equilibrium. This process of persuasion and oscillation between principles may be particularly marked in the presence of a pool of fatalists who have no consistent principle of their own to defend. Thus, although fatalists seemingly play little part in this account, it is their consent that holds the key to the final allocatory regime.

Another feature that should be noted is that the initial regime involving a mixture of hierarchy and parity did not arise out of a vacuum. The villagers had been involved in cooperative endeavours earlier and the initial regime essentially reflects their accumulated experience and interactions, involving both a process of accretion as well as a consensus about the specific principles to be applied in the present case. In this account of a relatively small village commons, we can thus see the interaction of the many ideas of fairness, each one linking burdens to benefits in a particular way, as also the different processes that are employed to choose from among them.

If it is such a contentious process rather than any commonality of beliefs, norms or interests that explains the working of the commons institution, what idea of partnership or fellow-feeling makes its members remain in the institution instead of leaving to pursue individual self-interest? What essentially binds individuals to the commons? Why, for instance, do those people who are against a specific allocatory principle not invariably defect when that principle is in fact adopted? In addressing these issues we now turn to a discussion of social capital.

The significance of social capital

Social capital refers to features of trust, norms of reciprocity and networks of engagement that improve the functioning of society by facilitating coordinated actions. The concept of social capital has been particularly useful in resolving a recurring conceptual dilemma of the commons. Cooperating with others involves additional costs of information, bargaining, monitoring, enforcement and risk. Although the expected benefits from cooperation may be greater than those from other options open to the individual, if such transaction costs are high or unpredictable this will effectively prevent individuals from cooperating.[16]

Where social capital is present, individuals know that they can trust other individuals and that their own contributions will provide a basis for reciprocal actions from others, thus lowering the transaction costs involved in cooperation. Social capital means 'a group whose members manifest trustworthiness and place extensive trust in one another will be able to accomplish much more than a comparable group lacking that trustworthiness and trust' (Coleman 1990: 304).

Stocks of social capital tend to be self-reinforcing and cumulative; successful collaboration in one endeavour help build connections and trust which become social assets that lubricate future collaboration in other, perhaps unrelated tasks (Putnam 1993). In recent years the concept of social capital has been used in the analysis of successful collective action and CPR situations, notably by Putnam in his seminal exposition of civic institutions in Italy (1992, 1993) and by Ostrom in her thoughtful analyses of CPR institutions (1990 and 1995).[17]

Over a century ago Durkheim (1893) observed that human societies can be built on *mechanical* solidarity, in which agents are bound to others because of similar roles and values, or on *organic* solidarity, in which agents are bound in ties of interdependence based on differentiated roles and specialized functions. Although Durkheim saw these processes in grand evolutionary terms, writers such as Rayner (1994) argue that more recent analytical approaches consider both forms to coexist in contemporary societies.

Correspondingly, empirical evidence suggests that commons institutions can be initiated by groups that are homogeneous in beliefs, preferences and capabilities and by groups that are not. For instance, Olson (1965) suggests that cooperation is more likely in groups with heterogeneous capabilities and interests than in homogeneous situations. He argues that in the former case those who have greater capabilities or stand to gain more from cooperation have incentives to provide a disproportionately higher share of contribution and initial organizational costs, making cooperation more likely than in cases involving equal provision.

Ostrom (1995) describes cases of local irrigation management in Nepal involving both homogeneous as well as heterogeneous capabilities, where investments of social capital took the form of bargaining over rules for the allocation of benefit and burden from the use of an irrigation channel. Such bargaining often involved negotiating the participants' contributions or inputs (such as the provision of labour for maintenance) in relation to the benefits derived by them. Ostrom observes that the final configuration of arrangements was frequently one that the participants believed to be 'fair', though the principles applied varied from parity in cases involving homogeneous contributions to some form of proportionality for heterogeneous contributions.[18]

Although collective action events can often be festive, involve singing and dancing and help to maintain cultural and emotional bonds, few analysts have noted that some of the benefits of collective action may be unrelated to outcomes. Such *process benefits* include participation in collective action as an activity important in itself, as a means of socializing and expressing solidarity with one's neighbours or building trust and making contacts that are useful in other, unrelated activities.

One implication of participation for process benefits that is generally missed is that originally heterogeneous groups of individuals may arrive at homogeneity of beliefs or preferences through continual interaction. Another, that 'process participation' may ultimately lead to a more substantial form of participation for outcome benefits.

Such dynamic processes may be seen especially where group boundaries are not rigidly or sharply defined, for example, in groups where inclusion is in some measure determined by beliefs and interests and is largely voluntary or spontaneous. But the fact that there are durable relationships and successful commons institutions does not in itself imply 'commonality'; only that there exists a pattern of reciprocity, trust and solidarity to engender cooperation. From all this we may conclude that society is inherently complex and that any implications of the notion of community in the commons must exist at a related level of meaning.

Studies of commons institutions in India frequently imply that social homogeneity, often viewed as a function of extended family, caste or tribe affiliations or a degree of social unity, is a necessary condition for successful institutional coordination (Chambers et al. 1989, Agarwal and Narain 1989). Admittedly, the Himalayan forest commons institution as well as the several village institutions responsible for watershed management in the Nada-Sukhomajri area of Himachal Pradesh (Sarin 1993, personal communication; Chopra et al. 1990) both involved groups constituting a single caste. In these as well as other cases, however, caste also determines the pattern of residential settlement. Since clearly demarcated boundaries based on the pattern of settlement is another proposed condition for the success of local resource management institutions (Agarwal and Narain 1989), and because caste and settlement are often (but not always) coincident, the contribution of these factors to successful commons institutions can in practice be hard to disaggregate.

Table 7.1: A Typology of Local Commons Institutions

Institutional Type	Norm of Fairness	Investment of Social Capital	Group Attributes	Form of Solidarity
1.	Parity	Coalition-building	Homogeneous beliefs and interests	Mechanical
2.	Priority	Selection from precedents	Shared beliefs; heterogeneous interests	Organic
3.	Proportion-ality	Bargaining	Heterogeneous beliefs and interests	Organic
4.	Externally prescribed	Ineffective	–	Mechanical

While caste may provide a pre-existing basis for group formation, there seems little evidence that social interaction within groups constituted of one caste is necessarily or significantly 'homogeneous'. As the conflicts in the case study outlined earlier have suggested, caste groups effectively possess as much heterogeneity of beliefs and interests as other kinds of groups. Instead of arguing that the presence of homogeneity is necessary for success in collective action, it is more plausible to suggest that different *kinds* of commons institutions are based on different levels of homogeneity, heterogeneity and forms of solidarity within the community. Relating this to the preceding discussion on principles of fairness, social capital and group attributes, we can distinguish between three or four types of commons institutions with some of their characteristic features (Table 7.1).

The analysis of institutional types involves different levels of commonality of beliefs and interests as an aspect of the constituent group. The norms of fairness associated with each institutional type correspond to the most frequently occurring or typical principle applied by groups possessing these attributes; they do not denote the varied notions of fairness that are represented by individual agents. Capabilities are excluded except in so far as they are reflected in the formation of interests through norms of fairness. It seems reasonable to assume that divergent capabilities especially if they produce regimes of heterogeneous provision will most often result in asymmetric distributions of interests and benefits, though the specific mechanism for negotiating outcomes may vary – as in types 2 and 3.

Type 4 is largely compatible with 'induced groups' involving a high degree of external influence and support (Chambers et al. 1989). At one extreme of this type, even the allocatory principle is externally prescribed and local decision making and social capital investment become marginal and ineffective. These may not properly be commons institutions at all. At the other extent, greater amounts of local self-reliance and initiative will suggest one of the other institutional types. Which one exactly this is will depend partly on the specific attributes and interactions of the group with respect to a particular resource management situation.

It should be evident that this classification identifies abstract institutional types along a continuum of possibilities rather than mimicking divisions in the real world. Real-life commons institutions will often show features belonging to more than one type, and (as we have seen in our case study) can be capable of transformation from one type to another.

Implications for the Management of the Commons

We have seen how fairness is related to the accumulation of social capital comprising the trust, norms and networks that facilitate the success of commons institutions. We have also seen how divergent notions of fairness result in complex social processes and selection mechanisms that are an aspect of the specific attributes of the group and its form of investment of social capital. The basic elements of this pattern can be summarized roughly as follows:

1. The experience of fairness in interactions and allocative decisions over time leads to trust, facilitating the norms of reciprocity and networks of social engagement that constitute the accumulation of social capital.
2. Social capital reduces the transaction costs of building institutions for the collective management of the commons.
3. Networks of social capital in turn lead to increased interaction and engagement in matters of fairness in a feedback loop. This process can be complex, and may involve composite principles, accretion, compromise and sequential variation in norms of fairness used for allocative decisions.

What we see here is the operation of a characteristic process in which agreements on fairness within interactions build trust and lead to a consolidation of social capital, resulting in extended community networks and potential for successful commons institutions. Even in cases of perceived unfairness *the norm of fairness may continue to operate*, for instance by generating obligations of future reciprocity.

The explanation quite evidently does not include why people are fair *in the first place*, that is, what gets the pattern going. To say that people are fair merely because of social interactions which are themselves mediated by processes of fairness would be to offer no substantive explanation at all. The sources of fairness are twofold. On the one hand, notions of fairness are to an extent autonomous, part of deeply held personal beliefs. In this sense, people are fair for reasons arising from functions of identity, personal values and experiences.

On the other hand, people are more likely to be fair in their interactions if they believe that others will reciprocate, or if they can expect some external benefits from being so (even though these benefits may in the first place be social, e.g. an accumulation of social capital). We have seen how such expectations of reciprocity join people in complex patterns of solidarity within which the exchange of goods and services becomes a basic form of social interaction determining the allocation of future entitlements (Mauss 1989, Douglas 1992, Rayner 1994). In this sense the operation of fairness is dependent on context, and related to everyday norms of reciprocity.

The point that is not entirely explained is the details of the process by which selection among contending principles of allocation is made. Here I can offer no simple rule or predictive theory. For details of this complex process I believe one must turn to specific contexts and cases relating 'who gets what, when, how'. Many commentators have noted that the reasons for variations in allocatory regimes are social as well as related to the management demands of different resources (Keohane and Ostrom 1995, Blaikie 1993).

Complex problems of divisibility and measurement as well as the presence of social inequality can lead to consensual decisions based on the 'salience' of the equality principle (Schelling 1960, Albin 1993) as was the case for irrigation water among farmers in Sukhomajri in India (Sarin 1993, personal communication). While water is the archetypal example of this kind of resource, other resources such as forests and pasture may be economic to manage only if the provision of inputs as well as the benefits are shared and coordinated collectively (i.e., if they are treated as indivisible). This is particularly so if the typical productivity of these resources is low.

Further, the technical management requirements of different resources can affect the principles of allocation adopted, as will prevailing social and legal institutions. We can think of two major types of resources with different management demands: those with fixed boundaries and stable groups of users, making possible the provision of predetermined inputs (forests, land, demersal fish, collectively maintained reservoirs to hold rainwater) and those that are random and stochastic in location, so that allocatory decisions cannot be made in relation to inputs (grass in semi-arid areas, pelagic fish) (Blaikie 1993). Insecurity of collective tenure, for instance where tenure is *de facto* and contested, can lead to the breakdown of the collective institutions that are the social context for decisions about fairness.

Clearly, we can expect no simple answers here. However, I hope this chapter has given some of the flavour of the complex social mechanisms responsible for decisions about fairness in the commons. Ultimately, what is considered fair by different actors or how negotiations about fairness will be conducted, are matters intimately associated with issues of identity, form and legitimacy in societies and institutions. Although it follows certain recurring principles and mechanisms, the role and pattern of fairness in quasi-autonomous community institutions cannot ultimately be separated from the deeper fabric in which its practice is embedded.

Notes

1   Two main streams of economic analysis applied to the commons can be distinguished. The first, rooted in neoclassical economics, relies heavily on the analysis of property rights, and consequently prescribes either the privatization or state control of common resources. The second, from which I borrow some concepts in this chapter, originates within the new institutional economics and is more sensitive to cultural variation and the effects of transaction costs on institutions, as discussed later.

2   Michael Thompson (in Chapter 8) argues that a theory that is both plural and precise cannot be considered weak. His reasoning seems to be that plurality is not a sign of theoretical inadequacy when it enriches understanding of human phenomena, an assertion with which I entirely agree. However, I see no way that a pluralist theory dealing with multiple specification and normative variation of the sort he is suggesting can be more than weakly *predictive*, therefore 'weak theory' or 'vague theory' in Elster's or Nussbaum's sense is an accurate description. Strength in theory is not the same thing as superiority, nor precision the same thing as accuracy. Some have even argued that in descriptions of complex natural and social systems one of these can only exist at the cost of the other because precision, involving quantification and mathematics, is a reductionist process in which information and accuracy are lost (Goldsmith 1993; Robert Mann, quoted in Goldsmith 1993).

3   This aspect of social exchange was pioneered by Durkheim (1957). Subsequently Mauss (1989) enriched our understanding of norms of reciprocity in his essay *The Gift*. For a more recent interdisciplinary analysis of exchange systems, see Cantor et al. (1992).

4   'Free-riders' are those who enjoy the benefits of collective action without contributing their share of costs or burdens.

5   The Himalayan Region has among the lowest figures for per capita income in the world, with Nepal, Bhutan and Afghanistan counting among the ten poorest countries (based on figures for 1991 and 1991–92 in UNDP 1994). Rural Garhwal and

Kumaon, the areas discussed in this section, have lower incomes than similar areas in the rest of Uttar Pradesh, which is one of the poorest states in India with an annual per capita income of Rupees 4,012 (US$155) and roughly 48 per cent of its rural people under the poverty line (income data for 1991–92, poverty for 1987–88; from Dreze and Sen 1995).

6 In this sense, perceived injustice and violation of the moral economy cannot be deduced simply from protests and other explicit forms of resistance. While the literature on social movements in India provides a good record of various protests and agitations, it pays less attention to the everyday patterns of resistance that are such a characteristic feature of relations between rural society and national elites.

7 Durkheim's disciple Marcel Mauss went further by suggesting that the 'glue' that binds society may actually consist of a running balance of *unfairness* in transactions, linking actors in continuing reciprocal networks of entitlement and obligation (Mauss 1989).

8 The rural poor in these studies were defined as smallholder or landless peasant families possessing less than two hectares of unirrigated or dry land. This includes over half of all Indian farmers.

9 The proportion of total fuel requirement obtained from the commons varied in the 7 states from an average of 66 per cent among poor households in Gujarat, to 84 per cent in Andhra Pradesh. For other, non-poor households it varied from 8 per cent to 32 per cent. The number of days of employment for the poor varied from 128 per year in Maharashtra to 196 per year in Gujarat, as compared with a range of between 31 and 80 days for other households. While Jodha's analysis pertains to 7 semi-arid states (Andhra Pradesh, Gujarat, Madhya Pradesh, Maharashtra, Rajasthan, Karnataka and Tamil Nadu), it may be taken broadly to approximate conditions in other marginal environments such as uplands, hill areas, etc., in India.

10 In official estimates the 'recorded forest area' formally under the charge of the Forest Department totals some 750,000 sq. km, or around 23 per cent of India's total area. Only some 85 per cent of this is believed to have any trees at all, and less than half has sufficient cover to qualify as good forest.

11 One of the major controversies was prompted by the first detailed interpretation of remote sensing data for India. This exercise estimated that the annual loss of forest cover might be as high as 13,000–15,000 sq. km. See J.B. Lal (1988) for one account of

the resulting debate between foresters, remote sensing specialists, NGOs and the national press.

12   As Oran Young, citing recent work by Jodha (1993), argues, the analysis of universal 'design principles' seems most suited to traditional, self-contained societies, while most contemporary situations are marked by 'complex mixes of traditional common-property arrangements and recent interventions stemming from the policy initiatives of modern states' (Young 1995: 40). Thus the formulation of such principles, he suggests, is applicable to a continually shrinking set of cases.

13   This happened when local authorities attempted to line the irrigation channels with concrete. The system no longer works because due to indifferent engineering the water course has disappeared *under* the concrete. This would have been repaired by the local institution earlier, but the official intervention ended the collective regime of maintenance that acted as a basis for strengthening social capital and collective action within the user community. In other words, the principal reasons for the collapse were social instead of technical; or rather, a misfit between technology choice and social organization. For an extended analysis of the role of social capital in irrigation systems in Nepal with a similar conclusion, see Ostrom 1995.

14   Cf., for example, Jon Elster who, in the *The Cement of Society*, distinguishes between the roles of rationality and social norms in collective action by arguing that the former is 'pulled' by the prospect of future reward, whereas the latter is 'pushed' from behind by quasi-inertial forces (1989a:97). He places fairness in the latter category, arguing that it should be seen primarily as a 'norm of cooperation'; that is as affecting only what people *do*, or contribute, not what they *get*, or otherwise derive in the way of benefits from cooperation (1989a:123, 187–92). While Elster bases his distinction on two views of human beings conveniently associated with Adam Smith and Emile Durkheim, it causes considerable complications for any explanatory scheme (including his own). I am not at all sure that the two views are necessarily compatible within the same scheme and do not consider this 'version' of fairness further.

15   Other principles might, for instance, include *no-envy, retribution, lottery, subtractive justice* and *precedent* (Albin 1993), as also *time-related* principles (queueing, waiting lists, seniority), *principles defined by status* (age, gender, ethnicity, residence), *principles defined by other properties* (need, contribution, efficiency) and

mixed systems (points systems, weighted lotteries, selection from a pool of eligibles) (Elster 1992).

16   The origin of transaction cost theory is generally attributed to Ronald Coase (1937) though Coase did not coin the term. The implications of transaction costs for various institutions including CPR institutions have been analysed by many authors, including North 1990; Williamson 1985; Ostrom 1990; Taylor and Singleton 1993; Feeny 1995, and Keohane and Ostrom 1995.

17   It is possible to object to such a description of social relationships and processes as a form of 'capital'. If a group of people meets in a coffee shop to discuss how to coordinate their actions and formulate rules for the management of some common resource, such social processes can surely be treated as an end in themselves, a final consumption good (Feeny 1995). While such interactions are certainly important in themselves, what is significant about the term social capital is that it demonstrates the centrality of social processes for effective collaboration and institutional formation.

18   The fact that the arrangements are frequently, but not always, thought to be fair is I think important for understanding the role of fairness in commons regimes. It should be evident that fairness is not a *condition* to be met for the success of the regime, but this does not discount its importance.

8

Style and Scale: Two Sources of Institutional Inappropriateness

Michael Thompson

In this chapter I present a Cultural Theory approach to the commons, an approach that highlights the institutional character of the commons, but is in sharp contrast to a popular theoretical framework called the New Institutionalism.[1] I argue that when the workings of the commons are misunderstood, so are the programmes and policies that are prescribed to 'fix' or manage them. Through a discussion of Cultural Theory, and a critique of New Institutionalism, this chapter presents a lens through which we can better understand the commons, wherever they may be. Since most of those who are interested in the commons will not have come across Cultural Theory, I should begin by saying a little about what it is and how its characterization of institutions differs from that of the New Institutionalists.

Robert Keohane and Elinor Ostrom are the chief architects of a New Institutionalist approach to the commons (Keohane and Ostrom 1995). They see the commons as flourishing in those places to which the nation-state's writ does not fully run. The nation-state's authority, they observe, often does not reach effectively to either the village level or the global level, where new international regimes are emerging to manage what they call 'the global commons' – enclosed coastal seas, ozone holes, whale populations and climates. The nation-state, according to Keohane and Ostrom, is hierarchical – that is, centralized and coercive – and the commons, which are voluntary and cooperative, are able to function only at the two extremes (the very small scale and the very large scale), the two places where the nation-state's authority is weak. That, essentially, is the New Institutionalism's characterization of the commons, local and global. 'What,' you may ask, 'is wrong with that?' 'Just about everything!' says Cultural Theory. Here's why:

- Centralization and coercion are *not* definitive of hierarchy; formal status distinctions, distribution by rank and station, asymmetry (trust in expert, certified knowledge, for instance) and accountability (the 'lowerarchs' right to bring into line those who are not acting in accordance with their proper role within the layered totality) are the sort of features that tell us we are dealing with a hierarchy (Gross and Rayner 1985).

- Cooperation and voluntariness are *not* definitive of the commons; market relationships are often (indeed are usually) voluntary, and many commons-managing institutions are hierarchical.

- Hierarchical relationships are to be found at *all* levels (not just within the effective grasp of the nation-state) and commons are to be found at *all* levels (not just those that are beyond the effective grasp of the nation-state). Scale, Cultural Theorists concede, does matter, but it plays no part in defining the commons. Nor does it play any part in defining those other transactional arrangements that are not commons. What, then, does define them?

The answer, I will be arguing, lies not in scale but in *style*: the different, and contending, arrangements for the promotion of social transactions that are to be found at all scale levels – from the household, through the village, the commune, the canton, the nation-state, to the sometimes global interactions of some of these actors. (And let us not forget to include corporations, large and small, and non-governmental organizations, local and far-flung.) If we are to sort out the various kinds of commons, and those various arrangements that are not commons (I'll call them 'privates'), then we are going to need a *typology of styles*. Cultural Theory provides such a typology that distinguishes those familiar arrangements – *markets* and *hierarchies* (the former promoting competition and instituting equality, the latter setting limits on competition and instituting inequality) – and then goes on to distinguish the less familiar arrangements, *egalitarianism* and *fatalism* (the former setting limits on competition and instituting equality, the latter enduring unfettered competition and inequality) that complete the permutational possibilities.

These four styles work themselves through in all sorts of ways: into the *patterns of social relationships* that both sustain and are themselves sustained by the transactions they carry; into the *myths of nature* (the convictions as to how the world is) that are shared by those who constitute each of these patterns of social relationships; into the *scopes of the knowledges* that are shaped by these different arrangements; into the *learning styles* that they adopt, into the *strategies vis-a-vis the environment* to which each way of knowing gives rise; and into the *ideas of fairness* by which each of these strategies is morally justified. It is the distinctive combinations of these key predictions from Cultural Theory that define the various styles and their manifestations on all the scale levels, in differing proportions and patterns of interaction.

I will be explaining much more about these concomitants of the various styles later in the chapter; for now, I will explore how this typology allows us to do two vital things. First, it will allow us to say precisely what the definitional ingredients of institutions – alternative arrangements for the promotion of social transactions – are. Second, it will allow us to sort out, at any scale level, the various forms of commons and the various forms of privates. Where the New Institutionalism has just a scale axis, with hierarchy in the middle and the commons at either extremity, Cultural Theory gives us a 'multi-layered template' in which all four styles are present at every scale level (Figure 8.1).

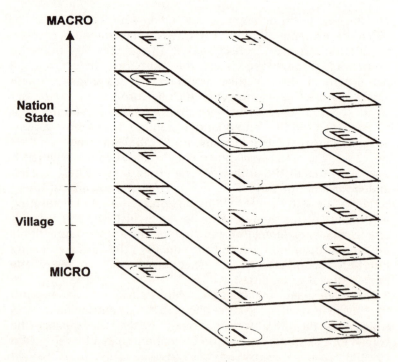

Figure 8.1 Cultural Theory's multi-layered template: four styles at every scale level

Scale and style are thus clearly distinguished, and we can use this template, in a very practical way, to tease out just why it is that things sometimes go right and sometimes go wrong. Institutional arrangements, like Tolstoy's happy and unhappy families, can be appropriate in just one way (right style, right scale) and inappropriate in three ways (right style, wrong scale; wrong style, right scale; and wrong style, wrong scale). This is a very simple idea, but not one that can be latched onto by way of the New Institutionalism, because the New Institutionalism conflates style and scale into a singular definition of the commons (and of the nation-state). It is, moreover, a simple idea that, as I hope to show, gets us quite a long way. But, before I set about demonstrating this simple idea's virtues, I need to explain something that may not be too immediately obvious: the way in which this approach fits with the conceptual framework that has been set out in Michael Goldman's Chapter 1 of this volume.

Cultural Theory and the Goldman Framing

Goldman begins by boldly capturing the past 20 or so years of work on the commons into a dialectic between those who accept the 'tragedy of the commons' explanation and those who systematically reject it. Those who accept this explanation are faced with a stark policy choice: either privatize the commons (a solution that is favoured by many development economists and much touted by libertarian think-tanks) or change human nature (a solution that is built into Aldo Leopold's 'earth ethic' and into the deep ecologists' insistence that we must develop 'a whole new relationship with nature'). 'Not so!' cry those who are ranked against them, 'the tragedy is not inherent to the commons': an argument that leads them, not to the stark choice, but to the painstaking elucidation of the conditions under which the tragedy of the commons does not occur (and Goldman lists the various 'development tribes', anthropologists amongst them, who have been beavering away at this task).

But Goldman discerns that something else is now beginning to happen. This dialectic, for all the disagreement that it contains, is ultimately contained within a wider area of agreement – that development is inevitable and desirable – that is now becoming the thesis in a new dialectic: a new dialectic in which the two original camps, joined together by their shared and unquestioned assumptions, are pitted against an antithesis that explicitly questions those assumptions. It is within this new questioning of the hitherto unquestioned that Goldman wishes to locate our project, and 'reflexivity' – the ability to take up a position from which it is possible to recognise the arguments of those for whom development is the solution *and* of those for whom it is the problem – is that project's crucial ingredient (Figure 8.2).

All this, of course, is pretty airy Hegelian stuff, but it does serve to point us in the right direction and to indicate, in very broad terms, what we should be doing. First, how do we achieve the 'requisite reflexivity'; second, how do we make that reflexivity operational – how do we bring it to bear, in a policy-relevant way, on the commons – and third, how do we translate that operational reflexivity into a do-able research programme for the facilitators of this book, Transnational Institute? 'By taking the Cultural Theory approach' is my answer!

I am, I confess, an anthropologist, which puts me into the first of Goldman's three 'tribes' that oppose the tragedy of the commons hypothesis. And I have done my share of the 'painstaking elucidation' that Goldman shows is the hallmark of these three tribes. But, unlike most anthropologists, I am an 'anti-particularist'. Unwilling to stop at 'thick description', I belong to that small band of anthropologists whose prime concern is to fashion some general and universally valid

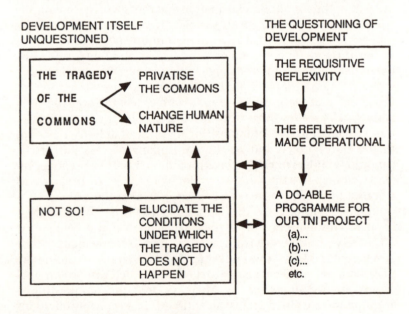

Figure 8.2 The Goldman framing

frame that will tell us just how similar and dissimilar all those 'thick descriptions' are. Nor do I see myself as fitting comfortably into the 'development community'. To do that one would have to buy into what postmodernists call 'the project of modernity' (or, even more portentously, 'the dark side of the Enlightenment') and British anthropology, to its great credit, never did that! As anti-particularists, many of us eschew the basic dualisms intrinsic to the development project, working under the banner 'What's Modern About Now and What's Traditional About Then?'

So try as we may (which, of course, we do not), we cannot fit ourselves into the 'development thesis' of Goldman's new dialectic. In other words, the anti-particularistic anthropological approach – that is, the Cultural Theory approach – is simply another way of arriving at the Goldman framing. And its great advantage, I will be claiming, is that its fourfold typology of styles provides us with Goldman's first essential: the requisite reflexivity. Cultural Theory's ideas of fairness, for instance, predict a willingness, among individualists and hierarchists, to go along with the notion of *Pareto optimality*, that is, an outcome in which the winners can fully compensate the losers, and still be better off than they were, is seen as preferable to the *status quo*. But egalitarians, Cultural Theory suggests, will likely prefer the opposite: a situation in which people are less well-off but more equal. Moving from one Pareto optimum to another, *ad infinitum*, is development; electing not to do that is something else! Ask those who elect not to follow this Pareto path what the opposite of development is and they will say, not 'stagnation', but 'hospitality'!

If the policy process is captured by those who, for all their admitted differences, share the development assumption then the egalitarians are going to find themselves excluded. Could this be the reason why the commons have been in such pronounced decline? If so, then there is no chance of our reinventing the commons, and including the egalitarian position in the policy process (the *sine qua non* for that reinvention), if we do not first place ourselves firmly within the antithesis of Goldman's new dialectic. Conventional approaches – painstaking elucidation, for instance, and the New Institutionalism – are not enough!

Why Institutions Have to be the Focus

Over the quarter-century that has elapsed since Garrett Hardin (1968) published his famous paper 'The Tragedy of The Commons', there are a number of lessons that have been (or, at any rate, should have been) learnt. One is that, when commons collapse, it is not because they are commons (any more than that, when privates – that is, markets – fail, it is because they are privates). Both commons and privates collapse because the institutional supports that are required to keep them in place are not up to the task. A related lesson is that, whilst an increase in population undoubtedly places a stress on that population's resource base, there is no direct relationship between population and environmental degradation. Again, it is the institutions that make all the difference. Hence the possibility of 'More People, Less Erosion' (Tiffen et al. 1994), a common phenomenon that makes such nonsense of the frequently invoked notion of 'carrying capacity'.

In other words, it is the institutional arrangements that are interposed between a human population and the resource base on which it draws that dramatically modify the sorts of limits that impinge so directly on non-humans. That the limits can be dramatically extended (and, in some circumstances, cut back) is the lesson; not that (as some gung-ho neoclassical economists insist) there *are* no limits.[2] If it is the institutions that make all the difference then it is with the institutions that we should concern ourselves.

The Himalayan Village[3]

There is, of course, no such thing as a typical Himalayan village. Nevertheless, Himalayan villages do have some common features, among which is the way in which they parcel out transactions among the four distinct institutional arrangements that the Cultural Theory typology identifies. Each parcelling-out, in consequence, is characterized by a distinctive management style, a state of affairs that is graphically represented by the village level 'sheet' (Figure 8.1) with its four styles – individualist, hierarchist, egalitarian and fatalist. As you enter this Himalayan village, the 'sheet' should help you understand what is going on. How, in other words, are the villagers interacting with one another and with their physical surroundings?

Agricultural land, you will find, is privately owned, whilst grazing land and the nearby forest are communally owned. But the grazing land and the village forest do not suffer the 'tragedy of the commons' because transactions in their products are under the control of a *commons managing institution*. Villagers appoint forest guardians, erect a 'social fence' (a declared boundary, not a physical construction) and institute a system of fines for those who allow their animals into the forest when access is forbidden, or take structural timber without first obtaining permission. If the offender is also a forest guardian the fine is doubled; if children break the rules their parents are penalized. Informal though they may seem, and lacking any legal status, these commons managing arrangements work well in the face-to-face setting of a village and its physical resources. Drawing on their 'home-made' conceptions of the natural processes that are at work (their *ethnoecology*), the forest guardians regulate the use of these common property resources by assessing their state of health, year by year or season by season. In other words, these transactions are regulated within a framework that assumes, first, that you can take only so much from the commons and, second, that you can assess where the line between 'so much' and 'too much' should be drawn. The idea of nature inherent to this transactional realm is that nature is bountiful within knowable limits. This, to make a link with the ecological theories of C.S. Holling (1986), is the myth of *Nature Perverse/Tolerant* (Figure 8.3).

With agricultural land, however, decisions are entirely in the hands of individual owners, and fields (unlike communally owned resources) can quite easily end up belonging to the moneylenders. In recent years, when forests and grazing lands have suffered degradation (for a variety of reasons which we will come to in a moment, but not the 'tragedy of the commons'), villagers have responded by shifting some of their transactions from one sphere to the other. For instance, they have allowed trees to grow on the banks between their terraced fields (thereby reducing the pressure on the village forest) and they have switched to the stall-feeding of their animals (thereby making more efficient use of the forest and grazing land *and* receiving copious amounts of manure which they can then carry to their fields).[4] In other words, transactions are parcelled out to the institutional modes that seem appropriate and, if circumstances change, some of those transactions can be switched from one mode to another.

Since they are subsistence farmers, whose aim is to remain viable over generations (rather than to make a 'killing' in any one year and then retire to Florida), their transactions within their local environment can be characterized as *low risk, low reward*. During those times of the year when there is little farm work to be done, many villagers engage in trading expeditions, or in migrant labour in India (Fürer-Haimendorf 1975). Trading expeditions are family-based and family-financed, and highly speculative: *high risk, high reward* (Thompson 1980). So the individualized transactions, when added together over a full year, constitute a nicely spread risk portfolio. The attitude here (and particularly at the high-risk end of the portfolio) is that 'Fortune favours the brave', 'Who Dares Wins', 'There's plenty more fish in the sea'. Opportunities, in other words, are there for the taking. The idea of nature here is optimistic, expansive and non-punitive: *Nature Benign* (Figure 8.3).

Social scientists in general, and institutional economists in particular, would see these two spheres as corresponding to their classic distinction between *hierarchies* and *markets*, and would have no difficulty in explaining the processes by which some transactions are switched this way or that (Lindblom 1977, Williamson 1975). But hierarchies and markets do not exhaust the transactional repertoire of the Himalayan villager. Some collectivized transactions do not involve formal status distinctions (such as those between forest guardians and ordinary villagers) and some individualized transactions are marked by the absence of bidding and bargaining (an essential characteristic of the market way of life). The plurality,

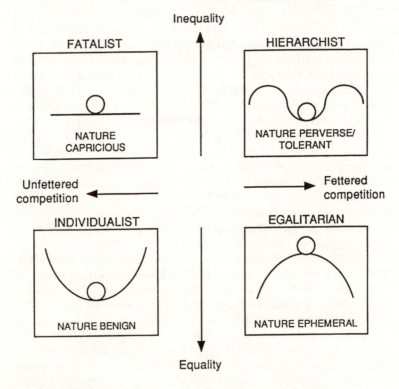

Figure 8.3 Myths of nature and their transactional realms

in other words, is fourfold, not twofold, and it is with this doubling of institutional variety that this chapter is concerned.

In many parts of the Himalaya (especially the Indian Himalaya), village autonomy is always under threat, because powerful outside actors are also laying claim to the forest resources that are so vital to Himalayan farming systems. One very effective response to this external threat has been the Chipko Movement. This is a grass-roots and highly *egalitarian* social movement, in which women (who are largely responsible both for fodder gathering and fuel-wood collection) predominate. 'Chipko' means 'to stick', and the Gandhian strategy is to physically hug the trees, thereby preventing them from being appropriated. Those villagers of a slightly less nonviolent disposition actually chase the logging contractors (and the government forestry officers who have been corrupted by the contractors) out of the forest with their *kukris* (long curved knives). In the Narmada Valley, further to the south, they have now done the same to the representatives of the World Bank.

So far as these threatening external transactions are concerned, it is certainly not a case of 'plenty more fish in the sea', nor is there even a 'safe limit' within which the commercial extraction of timber would be sustainable. *All* external predation is seen as catastrophic in its consequences. Hence the spectacularly uncompromising collectivist response of the tree-huggers, whose idea of nature is one in which any perturbation of the present low-key regime is likely to result in irreversible and dramatic collapse: *Nature Ephemeral* (Figure 8.3).

Finally, in every village, we may be sure, there will always be some people who sneak produce from the forest when no one is looking, or who can never quite get together the capital, the contacts and the 'oomph' to go off on trading expeditions, and who manage somehow not to be around when it's all hands to the tree-hugging. These are the *fatalists*: people whose transactions are somehow dictated by the organizational efforts of those who are not themselves fatalists. Theirs is a life in which the world is always doing things to them – sometimes pleasant, sometimes unpleasant – and in which nothing that they do seems to make much difference. 'Why bother?' is the not unreasonable response of the fatalist. If that is how the world is, then learning is not possible and, even if it were, there would be no way of benefiting from it. The idea of nature here is one in which things operate without rhyme or reason: a flatland in which everywhere is the same as everywhere else – *Nature Capricious* (Figure 8.3).

The Himalayan village, with its transactions parcelled out in these four very different ways, is impressively plural. More than that, as shown by the examples of stall-feeding and trees on private land, it has the ability to switch transactions from one way to another whenever it seems likely that this might be more appropriate. Since the behaviour of the villagers is continuously altering the resource base on which they depend, this is, to put it mildly, a useful in-built mechanism. The jurist, Michael Schapiro (1988), has dubbed this sort of set-up (in which each conviction as to how the world is – each myth of nature – is given some recognition) a *clumsy institution*. This is in contrast to those more elegant, and more familiar, arrangements in which just one conviction holds sway. The terminology is deliberately counter-intuitive: clumsy institutions have some remarkable properties that are not shared by their unclumsy alternatives.

To understand just how remarkable this particular clumsy institution is, imagine for a moment that you are some God-like experimenter, able to reach out and change this or that variable in a village's environment, or to move it bodily east or west, north or south, across the Himalayan landscape. As you bring in the logging contractors, or take it a hundred miles eastwards or 1,000 metres higher, the village will shift its transactions this way or that between its four options until it has adapted itself to its changed circumstances. In other words, it will maintain its *resilience* thanks to the very practical learning system that is part-and-parcel of its fourfold plurality.[5] But, if it did not have this plurality, and was an elegant and unclumsy institution – such as, for instance, many national forestry services – it would not be able to do this. Something along these imaginary lines, it turns out, is what has actually happened (and is still happening).

As we go from one Himalayan village to another, the relative strengths of the four ways of organizing vary. Egalitarianism, for instance, is strongest in those parts of the Himalaya that are most prone to commercial logging. As one moves eastwards, from India (with its powerful centre and its colonial heritage of Reserved Forests) into Nepal and Bhutan, so the Chipko Movement becomes less of a force to be reckoned with. If the inequitable external threat is absent then so too, it appears, is the communitarian response to it. The most dramatic of these variations is that between the strongly individualized Buddhist villages (those of the Sherpas of Khumbu, for instance, whom we will meet presently) and the strongly grouped Hindu villages just a day or two's walk downstream. These are Fürer-Haimendorf's (1975) 'adventurous traders' and 'cautious cultivators', respectively, and he has shown how the distinctive strategy of each makes viable the other's. For instance, the Sherpas of Khumbu (the high valley just below Mount Everest) used to buy the small agricultural surpluses of their Hindu neighbours which then became the payloads of their yaks on the perilous, but highly profitable, journey over the Nangpa La (a 19,000-foot pass) into Tibet. On the return journey the yaks carried salt (of which there are ample deposits on the Tibetan Plateau) that was then sold, again profitably, to the Sherpas' stay-at-home Hindu neighbours. Nowadays many Sherpas earn good money as mountain guides and high-altitude porters, whilst their Hindu neighbours remain below the snowline, contentedly carrying their produce (including pigs) on the short and comparatively safe journey up to the ever-expanding Sunday market in Namche Bazaar, the Sherpa capital. In other words, each village, in adjusting to its circumstances (which include the other villages), creates and takes its place in a social and cultural 'ecosystem', in which the marked divergence of the parts sustains the whole.

This is not a fanciful analogy. Anthropologists and ecologists have shown that the 'adventurous trader's' strategy matches that of what biologists call the omnivorous and opportunistic 'r-selected species'; the 'cautious cultivator's' strategy matches that of the biologists' specialized and niche-dependent 'K-selected species'; the fatalists do for social systems what compost does for natural systems (provides a generalized resource for renewal); and the egalitarians, through their small-scale communal fervour, are creating enclaves of low-level energy (what Marx called 'primitive capital') in places where neither the r-selected nor the K-selected species can make any impression (Holling 1986, Thompson et al. 1990, Holling et al. 1993).

So the hypothesis I am sketching here is very different from the way people usually think about the interaction of social and natural systems. There is, in my view, no way of ever getting it 'right' – of bringing the social into long-term harmony with the natural. Instead, each is a fourfold and plurally responsive system, and their time-lagged interactions ensure that there can be no steady-state outcome. The whole thing is in a perpetual *un*steady state: changes at each level – the social and the natural – adapting to the other and changing it in the process, thereby setting in motion another set of changes. On and on.

These changes are not at all predictable, as they would be if each level had only two states to be in: hierarchies and markets at the social level, and pioneer and climax communities at the natural level. In other words, bumping up the plurality from two to four takes both social and natural systems out of the well-understood realm of 'Newtonian science', in which once you have identified the key variables and written and solved the equations expressing their cause-and-effect relationships, you can predict the future states of the system. It forces the analysis into a 'non-Newtonian' realm that is characterized by complex systems – systems that are non-linear, highly sensitive to initial conditions, far from achieving equilibrium and inherently unpredictable. Order without predictability is what complex systems give us, and my argument is that, when we are talking about institutions, we will be seriously wide of the mark if we assume (as pretty well all of current thinking does assume) that they are simple.

What this means, in practical terms, is that *elegant institutions* – solutions that begin by defining the problem in terms of just one of the myths of nature and then try to put all our transactions on to the pattern of social relationships that is supported by that myth of nature – are wholly inappropriate for complex systems. In their place we need much messier arrangements: set-ups in which each myth of nature is granted some legitimacy, and in which transactions are tentatively distributed among the various institutional bases. Policies designed in this way are *non-hubristic* (because they fully acknowledge the extent of our ignorance), *high in consent* (because all the 'contradictory certitudes' are granted some validity), *quick learners* (because they do not set off by discarding three-quarters of the experience and wisdom from which they could learn) and *highly adaptive* (because, by covering all the bases, they allow us to continuously reassess the appropriateness of our initial distribution of transactions and to switch those that are not working well on to more promising alternatives).

In other words, if you're having to ask who's right you're wrong! *Of course* we need the commons; *of course* we need the markets. It is never a matter of one or the other; always a question of what is best handled by which. Nor (and this is the crux of the complex-not-simple realization) is it ever a straightforward, twofold allocation: this to the commons, that to the markets. Rather, there is a double bifurcation: the commons come in two very different forms – hierarchy and egalitarianism – and the 'privates' come in two very different forms – individualism (the form that is supported by market relations) and fatalism.

It is Style, not Scale, that Distinguishes the Institutions

Cultural Theory, in marked contrast to the New Institutionalism that informs most of the recent work on the commons, focuses on style and ignores scale. The underlying idea in Cultural Theory is that there is no need to make the dichotomy between micro and macro, between the individual and society. To do so would be to slice right through the 'meso-level' – the various viable patterns of social relationships, which is Cultural Theory's point of departure. These patterns, Cultural Theory argues, work their way down into the village, into the household and even into the individual (individuality being something that, to a considerable extent, we get from others). And, in the other direction, these patterns manifest themselves in the corporate cultural differences between multinationals (Procter & Gamble, for instance, and Unilever, the former opting for global products, the latter for 'harmonization') and in the political cultural differences between nation-states (Ireland, for instance, is currently the most hierarchical country in Europe, France the most fatalist, Germany the highest on both individualism and egalitarianism). The four styles, you could say, are like the letters in a stick of Blackpool rock: no matter where you happen to break it – at the village or nation-state, household or international organization – they are always present![6] (See Figure 8.1.)

With scale placed in the background, we can see that both village-level commons managing institutions and nation-level state institutions can be stylistically identical: both can be hierarchical. Both are often founded on formal status distinctions, both place their trust in expert certified knowledge and both subscribe to a view of the world (Nature Perverse/Tolerant) as a place that is forgiving of many interventions but vulnerable to the occasional knocking of the ball out over the rim. Both also hold to a view of human nature as originated in sin but redeemable by firm, long-lasting and nurturing institutions. Steering a careful path between the egalitarians (who see people as essentially caring and cooperative until corrupted by coercive and unjust institutions) and the individualists (who see people as inherently competitive and self-seeking) hierarchists are committed to wise guidance and far-sighted stewardship.

Everything, therefore, hinges on their discovering just where the limits are and then ensuring (by statutory regulation, in the case of the nation-state, and by more homely, face-to-face sanctions, in the case of the Himalayan village) that everyone stays on the right side of them. Whenever we hear talk of 'safe limits', 'assimilative capabilities', 'tolerable risks' and 'carrying capacities' – and we hear such talk in both global and local forums – we are in the presence of hierarchy.

Individualists, however, do not talk like this. They put their trust in those institutional arrangements – markets – that harness people's self-seeking nature to the benefit of all. Adam Smith's 'hidden hand', individualists feel, is all the guidance they need, and they note that its track record in terms of wealth creation and technological innovation has not yet been brought to a halt by any natural limit. Others such as the egalitarians are aghast at this business-as-usual complacency, and would likely point out that the individualist's true predicament is akin to that of the man who, having fallen off the top of a skyscraper, remarks 'So far, so good' as he passes each floor. Nor are the egalitarians prepared to stop off at the hierarchists' halfway-house. Nature, they are convinced, allows us no safe limits, and they are deeply distrustful of the sort of 'bench science' that is so relied on by the hierarchists. Holism, or the insistence that 'you can never change just one thing' (which, of course, is what bench science claims to do), is the bedrock of the egalitarian's science.

One of the attractions of Cultural Theory is that it gets to grips with the problem of *irreducible ignorance*. Science, it tells us, will never be able to decide, once and for all, whose science is right. Each, rather, will be valid at times and in places; hence the desirability of not choosing just one and discarding the others. To say, as is so often said, that knowledge is power is to miss the pluralistic point, and to avoid posing the really important questions: 'Whose knowledge?' and 'Power to do what?' Cultural Theory shows how the different knowledges continually emerge and reconstitute themselves as the different myths of human and physical nature get to work on whatever it is that each new day brings (a considerable proportion of that historical change being, of course, the consequence of earlier actions based on those knowledges). When acted upon, each knowledge gives those who act on it the power to extend their preferred way of organizing – their preferred pattern of social relationships – at the expense of others.[7] In other words, the styles are far from superficial; they cut deep. Styles can define the entire repertoire of institutional arrangements that are available to us.[8] One practical consequence of this stylistic depth is a fourfold typology of *ideas of fairness*. Every policy debate – local and global – is a debate over fairness, yet nearly all policy analysis is couched in the purportedly neutral terms of economic efficiency. Something, for sure, is wrong here, and Cultural Theory can tell us what it is.

A recent book on business ethics (Sternberg 1994) defines as fair a system of distribution in which the rewards are in proportion to the contributions made to the business. Those who put most in should get most out, a state of affairs that would meet with the approval of our Himalayan villager as he or she sets off on a trading expedition, and that is consistent both with the notion of equality of opportunity and with the criterion of economic efficiency. But this idea of fairness cannot be reconciled with the notion of equality of outcome, in which everyone gets exactly the same regardless of contribution (as happens when the tree-hugging successfully repels those who would appropriate the villagers' forest). Nor is it consistent with the notion that distribution should be by rank and station, as in the cases when brahmins insist they should receive more water because they are more easily polluted than those who are lower in the caste hierarchy or when leaders of developed countries insist their populations should have higher carbon quotas because their economies are more energy-intensive than those of less developed countries. Nor is it consistent with the idea that distribution should be by lottery: that people's efforts, be they cooperative or competitive, equalized or stratified, are irrelevant in a haphazard world that is everywhere presided over by Lady Luck. Since it is an easy matter to find people and situations in which one or other of these four ideas of fairness are passionately adhered to and morally justified (in our Himalayan village the people stay the same and only their situations vary), any approach that assumes just one idea of fairness is going to make sense of only a fraction of what is going on. Cultural Theory offers another way around this serious disability.

Distribution in proportion to contribution, we can now see, is supportive of the ego-focused networks that characterize markets, but would quickly destroy the status distinctions that are so vital a part of hierarchy. And such an idea of fairness, by introducing marked inequalities of outcome, would soon undermine the distributive arrangements (strict parity) that keep the members of an egalitarian group equal and united. Conversely, a fatalist who worked out that life's lottery was not in fact random would likely expect to retain the rewards received as a result of intellectual efforts, thereby opening up an achievement gap between him or herself and fellow fatalists. And, if he or she kept that up, then they would inevitably find themselves making the transition to market individualism: the pattern of social relationships whose supporting idea of fairness comports with their new-found transactional reality.

And so it goes, each way of organizing – each pattern of social relationships together with its supporting myth of nature – continually competing with the others for adherents, and all the time holding itself together with its particular brand of social glue: its distinctive idea of fairness.

Cultural Theory aims for something quite modest: the offering-up of Cultural Theory's plural framework of predictions as a first step towards untangling all the different things that are simultaneously going on in our transactions with one another and with our physical surroundings. Cultural Theory, I should mention, makes a great many fourfold predictions, but the ones most relevant for present purposes are the ones I have already mentioned.[9] They can be assembled (Table 8.1) into a handy exploratory tool: a tool that, if it does nothing else, enables us to achieve the first essential, the avoidance of capture by just one of the positions that it maps.

What is Unfamiliar in this Approach?

The fact that the Himalayan villagers' forest and grazing land is communally owned puts these resources firmly on the commons side (the right-hand side) of the Cultural Theory diagram (Figure 8.3), and the fact that agricultural land is privately owned puts this resource firmly on the privates side (the left-hand side). There is, as I have already pointed out, nothing outlandish about this assignment: it corresponds to the conventional markets-and-hierarchies distinction (though at what Oran Young (1995) has called the 'nano-level'). But the diagram shows us that this assignment takes account of only two of the four quadrants: the hierarchists' and the individualists', respectively. The other two quadrants – one (the egalitarians') on the commons side, the other (the fatalists') on the privates side – are not covered by this hierarchies-and-markets distinction.

Table 8.1: Some of Cultural Theory's Key Predictions

	HIERARCHIST	EGALITARIAN	INDIVIDUALIST	FATALIST
PATTERN OF SOCIAL RELATIONSHIPS	Ranked groups	Unranked groups	Ego-focused networks	Margins of organized patterns
MYTH OF NATURE	Perverse/ Tolerant	Ephemeral	Benign	Capricious
SCOPE OF KNOWLEDGE	Almost complete and divided up	Incomplete but holistic	Sufficient and timely	Irrelevant
LEARNING STYLE	Anticipation	Trial without error	Trial and error	Luck
STRATEGY w.r.t. THE ENVIRONMENT	Control	Harmony	Exploitation	Happenstance
IDEA OF FAIRNESS	Distribution by rank and station	Equality of outcome	Equality of opportunity	Not on this earth!

Moreover, some of the Himalayan villagers' resources do not fall clearly on one side or the other: the water that several farmers have to share to irrigate their private fields, for instance. Is that a commons? Or, since it is going to flow down the hillside anyway, is it privately owned and simply waiting to be divided up in an effective way? Certainly the farmers have to cooperate if each is to get the irrigation they need, but cooperation, by itself, does not imply a commons. Individualists can cooperate; indeed they are famous cooperators, provided it is in each one's interest to cooperate. If this was all that was involved in the commons (as Keohane and Ostrom (1995), for instance, come perilously close to saying) then there would be little point in reinventing them![10] Fortunately, it is not all that is involved.

Every day, during the growing season, thousands of tiny meetings take place across the Nepalese landscape as groups of farmers sort out the sequences and timings by which each will receive their share of the water. Often enough, they also have to determine what will have to be done, and who will do it, by way of maintaining, and perhaps extending, the shared system of channels and flumes by which the water is brought from the stream-bed to their part of the hillside. But only if they were *un*cooperative would we know, for sure, where they fitted on the Cultural Theory diagram. Only fatalists are uncooperative; people, they insist, are not to be trusted and, anyway, what would be the point of going to all that trouble if nothing you did was going to make any difference! In other words, cooperation, by itself, tells you very little: only that you are not dealing with fatalism. What *is* diagnostic is the moral basis for the cooperation: individualists cooperate only when each judges that he or she will do better by cooperating than by going it alone; hierarchists cooperate in a way that subordinates and, if needs be, sacrifices the individual to the higher claims of the totality (a stratified totality in which the members of each rank are expected to perform their allotted role – *noblesse oblige*, for instance, for the upper-class officers as they lead their deferential working-class troops 'over the top'), and egalitarians cooperate, all on an equal footing, for the benefit of their unstratified collectivity ('All in the same boat', as it were, and all, in the absence of any distinctions of rank and function, 'pulling together').[11]

So it is only by careful observation – observation aimed at discovering what metaphors are being used, which ideas of fairness are being appealed to, whether status distinctions are being upheld or resisted, and what myths of nature are being granted credence – that we can tell, in situations such as the sharing of the Himalayan waters, with which institutional style we are dealing. That there is cooperation tells us only that this is not fatalism. If it is individual-istic cooperation then we are not dealing with a commons, if it is hierarchical cooperation then we are dealing with a commons in what is now the conventional sense of the word, and if it is egalitarian cooperation then we are dealing with a commons in a sense that is either not conventionally recognized or uncritically merged with the conventional sense.

The essential point is that you can say nothing about the appro-priateness or inappropriateness of a particular situation until you have a sufficiently varied typology of institutional styles, and you do not arrive at such a typology simply by invoking differences of scale (nation-state versus village) even though differences of scale (as we will see in a moment) do make a difference. The important lesson we should draw from the story of the Himalayan village is that the villagers are making these stylistic distinctions all the time: using the appropriate metaphors, myths of nature and ideas of fairness in each of their transactional realms and, wherever a particular allocation appears not to be working too well, reassessing its appro-priateness in comparison with the other styles that are available. This is pretty sophisticated stuff (especially when you realize that most of these villagers cannot read or write) and not something that you see happening every day in ministerial deliberations, say, or being taught in the economics departments of the developed world's finest universities, or being promoted in the policy think-tanks of Washington and London, Berlin and Vienna. Changing all that – getting the North to catch up with the South – it seems to me, would be an excellent reason for reinventing the commons.

So How Do We Do It?

A moment's reflection will confirm that it is not just Himalayan villagers who parcel out their transactions to different institutional arrangements, each with its supporting idea of fairness and myth of nature; we all do it. In Britain, if we want a cup of coffee or a loaf of bread, we get it through the market, but if we need a kidney transplant we rely on a hierarchical arrangement: health authorities, organ donor cards, committees of experts and professional medical judgements as to whether we are suitable cases for treatment. When we want to stop our inner-city street from becoming a rat-run for through traffic, we soon discover that sealing it off by the direct action of all the residents is the most effective recourse. Of course, the lines get drawn at different places in different countries. Cups of coffee used not to come through the market in centrally planned places such as Bulgaria (with the result that they seldom came) and being an expert (that is, owning a pen) was not a respected station in Pol Pot's Cambodia. Even within one country, there is always plenty of disagreement as to just what goods and services should be promoted by which institutional arrangement. The point, however, is that these institutional bases *are* there (they could not not be) and people are concerned not over which one is right, everywhere and always, but with their appropriateness for some transactions and with their inappropriateness for others.

Small wonder, then, that policy advice based on just one idea of fairness (economic efficiency, for instance) and just one myth of nature (Perverse/Tolerant, for instance) is so often a disappointment.[12] The simple fact is that the neatness of its single metric is no match for the plurality of the system it seeks to improve. It lacks the requisite variety, and the task, as I see it, of the project we are engaged in is to make good that deficiency.

In suddenly jumping out of the Himalayan village and into developed world transactions over cups of coffee, kidney transplants and traffic-calming devices, I am, perhaps, pushing anti-particularism further than many readers will be prepared to go. But it is only by doing this that we can pursue the aim I have just identified: getting the North to catch up with the South. If the Himalayan villagers' resilience derives from the kind of messy wisdom that those who seek to bestow development upon them have been hell-bent on ridding themselves of, then a bout of shock treatment may be the only remedy. The shock, of course, lies in the claim that the three-dimensional picture (Figure 8.1), in which the cultural dynamics (the interplay of the four management styles) are independent of social scale (the various levels: individual to supranational regime), applies to any human system: industrial or hunting-and-gathering, ancient or modern, G7 or G77, North or South. Institutional inappropriateness, Cultural Theory insists, is no respecter of these much-respected distinctions; it occurs, has occurred and will occur across them all.

A Three-Dimensional Template for Assessing Appropriateness

There are two distinct sources of institutional inappropriateness – style and scale:

- Transactions at the village level, or at the level of the nation-state (or at any of the intervening levels of canton, county or

whatever) may be parcelled out in ways that are stylistically inappropriate.
- Transactions that are parcelled out to the appropriate institutional style may still be inappropriate, because they are pitched at the wrong point along the local to global scale.
- Transactions may be inappropriate on both counts: style and scale.

This way of framing the task we face – sorting out the more appropriate from the less appropriate – takes us a long way from the conventional either/or frameworks: markets or hierarchies, privates or commons, local or global, coercive or voluntary, top-down or bottom-up, centralized or decentralized, cooperative or competitive and so on. Instead, we have a 'template' with four holes in it (one for each institutional style) only one of which will be appropriate in any instance. On top of that, this template also extends along another dimension – scale – and at each scale level there are four more holes (again, one for each style) (Figure 8.1). Within this three-dimensional template, only one hole is going to be appropriate and all the rest are going to be inappropriate. Of one thing we can be sure: we are not going to get it right first time, every time!

By way of a conclusion, let me lay out a few examples, spread out along both the style and scale dimensions, some of which show a happy zeroing-in on appropriateness, others the reverse.

Inappropriatenesses of style

Himalayan villagers letting trees grow on private land, and switching to the stall-feeding of their animals, are nice examples of transactional changes in response to an awareness that things are no longer so appropriate as they once were. Trees on private land work well, not because they replace the commons – the village forest – but because they supplement it: taking some of the pressure off the village forest and thereby enabling it to increase its sustainable yield. Something similar happens in the case of stall-feeding. The fodder is cut from the commons but the animals have to eat what they are given, rather than eating what they prefer, which is what they do if they are out on the commons. Stall-feeding is more labour-intensive, but this is offset by the animals not having to be watched while on the commons and by their depositing all their manure in one place. And, as with the trees on private land, what we have here is an intensification of land use that is achieved by exploiting interdependencies between commons and privates.

What is so instructive about these two examples is that they do not conform to the only solutions that follow from the 'tragedy of the commons' hypothesis: privatize the commons or change human nature! What is more, according to the Cultural Theory hypothesis, neither of these extreme positions *could* constitute a solution; all the possibilities lie in between. The Himalayan villagers, it would seem, have worked that out for themselves![13]

The fourfold allocation of transactions is also found in the Swiss Alps, again with agricultural land being privately owned and grazing land (and sometimes the forest) being communally owned.[14] But unlike Himalayan villagers, the Swiss forests are physically sandwiched between the high pastures (communally owned) and the valley floor (privately owned fields, houses and hotels). Over the centuries that the Davos valley has been settled, for instance, both the fields and the grazing land have expanded at the expense of the forest, but the trees on the steeper slopes have stayed in place, acting both as a source of timber and as a barrier against avalanches. It is difficult to achieve both these functions simultaneously and, in managing the forest for timber production, the Davosers have often set in train changes in the forest's age structure which, decades later, have resulted in exceptional avalanches reaching the valley floor and threatening the destruction of the entire community.

Every time this unpleasant surprise has befallen them the Davosers have responded by switching their forest management on to the all-in-the-same-boat, egalitarian style. Later, it has sometimes shifted to the hierarchist style, often to the individualist style (with farmers owning long thin strips of forest running all the way from valley floor to alpine pasture), and sometimes to the fatalist style (as happened, for instance, when the avalanche danger was clearly perceived yet extraction continued in response to the demands of various mining booms and, in more recent years, the demand for ski-runs).

Surely, you might think, they would have got it right by now. But to think that is to assume that there *is* one right way, and that is not the case. There is no way of ever getting it right, because managing one way inevitably changes the forest, eventually to the point where that way of managing is no longer appropriate. This would happen even if there were no exogenous changes (like the mining and tourist booms) which, of course, there always are (even in seemingly remote places like the Himalaya). Viability can only be achieved, therefore, by 'covering all the bases': by the villagers ensuring that they have the full repertoire of management styles, and by their being prepared to try a different one whenever the one they are relying on shows signs of no longer being appropriate. The Davosers, like their

Himalayan counterparts, have now been in their valley for more than 700 years, without destroying either themselves or their valley in the process: an achievement that would not have been possible if they had opted for just one (or even a mixture of two) institutional styles.

Inappropriatenesses of scale

Many of Nepal's forests have, over the past 30 years or so, gone into serious decline. Some have seen this as proof of the 'tragedy of the commons' hypothesis: an explanation, however, that cannot cope with the fact that this decline has only happened now while the village forests have existed for centuries. To get around this obstacle we need to ask whether, a few decades ago, there were any major institutional changes in the way these forests were managed. Indeed there were. In the 1950s, following the overthrow of the semi-feudal Rana regime, all the forests were nationalized and control vested in regionally-based Forestry Officers.

Since a Sherpa in Khumbu, to take a specific instance, now had to go on a four-day walk to Paphlu (the local administrative centre) to obtain permission to fell a tree for a new roof-post, instead of just popping round to the house of the fellow-villager who happened that year to be the forest guardian, and since the official in Paphlu could not see what was happening in Khumbu (there being some rather large mountains in the way), the old commons managing institution was destroyed and the new one did not work. Both institutions, however, were hierarchical; it was the scale of the new one that was inappropriate.

With the gentle but firm controls of the old system no longer operational, people began to slide into fatalism, taking too much from the nearby forest and not enough from further afield, thereby setting in motion the 'nibble effect', which can easily remove an entire forest even though the extraction rate may be far below the rate at which the forest itself is growing. It is this shift from an appropriate way of doing things to an inappropriate way, and the resulting fatalization of those who are on the receiving end, and not the 'tragedy of the commons', that explains the recent decline of the Nepalese forests.

There is a sophisticated theory of political development that argues that, even so, this drastic centralization of the forests was desirable. The idea is that it is only appropriate for a state to decentralize its power once it has gathered into itself enough power to make this possible. But, even if that is so, there was surely no need for the state to be so destructive of the village-level institutions. Ultimate title had long been vested in the Nepalese monarch, so the Forestry Service could have based their centralization on that – there are vast tracts of forest in Nepal that are not village forests – and done nothing more than kept a helpful professional eye on what was happening in the villages.

This, I am pleased to be able to report, is what the Nepalese Forestry Service is now doing: handing the forests back to the villages and helping them to reinvent their commons managing institutions. All in all, it is not dissimilar to what happened with London's Location of Offices Bureau. For many years this hierarchical outfit dutifully carried out its mandate – to encourage offices to move out of the capital – and it went on doing this until, one day, it was realized that there were no longer any jobs for Londoners. The mandate was therefore changed, and the bureau (without even having to alter its name) set about its new task: encouraging offices to move into London!

Hierarchies are often rather unloved, but they do have this wonderful ability to execute complete U-turns, without even changing step. The result, in Nepal, is that hierarchical management institutions are now in place at two points along the local-to-global scale – the village and the state – and each it would seem, on present evidence, is performing appropriately. The Forest Service, now, is careful not to arrogate to itself management functions that can be (and are being) carried out at the village level. Researching (in collaboration with Australian foresters) ways of regenerating forests on the seriously denuded and exposed slopes that are found in many parts of the Middle Hills – something that, as yet, is not within the villagers' competence – is the sort of task the Forest Service concentrates on.

Forests, of course, are now seen as desirable, not just for the villages and the nations that contain those villages, but for the totality: the global community. Keeping the trees in place and, if possible, increasing their size and quantity is one major part of the solution to the problem of global climate change (not to mention another global commons, biodiversity). So it is worth speculating, for a moment, what institutional arrangements would be most appropriate at this supranational level.

One essential is that this global institution not destroy those arrangements that are already doing a good job at lower scale levels: the Nepalese village and the Nepalese state, for instance. So there needs to be a sort of *subsidiarity principle*: anything that is being done (or could be done) at a lower level should not be done at a higher level.[15] That individualistic management (trees on private land, for instance) is a vital part of the stylistic mix at the village level, alerts us to the inappropriatenesses that are built into the present insistence (GATT, for instance) that markets be global. Some markets, yes, but all cannot be right. That would be saying that just one hole in the template – the individualist-style/global-level hole – is appropriate for everything and all the other holes for nothing! The informal sector, for instance, almost by definition, is local, and in Nepal it accounts for something like 80 per cent of all economic activity. Sweeping that away, which is what would happen if the World Trade Organization (as GATT is now called) was able to get its hands on it, would be a truly sensational act of institutional inappropriateness. That really *would* remove every last tree from the Himalaya.

A second essential is *clumsiness*; if the fourfold plurality is vital for the resilience of the mountain village vis-a-vis its environment then it would be surprising indeed if it were not also vital at the global level. There is not space here to go into precisely what this would involve, but one thing is certain: the requisite plurality will not be achieved if the problem is defined (as the IPCC, The Intergovernmental Panel on Climate Change, has at present defined it) entirely in terms of just one cultural perspective: just one of the four myths of nature.[16]

Inappropriatenesses of style and scale

Throughout the 1950s and 1960s, the provision of housing in London was almost totally in the hands of the hierarchists – the planners – and one of their main concerns was the renewal of the worn-out fabric of the inner city.[17] One of their number, Harold P. Clunn, put it like this:

> London . . . is marching on to a destiny which will make it the grandest city in the whole world . . . London must be allowed to grow upwards and the straggling villas and small houses of Highbury, Barnsbury, Stoke Newington, Hackney, Maida Vale and St John's Wood [virtually the entire inner suburbs of London north of the Thames] must give way to new blocks of flats.

Much of London did indeed give way to new blocks of flats and, if the planners had had it all their way, and if enough money had been made available to them, their algorithms for determining just when a section of the built environment had become 'optimally demolishable' (their terminology) would have ensured that every urban acre underwent its 'comprehensive re-development' (again, their terminology).

Fortunately, a creative and motley assortment of owner-occupiers, who saw these eighteenth- and nineteenth-century houses as sadly neglected heritage not rat-infested slums (the official perception), were able, through their myriad individual and uncoordinated efforts, to derail the planners' singular and unrelenting vision of the New Jerusalem. It was this anarchic and innovative bunch who, in effect, privatized the despised communal burden, revalued it (just one of those 'straggling villas' could now set you back a million pounds or more) and put it into the healthy and highly liveable state in which we now see it. This conceptual (as opposed to physical) recycling of the built environment is now something that continues apace in almost every European city, but it would never have happened if control had remained in the hands of the hierarchists.

Again, as with the Himalayan village, the lesson is not that the North's built environment should be entirely privatized. Rather, it is that a vigorous individualistic component is an essential feature of any sustainable city. So too (to anticipate the next example) is the egalitarian component: the recognition that the city, the borough, the neighbourhood and the street belong to those who live there, and the insistence that there are some rights (above and beyond those of the individual property owners and the local authorities) that are held in common. These rights may not be easy to define, but we soon know when we have not got them!

Conclusion: The Commons most Social Science Ignores

The egalitarian commons is not something that is bestowed from on high, nor does it come with the security-fenced housing developments that are so common in the United States and are now catching on in Britain. The egalitarian commons is rooted in the low-key notion of *decency*, and is created among ordinary people as they go about their daily lives. Often it consists of little more than the occasional taking-in of a delivery for the people next door, or the feeding of their cat while they are away for a couple of days, or the pulling of a fellow-shopper from the path of an oncoming bus. That is why it is so hard to define and quantify, and why it is so easily destroyed. The fact that, as has happened in India with the Chipko Movement, it can escalate into a major political force suggests that the egalitarian commons is a vital component in any healthy civic culture.

Michael Jacobs (1995) has provided a nice account of how the egalitarian commons differs from the other commons (and from the privates), and he has gone on to suggest how this particular institutional style should coexist with those with which we are more familiar:

> Geographical communities are important because we cannot avoid living in them. However 'creatively individual' we may be, with whatever networks of friendships and 'communities of interests', we are dependent on the other people, mostly strangers, with whom we share physical and political space.

Ego-focused networks (individualism, that is), he concedes, have their place in our lives but they are not sufficient:

> We are dependent on such strangers to cooperate in a shared moral and legal order; when they don't, this is called crime, and it affects us all. If the relationship between people in society is insufficiently equal (economically and politically) to allow participation in a shared culture, the result is social disintegration and violent conflict, and it damages everyone.

Destroy egalitarian relationships, Jacobs is arguing, and you open the floodgates of fatalism: neighbours stealing from you instead of looking out for you(!):

> Only with the mutual involvement of neighbouring strangers can individuals take part in democracy, electing and influencing governments. None of these things can be wholly determined by government: they depend on voluntary membership of, and informal association in, society. They depend on the bonds of community.

Fatalists, he rightly observes, do not vote ('It doesn't matter who you vote for,' the fatalist rationalizes, 'the government always gets in') and government (that is, hierarchy) cannot itself provide that which is essential to its viability: the egalitarian commons, those common goods that, as Jacobs puts it, 'we share with others, with strangers' (Jacobs 1995:17–18).

It is precisely these common goods, my next (and final) example suggests, that have been swept away by the public-private partnerships that, in recent decades, have been promoted as the panacea for the ills of the American city.

The argument, as originally propounded by Robin Paul Malloy (1992), is that these public-private partnerships function in a way that does not comport with the classic liberal values. Classic liberalism, according to Malloy, seeks to maximize freedom, individual liberty and human dignity through capitalism and the free market as counterbalanced by a limited state. He finds markets and hierarchies, with hierarchies doing little more than keeping the peace, repelling enemies and enforcing the law of contract. The public-private partnerships, Malloy points out, transgress this ideal, becoming exercises in 'state capitalism' and 'urban socialism', components in an 'ever increasing trend towards central planning, communitarianism, and statism'. In other words, it is too much hierarchy and not enough individualism that is the trouble. Additionally, hierarchy and individualism are supposed to be pitted against one another, not cuddled up together in the same bed.

Denis Brion (1992), however, points out that Malloy's analysis (in common with 'two destination' social theory) ignores communalism, 'an alternative world view that also has strong roots in American culture'. After all, there must be something – neither hierarchy nor individualism – that keeps hierarchy and individualism apart and which, when it is excluded, results in their coming together. Cultural Theory, Brion asserts, and in particular its recognition of egalitarianism as a distinct institutional form, 'explains what has in practice happened in the United States'. He supports this assertion with a mass of recent lawsuits, e.g. Ollie's Barbecue in Birmingham, Alabama and Morris's Department Store in Washington, DC, which he further strengthens by a lengthy excursion into the theory of place. Since there is not time to go into all these Northern counterparts of the Chipko Movement and the village forest, I will simply lay out the bare bones of his argument for not ignoring egalitarianism.

Cultural Theory shows how it is 'that a society that values individualism highly nevertheless can readily evolve into one with a substantial element of hierarchy as well'. The resulting tacit coalition of individualists and hierarchists leaves the mass of society in a position of 'atomized, alienated subordination and systematic exploitation' (i.e., fatalism). The result is an increasingly contradictory and unstable situation in which a society that in concept values individual liberty highly is, in practice, made up largely of powerless individuals. Though communitarianism is usually seen as being the antithesis of individualism, Cultural Theory reveals how it is that 'egalitarian communalism can act as a leaven within society in a way that derivatively serves individualistic values'.

In other words, the egalitarian commons are *essential* to the American way of life, and Brion, having explained in some detail why this is so, then argues that this leavening power 'provides the judiciary with the justification for facilitating, rather than preventing, the emergence of egalitarian communities'. If they did that they would be promoting, rather than suppressing, the requisite plurality.

So here – not on the remote and economically marginal Himalayan hillside but at the heart of the once great and now greatly troubled US city – is the most exciting and surprising of all arguments for reinventing the commons: if we don't, capitalism itself will collapse!

Notes

1   Nor is this approach in agreement with other New Institutionalists such as March and Olsen (1989), Powell and DiMaggio (1991) or North (1990), but I will not discuss these other versions here.

2   Meadows et al. (1992:123) describe the various ways in which a population can approach its limits. At one extreme (where the limits are very close and incapable of recovering quickly if breached) we get overshoot and collapse. At the other extreme (where the limits are far away) we get an 'onwards and upwards' curve. In between (where the limits are not too close and are capable of recovering, provided the population's behaviour is not too exuberant) we get an asymptotic approach to the limit (or a series of steadily diminishing overshoots and their accompanying fall-backs). It is the second (the remote limits) of these ways – a way which Meadows et al. are convinced does not fit our present situation, but which their critics are convinced does – that is closest to the assumptions that are built into neo-classical economics. To insist that there are no limits is to allow the possibility that eventually umpteen billion of us will be living the life of Reilly on just one molecule!

3   Much of this section is borrowed from Price and Thompson (1997); please consult that version for many of the details and references left out of this chapter.

4   As well as being a source of fuel-wood, the forest provides much of the animals' fodder. The increase in efficiency comes about because the stall-fed animals have to eat what they are given. Loose on the pasture or in the forest, they ignore the less palatable vegetation.

5 I use the word resilience, rather than sustainability, because sustainability is too stable a notion and implies that human and natural systems can, if they get it 'right', settle down into some harmonious, long-term balance.

6 Blackpool is a seaside resort in the north of England, and Blackpool rock is a long cylinder of white candy with the word 'Blackpool' running all the way through it in red letters.

7 Just how much power will depend, of course, on the extent to which the world is indeed the way the chosen myth of nature insists it is. And, since our acting in the world often alters the way it is, the equation between knowledge and power can often go into reverse. Surprises, like the poor, are always with us!

8 I am referring to the basic building blocks. Specific institutions can be more complex and varied, but all are put together from these fundamental elements.

9 These are assembled, in the form of a chart covering several pages, in Thompson (1992).

10 A Cultural Theoretic reading of the introductory chapter of Keohane and Ostrom (1995) picks up a host of characteristics of institutional arrangements for the management of common-pool resources that comport with individualism rather than with either of the quadrants on the commons side of the diagram: 'productive cooperation', 'reciprocity rather than hierarchy', the 'positive advantage' of 'self-help', 'self-monitoring and self-enforcing patterns of human interaction', arrangements that 'increase the availability of information and reduce transaction costs' and their 'existence in a world without clear hierarchies or centralised enforcement'. All of these can be found in the first two pages of their book.

11 The difference in Nepal is between a high yield from an irrigated field (*khet*, as it is called) and a lower yield from a rain-fed terrace (*bari*, as it is called). This potential gain, however, has to be balanced against the risk that the field, if irrigated, might become more prone to landslip. And if it does slip the liability is the individual's who cannot rely on the community to help make good the loss.

12 I mention these two (the first individualist, the second hierarchical) because so much of policy analysis is captured by this particular cultural alliance.

13 This, I now realize, is probably the main theme of my early work (Thompson et al. 1986) on the Himalaya and their commons.

14 The Swiss example is set out in much greater detail in Price and Thompson (1997).

15   For a detailed account of the important concept of subsidiarity, and of its career, see Blichner and Sangolt (1994).

16   The IPCC scenarios of climate change, it has now been shown (as part of the Battelle-initiated State of the Art Report on Social Science and Global Climate Change) are all hierarchical scenarios. The egalitarians and the individualists have been excluded. The State of the Art Report is not yet published, but much of the evidence concerning the IPCC scenarios (together with suggestions as to how the IPCC process might be made sufficiently clumsy) is contained in van Asselt and Rotmans (1995).

17   While I have not provided any references for this example, readers interested in going more deeply into this approach to the built environment are directed to Thompson (1979) and Thompson (1987).

Bibliography

Acevedo, R. and E. Castro (1993) *Negros do Trombetas: guardiáts de matos e rios* (Belém: UFPA/NAEEA).

Agarwal, Anil, and Sunita Narain (1989) *Towards Green Villages: A Strategy for Environmentally Sound and Participatory Rural Development* (New Delhi: Centre for Science and Environment).

Agarwal, Anil, and Sunita Narain (1991) *Global Warming in an Unequal World* (New Delhi: Centre for Science and Environment).

Albin, Cecilia (1993) 'Negotiating the Acid Rain Problem in Europe: A Fairness Perspective', paper presented to the Workshop on Risk and Fairness, International Institute for Applied Systems Analysis, Laxenburg, Austria, 20–22 June.

Aldhous, Peter (1991) 'Hunting licence for drugs', *Nature* 353.

Allegretti, M. (1987a) *Reservas Extrativistas: Uma Proposta De Desenvolvimento Da Floresta Amazônica* (Curitiba: IEA).

Allegretti, M. (1987b) *Extractive Production and the Rubber Tappers' Movement* (Washington, DC: Environmental Defense Fund).

Alston, Dana (ed.), (1990) *We Speak for Ourselves: Social Justice, Race and Environment* (Washington, DC: Panos Institute).

Altvater, Elmar (1993) *The Future of the Market: An Essay on the Regulation of Money and Nature after the Collapse of 'Actually Existing Socialism'* (London: Verso).

Anderson, Benedict (1983) *Imagined Communities: Reflections on the Origins and Spread of Nationalism* (New York: Verso).

Anderson, R.F. and M.R. Greening (1982) 'Hazardous Waste Facility Siting: A Role of Planners', *Journal of the American Planning Association* 48 (Spring).

Anthony, Carl (1990) 'Why African Americans Should Be Environmentalists', *Earth Island Journal* 5 (Winter).

Anthony, Carl, (1995) 'Ecopsychology and the Deconstruction of Whiteness', in Theodore Roszak et al. (eds) *Ecopsychology: restoring the earth, healing the mind* (San Francisco: Sierra Club Books).

Aryal, Manisha (1994) 'Axing Chipko', in *Himal* 7:1.

Ayres, D. and J.M. Ayres (1993) 'A implantação de uma unidade de conservação em área de várzea: a experiência de Mamirauá', in *Interdisciplinary Approaches to Biodiversity Conservation and Land Use Dynamics in the New World*, Atas do Congresso International (Belo Horizonte, Brazil).

Baitenmann, Helga (1995) 'Local responses to government discourse on rural property: The case of Central Veracruz 1914–1920', presented at the 19th International Congress of the Latin American Studies Association, Washington, DC, 25–27 September.

Barratt Brown, Michael and Pauline Tiffen (1992) *Short Changed: Africa and World Trade* (London: Pluto Press).

Barry, Tom (1995) *Zapata's Revenge: Free Trade and The Farm Crisis in Mexico* (Boston: South End Press).

Barton, John H. and Wolfgang E. Siebeck (1994) 'Material transfer agreements in genetic resources exchange: the case of the International Agricultural Research Centres', *Issues in Genetic Resources 2* (Rome: IPGRI).

Bartra, Roger (1982) 'Capitalism and Peasantry in Mexico', *Latin American Perspectives* 9(1):36, Winter.

Beck, Ulrich (1992) 'From Industrial Society to the Risk Society: Questions of Survival, Social Structure and Ecological Enlightenment', *Theory, Culture & Society* 9:1.

Berkes, Fikret (ed.) (1989) *Common Property Resources: Ecology and Community-based Sustainable Development* (London: Belhaven Press).

Bernstein, Henry (1990) 'Agricultural "Modernisation" and the Era of Structural Adjustment: Observations on Sub-Saharan Africa', *Journal of Peasant Studies* 18:1 (October).

Berry, Sara (1984) 'The Food Crisis and Agrarian Change: A review essay', *African Studies Review* 27:2 (June).

Bifani, Paolo (1989) 'International Property Rights and International Trade', in UNCTAD (ed.) *Uruguay Round: Papers on Selected Issues* (New York: United Nations Conference on Trade and Development).

Blaikie, Piers (1993) 'Common Property Resource Management: New Directions and New Cul-de-Sacs', in Henrik Secher Marcussen (ed.) *Institutional Issues in Natural Resource Management,* Occasional Paper No. 9, International Development Studies (Roskilde, Denmark: Roskilde University).

Blichner, L.C. and L. Sanglot (1994) 'The concept of subsidiarity and the debate on European co-operation: pitfalls and possibilities', *Governance* 7:3.

Blum, Elissa (1993) 'Making Biodiversity Conservation Profitable, A Case Study of the Merck/INBio Agreement', *Environment* 35 (4).

Bourdieu, Pierre and Loic Wacquant (1992) *An Invitation to Reflexive Sociology* (Chicago: University of Chicago Press).

Brion, D.J. (1992) 'The meaning of the city: urban redevelopment and the loss of community', *Indiana Law Review* 25:3.

Brockway, Lucille (1979) *Science and Colonial Expansion: The Role of the Royal Botanic Gardens* (New York: Academic Press).

Bromley, Daniel (ed.) (1992) *Making the Commons Work: Theory, Practice and Policy* (San Francisco: Institute for Contemporary Studies Press).

Bromley, Daniel and Michael Cernea (1989) 'The Management of Common Property Natural Resources: Some Operational Fallacies', World Bank Discussion Papers series #57 (October).

Brown, Lester (1981) *Building a Sustainable Society* (New York: Norton).

Brown, Phil and Edwin J. Mikkelsen (1990) *No Safe Place: Toxic Waste, Leukemia, and Community Action* (Berkeley: University of California Press).

Brush, Stephen and Doreen Stabinsky (eds) (1996) *Valuing Local Knowledge: Indigenous People and Intellectual Property Rights* (Washington/Covelo: Island Press).

Bullard, Robert (1990) *Dumping in Dixie: Race, Class, and Environmental Quality* (Boulder, CO: Westview Press).

Bullard, Robert (1993) *Confronting Environmental Racism: Voices from the Grassroots* (Boston: South End Press).

Bullard, Robert and Beverly Wright (1987) 'Environmentalism and the Politics of Equity', *Mid-America Review of Sociology* 12 (Winter).

Cameron, Kenneth Neill (1992) *Atmospheric Destruction and Human Survival* (Santa Cruz, CA: Center for Political Ecology).

Campbell, Bonnie K. and John Loxley (eds) (1989) *Structural Adjustment in Africa* (London: Macmillan).

Cantor, Robin, Stuart Henry and Steve Rayner (1992) *Making Markets: An Interdisciplinary Perspective on Economic Exchange* (Westport, CT: Greenwood Press).

CCRI (Comité Clandestino Revolucionario Indígena, Comandancia General del Ejército Zapatista de Liberación Nacional) (1994a) 'Votán Zapata', #57 Communique, *Anderson Valley Advertiser (AVA)* 42(31):16.

CCRI (1994b) 'Zapata will not die by Arrogant Decree,' #58 Communique, *AVA* 42(31):16.

CCRI (1994c) 'Demands at the Dialogue Table', *AVA* 42(31): 13, August 3.

CEDI/CONAGE (1989) *Empresas de Mineração e terras Indígenas na Amazônia* (São Paulo, 1988).

CEDI/Museu Nacional (1987) *Terras Indigenas do Brasil* (Rio de Janeiro).

Cernea, Michael (1985) *Putting People First: Sociological Variables in Development* (New York: Oxford University Press).

Chambers, Robert, N.C. Saxena and Tushaar Shah (1989) *To the Hands of the Poor: Water and Trees* (New Delhi: Oxford and IBH Publishing Company).

Chauvet, Michel and Louis Olivier (1993) *La biodiversité enjeu planétaire* (Paris: Sang de la terre).

Chopra, Kanchan, Gopal Kadekodi and M.N. Murty (1990) *Participatory Development: People and Common Property Resources* (New Delhi: Sage).

Churchill, Ward (1993) *Struggle for the Land* (Monroe, Maine: Common Courage).

CIMA (1991) *Subsídios Técnicos para a elaboração do Relatório Nacional do Brasil para a CNUMAD* (Brasilia).

Ciriacy-Wantrup, S.V. and Richard Bishop (1975) '"Common Property" as a Concept in Natural Resources Policy', *Natural Resources Journal* 15 (October).

Clifford, James (1988) *The Predicament of Culture* (Cambridge, MA: Harvard University Press).

Clifford, James and George Marcus (eds) (1986) *Writing Culture: The Poetics and Politics of Ethnography* (Berkeley: University of California Press).

CNPT/IBAMA/Banco Mundial/ECOTEC (1994) *Estudo Pré-investimento Projeto Reservas Extrativistas* (Brasilia: In Brasileiro do Meio Ambiente).

Coase, R.H. (1937) 'The Nature of the Firm', *Economica* 4:16.

Cockcroft, James (1983) *Mexico: Class Formation, Capital Accumulation, and the Mexican State* (New York: Monthly Review Press).

Coleman, James (1990) *Foundations of Social Theory* (Cambridge, MA: Harvard University Press).

Collier, George A. with Elizabeth Lowery Quaratiello (1994) *Basta! Land and the Zapatista Rebellion in Chiapas* (Oakland, CA: Food First Publications).

Comaroff, John and Simon Roberts (1981) *Rules and Processes: The Cultural Logic of Dispute in an African Context* (Chicago: University of Chicago Press).

Commission for Racial Justice (1987) *Toxic Waste and Race in the United States: A National Report on the Racial and Socioeconomic Characteristics of Communities with Hazardous Waste Sites* (New York: United Church of Christ).

Correa, Guillermo, Salvador Corro and Julio César López (1994) 'Campesinos e indígenas de todo el país apoyan las demandas del EZLN y marchan hacía la capital', *Proceso* 910: 36–40, 11 Abril.

Cowen, Michael and Robert Shenton (1995) 'The Invention of Development', in Jonathan Crush (ed.) *Power of Development* (London: Routledge).

Cronon, William (1991) *Nature's Metropolis: Chicago and the Great West* (New York: Norton).

Cronon, William (1996) *Uncommon Ground: Rethinking the Human Place in Nature* (New York: W.W. Norton).

Cunningham, A.B. (1993) *Ethics, Ethnobiological Research, and Biodiversity* (Gland: World Wide Fund for Nature).

de Groot, Wouter et al. (1995) 'Drawing the Boundary: An Explorative Model of the Defence of the Common', in J.P.M. van den Breemer et al. (eds), *Local Resource Management in Africa* (London: Wiley).

Deutsch, Morton (1975) 'Equity, equality and need: What determines which value will be used as the basis of distributive justice?', *Journal of Social Issues* 31.

Diamond, Irene and Gloria Orenstein (1989) *Revealing the World: The Emergence of Ecofeminism* (San Francisco Sierra Club Books).

Diegues, Antonio (1992a) *The Social Dynamics of Deforestation in the Brazilian Amazon* (Geneva: UNRISD).

Diegues, Antonio (1992b) 'Sustainable development and people's participation in wetland ecosystems conservation in Brazil: two comparative studies', in D. Ghai and J. Vivian (eds) *Grassroots environmental action* (London: Routledge).

Diegues, Antonio (1992c) 'Human Occupation of Wetlands in Amazonia', in L. Kosinski (ed.) *Ecological Disorder in Amazonia: Social Aspects* (Paris: UNESCO/ISS/EDUCAM).

Diegues, Antonio (1994) *Desmatamento e modos de vida na Amazônia Brasileira* (São Paulo: NUPAUB-USP).

Diegues, Antonio (1996) *O mito moderno da natureza intocada* (São Paulo: Huicitec).

Douglas, Mary (1992) 'Muffled Ears', in *Risk and Blame: Essays in Cultural Theory* (London: Routledge).

Dreze, Jean and Amartya Sen (1995) *India: Economic Development and Social Opportunity* (Delhi: Oxford University Press).

Dudley, Nigel, Jean-Paul Jean Renaud and Francis Sullivan (1995) *Bad Harvest? The Timber Trade and the Degradation of the World's Forests* (London: Earthscan).

Durkheim, Emile (1893) *De la Division du Travail Sociale: Etude sur L'Organization des Societes Superieurs* (Paris: Alcan).

Durkheim, Emile (1957) *Professional Ethics and Civic Morals* (London: Routledge).

Edelstein, Michael (1988) *Contaminated Communities* (Boulder, CO: Westview Press).

Eglin, J. and H. Thery (1982) *Le pillage de l' Amazonie* (Paris: Masapero).

Elster, Jon (1989a) *The Cement of Society: A Study of Social Order* (Cambridge: Cambridge University Press).

Elster, Jon (1989b) *Nuts and Bolts for the Social Sciences* (Cambridge: Cambridge University Press).

Elster, Jon (1992) *Local Justice: How Institutions Allocate Scarce Goods and Necessary Burdens* (New York: Russell Sage Foundation).

Environmental Health Coalition (1993) 'Principles of Environmental Justice', *Toxic-Free Neighborhoods: Community Planning Guide* (San Diego).

Escobar, Arturo (1995) *Encountering Development: The Making and Unmaking of the Third World* (Princeton, NJ: Princeton University Press).

Faber, Daniel (1992) 'Imperialism, Revolution, and the Ecological Crisis of Central America', *Latin American Perspectives* 19(1):17–44.

FAO CPGR (1995) *Documents of the Sixth Session of the Commission on Plant Genetic Resources* CPGR/6/95/1–8 (Rome: Food and Agriculture Organization).

Farren, M. (1989) 'Social dimensions of Amazonian Ecological Disorder', from a seminar, *Desordem Ecológica da Amazônia*, Rio de Janeiro, 27–31 August.

Fearnside, Paul (1989) 'Extractive Reserves in Brazilian Amazonia', *Bioscience* June.

Feder, Ernest (1977/78) 'Campesinistas y Descampesinistas, Tres Enfoques Divergentes (No Incompatibles) Sobre La Destrucción Del Campesinado', *Comercio exterior*, 27:12 and 28:1.

Feeny, David (1995) 'Optimality, Sub-optimality, Nirvana, and Transaction Cost: Foraging on the Commons', *Book of Abstracts of the Fifth International Common Property Conference* (Bloomington, IN: International Association for the Study of Common Property).

Feeny, David, Fikret Berkes, Bonnie McCay and James Acheson (1990) 'The Tragedy of the Commons: Twenty-two Years Later', *Human Ecology* 18.

Feld, Steven (1991) 'Voices of the Rainforest', *Public Culture* 4:1.

Ferguson, James (1994) *The Anti-Politics Machine: 'Development', Depoliticization, and Bureaucratic Power in Lesotho* (Minneapolis: University of Minnesota Press).

Flitner, Michael (1995) *Sammler, Raeuber und Gelehrte. Die politischen Interessen an pflanzengenetischen Ressourcen 1895–1995* (Frankfurt/New York: Campus).

Foley, Michael (1995) 'Privatizing the Countryside: The Mexican Peasant Movement and Neoliberal Reform', *Latin American Perspectives* 22:1 (Winter).

Foucault, Michel (1979) *Discipline and Punish: The Birth of the Prison* (New York: Vintage).

Fowler, Cary and Pat Mooney (1990) *Shattering: Food, politics and the loss of genetic diversity* (Tucson: University of Arizona Press).

Fowler, Robert Booth (1991) *The Dance with Community: The Contemporary Debate in American Political Thought* (Lawrence: University Press of Kansas, 1991).

Fox Keller, Evelyn (1985) *Reflections on Gender and Science* (New Haven, CT and London: Yale University Press).

Friedland, Roger and Robert Alford (1991) 'Bringing Society Back In: Symbols, Practices, and Institutional Contradictions', in Walter Powell and Paul DiMaggio (eds) *The New Institutionalism in Organizational Analysis* (Chicago: University of Chicago Press).

Frankel, Otto H. and Erna Bennett (eds) (1970) *Genetic Resources in Plants – Their Exploration and Conservation*, IBP Handbook II (Oxford and Edinburgh: Blackwell Scientific Publishers).

Fürer-Haimendorf, C. Von (1975) *Himalayan Traders: Life in Highland Nepal* (London: John Murray).

Gall, N. (1978) 'Letter from Rondonia', American University Field Staff Reports, n. 9–13.

García de León, Antonio (1994) 'La Vuelta del Katun (Chiapas: a 20 años del Primer Congreso Indígena)', *Perfil de la Jornada*, October 12.

Gartlan, Steve (1989) *La Conservation des Ecosystèmes Forestiers au Cameroun* (London: IUCN).

GEF, Scientific and Technical Advisory Panel (1991) 'Criteria for Eligibility and Priorities for Selection of Global Environment Facility Projects' (Washington, DC: GEF).

George, Susan and Fabrizio Sabelli (1994) *Faith & Credit: the World Bank's Secular Empire* (Boulder, CO: Westview).

Gettkant, Andreas (1995) 'Auf der Suche nach den grünen Diamanten', J. Wolters (ed.) *Leben und Leben lassen* (Giessen: Focus).

Gibbs, Lois (1982) *Love Canal: My Story* (Albany: State University of New York Press, 1982).

Golden, Tim (1994) 'Mexican Rebel Sees No Quick Settlement' *New York Times*, February 24.

Goldsmith, Edward (1993) *The Way: An Ecological World-view* (Boston, MA: Shambhala).

Goodland, Robert and H. Irwin (1988) 'A selva amazônica: do inferno verde ao deserto vermelho' *Itatiaia*.

Goodwin, Neva (1991) 'Introduction', *World Development* (19:1).

Gordon, H.S. (1954) 'The Economic Theory of a Common-Property Resource: The Fishery', *Journal of Political Economy* 62.

Gottlieb, Robert (1993) *Forcing the Spring: The Transformation of the American Environmental Movement* (Washington, DC: Island Press).

Gottlieb, Robert and Helen Ingram (1988) 'The New Environmentalists', *The Progressive* August.

Gould, Stephen J. (1981) *The Mismeasure of Man* (New York: Norton).

Grall, Jacques and Bertrand R. Lévy (1985) *La Guerre des Semences: Quelles moissons, quelles sociétés?* (Paris: Fayard).

Gross, J. and S. Rayner (1985) *Measuring Culture: A Paradigm for the Analysis of Social Organisation* (New York: Columbia University Press).

Grossman, Karl (1992) 'From Toxic Racism to Environmental Justice', *E Magazine*, May–June.

Guha, Ramachandra (1989) *The Unquiet Woods: Ecological Change and Peasant Resistance in the Himalaya* (Delhi: Oxford University Press).

Guha, Ranajit (ed.) (1981–88) *Subaltern Studies, Volumes I–VI* (Delhi: Oxford University Press).

Haavelmo, Trygve and Stein Hansen (1991) 'On the strategy of trying to reduce economic equality' in Robert Goodland et al. (eds) *Environmentally Sustainable Economic Development: Building on Brundtland* (Paris: UNESCO).

Hagemann, Helmut (1995) *Banken, Brandstifter und Tropenwälder. Die Rolle der Entwicklungszusammenarbeit bei der Zerstörung der brasilianischen Tropenwälder* (Giessen: Focus).

Hall, A. (1989) *Amazônia, desenvolvimento para quem? Desmatamento e Conflito Social no Programa Grande Carajás* (Rio de Janeiro: Zahar Editora).

Hammond, Allen (1990) 'Accountability in the Greenhouse', *Nature* 347 (25 October).

Hammond, Allen (ed.) (1991) *World Resources 1990–1991* (Washington, DC: WRI).

Haraway, Donna (1989) *Primate Visions: Gender, Race, and Nature in the World of Modern Science* (New York: Routledge).

Haraway, Donna (1991) *Simians, Cyborgs, and Women: the reinvention of nature* (New York: Routledge).

Haraway, Donna (1997) *Modest-Witness@ Second-Millenium, Female Man-Once a Mouse* (New York: Routledge).

Hardin, Garrett (1968) 'The Tragedy of the Commons', *Science* 162.

Hartmann, Betsy (1987) *Reproductive Rights and Wrongs: The Global Politics of Population Control and Contraceptive Choice* (New York: Harper & Row).

Hartman, W. (1989) 'Conflitos de pesca em águas interiores da Amazônia e tentativa pra a sua solução', *II Encontro de Ciências Sociais e o Mar* (São Paulo: NUPAUB).

Harvey, Neil (1992) 'La Unión de Uniones de Chiapas y los retos políticos del desarollo de base,' in Julio Moguel, Carlota Botey and Luis Hernández (eds) *Autonomía y Nuevos Sujetos Sociales en el Desarrollo Rural* (Mexico City: Siglo XXI Editores and Centros de Estudios Históricos del Agrarismo en México).

Harvey, Neil (1994) 'Rebellion in Chiapas: Rural Reforms, Campesino Radicalism and the Limits to Salinismo', *Rebellion in Chiapas*, Transformation of Rural Mexico Series, No. 5 (La Jolla: Center for U.S.-Mexican Studies, University of California).

Hecht, Susanna (1982) Cattle Ranching in the eastern Amazon: Evaluation of a development Strategy', PhD dissertation, University of California-Berkeley.

Hecht, Susanna and Alexander Cockburn (1990) *Fate of the Forest* (New York: Harper & Row).

Hermitte, M.-A. (1991) 'Les aborigènes, les "chasseurs de gènes" ...et le marché', *Le monde diplomatique* 12.

Hernández Navarro, Luis (1994) 'The Chiapas Uprising', *Rebellion in Chiapas,* Transformation of Rural Mexico Series, No. 5 (La Jolla: Center for U.S.-Mexican Studies, University of California).

Hess, Charlotte (1996) *Common-pool Resources and Collective Action: A Bibliography*, Volume 3 (Bloomington: Indiana University, Workshop in Political Theory and Policy Analysis).

Hindley, Jane (1995) 'Towards a Pluricultural Nation: The Limits of Indigenismo and Article 4', in Rob Aiken et al. (eds) *Dismantling the Mexican State* (London: Macmillan).

Hofrichter, Richard (ed.) (1993) *Toxic Struggles: The Theory and Practice of Environmental Justice* (Philadelphia: New Society Publishers).

Holdgate, Martin and Bernard Giovannini (1994) 'Biodiversity Conservation: Foundations for the 21st Century', in A. Krattiger et al. (eds) *Widening perspectives on biodiversity* (Gland: IUCN).

Holling, C.S. (1986) 'The resilience of terrestrial ecosystems: local surprise and global change', in W.C. Clark and R.E. Munn (eds) *Sustainable Development of the Biosphere* (Cambridge: Cambridge University Press).

Holling, C.S., L. Gunderson and G. Peterson (1993) *Comparing Ecological and Social Systems*, Beijer Discussion Paper Series No. 36 (Stockholm: Beijer International Institute of Ecological Economics).

Hummon, David M. (1990) *Commonplaces: Community Ideology and Identity in American Culture* (Albany: State University of New York Press).

INPE (1988, new edn 1995) *Dados sobre o desmatamento na Amazônia* (São Paolo: São José dos Campos).

IUCN, WRI, WWF-US and The World Bank (1990) *Conserving the World's Biodiversity* (Gland and Washington: World Bank and IUCN).

Jacobs, M. (1995) 'Inescapable community', Letter to *New Statesman and Society*, 24 March.

Janzen, Daniel H. et al. (1993) 'The Role of Parataxonomists, Inventory Managers, and Taxonomists in Costa Rica's National Biodiversity Inventory', in Walter Reid et al. (eds) *Biodiversity Prospecting* (Washington, DC: World Resources Institute).

Jodha, N.S. (1986) 'Common Property Resources and Rural Poverty in Dry Regions of India', *Economic and Political Weekly* 21:27 (July 5).

Jodha, N.S. (1993) *Property Rights and Development* (Stockholm: Beijer Institute).

Jodha, N.S. (1995) 'Common Property Resources and the Dynamics of Rural Poverty in India's Dry Regions', *Unasylva* 46(1).

Juma, Calestous (1989) *The Gene Hunters: Biotechnology and the Scramble for Seeds* (London: Zed Books).

Karsenty, Alain (1996) Maîtrises foncières et gestion forestière', in Etienne Le Roy et al. (eds) *La sécurisation foncière en Afrique* (Paris: Khartala).

Kay, Jane (1991) 'Women in the Movement', *Race, Poverty and the Environment* 1:3, Winter.

Keohane, Robert (1984) *After Hegemony: Cooperation and Discord in the World Political Economy* (Princeton, NJ: Princeton University Press).

Keohane, Robert (ed.) (1993) *After the Cold War* (Cambridge, MA: Harvard University Press).

Keohane, Robert and Elinor Ostrom (eds) (1995) *Local Commons and Global Interdependence: Heterogeneity and Cooperation in Two Domains* (London: Sage).

Kiss, Alexandre (1989) *Droit international de l'environnement* (Paris).

Kloppenburg, Jack R. (1988) *First the seed: The political economy of plant biotechnology 1492–2000* (Durham, NC: Duke University Press).

Kloppenburg, Jack R. and Daniel Lee Kleinman (1988) 'Seeds of Controversy: National Property Versus Common Heritage,' in J. R. Kloppenburg (ed.) *Seeds and Sovereignty: The Use and Control of Plant Genetic Resources* (Durham, NC: Duke University Press).

Lal, J.B. (1988) *India's Forests: Myth or Reality*? (Dehradun, India: Natraj Publishers).

Lappé, Frances Moore and Rachel Schurman (1988) *Taking Population Seriously* (San Francisco: IFDP).

Lee, Charles (1993) 'From Los Angeles, East St. Louis and Matamoros: Developing Working Definitions of Urban Environmental Justice', *Earth Island Journal* 8:4.

Legler, Thomas (1995) 'Contending Approaches to the Politics of Economic Restructuring in Rural Mexico', presented at the 19th International Congress of the Latin American Studies Association, Washington, DC, 25–27 September.

Leskien, Dan and Michael Flitner (1997) *Intellectual property rights and plant genetic resources: options for a sui generis system* (Rome: IPGRI).

Lindblom, Charles (1977) *Politics and Markets: The World's Political-Economic System* (New York: Basic Books).

Lipton, Michael (1994) 'Institutional Issues in Poverty Reduction', in *Poverty Reduction and Development Cooperation*, CDR Working Paper No. 94.6 (Copenhagen: Centre for Development Research).

Lohmann, Larry (1991) 'Who defends Biological Diversity?' in *Biodiversity – Social and Ecological Perspectives* (Penang: World Rainforest Movement).

Lomas, Emilio (1994) 'Salinas: no habrá retrocesos en las reformas a favor a campo', *La Jornada* 11 Abril.

Loureiro, V. (1991) 'Amazônia: pequenos produtores rurais e a questão ambiental', *Proposta* n. 48, Março.

Luke, Timothy (1994) 'Worldwatching at the Limits of Growth', *Capitalism, Nature, Socialism* 5:2 (June).

Lynch, Barbara Deutsch (1993) 'The Garden and the Sea: U.S. Latino Environmental Discourses and Mainstream Environmentalism', *Social Problems* 40.

Malloy, R.P. (1992) 'Planning for serfdom: an introduction to a new theory of law and economics', *Indiana Law Review* 25:3.

March, J.G. and J.P. Olsen (1989) *Rediscovering Institutions: The Organisational Basis of Politics* (London: Macmillan).

Marsh, David (1993) 'A Win-Win Scenario for Natural Resources Access', *Biotechnology* Vol. 11, October.

Martin, Fenton (1989) *Common-pool Resources and Collective Action: A Bibliography*, Volume 1 (Bloomington: Indiana University, Workshop in Political Theory and Policy Analysis).

Martin, Fenton (1992) *Common-pool Resources and Collective Action: A Bibliography*, Volume 2 (Bloomington: Indiana University, Workshop in Political Theory and Policy Analysis).

Mauss, Marcel (1989) *The Gift* (London: Routledge, original edn 1925).

McCay, Bonnie and James Acheson (1987) *The Question of the Commons: The Culture and Ecology of Communal Resources* (Tucson: University of Arizona Press).

McGinnis, M. and E. Ostrom (1993) 'Design Principles for Local and Global Commons' in R. Keohane et al. (eds) *Proceedings of a Conference on Linking Local and Global Commons* (Cambridge, MA: Center for International Affairs, Harvard University).

McNeeley, Jeffrey (1984) 'Global Environment Facility: Cornucopia or kiss of death for biodiversity', *Canadian Biodiversity* 2.

Meadows, D.H., D.L. Meadows and J. Rander (1992) *Beyond The Limits* (London: Earthscan).

Mellor, Mary (1997a) 'Feminist, Green, Socialism: Theory into Practice', presented at the seminar 'What is Ecological Socialism?' at University of California-Santa Cruz, May.

Merchant, Carolyn (1980) *The Death of Nature: Women, Ecology, and the Scientific Revolution* (San Francisco: Harper and Row).

Merchant, Carolyn (1989) *Ecological Revolutions: Nature, Gender, and Science in New England* (Chapel Hill: University of North Carolina Press).

Mies, Maria (1992) 'Moral Economy' in R. Rilling et al. (eds) *Challenges: Science and Peace in a Rapidly Changing Environment*, Schnftenreïhe Wissenschaft und Frieden, Vol. 1 (Marburg: Bund demokratischer Wissenschaftler).

Ministere du Plan et de l'Amenagement du Territoire (1991) 'Rapport sur l'Etat de l'Environnement et du Developpement au Cameroun', (Yaoundé, November).

Moguel Viveros, Reina and Manuel Parra Vasquez (1995) 'El problema agrario en Chiapas: nudo gordiano para el Procede', *La Jornada* June 27.

Mooney, Pat (1979) *The Seeds of the Earth: A Private or Public Resource?* (Ottawa: Inter Pares).

Mooney, Pat (1988) 'The Law of the Seed', *Development Dialogue* 1–2.

Moore, Richard (1992) 'Confronting Environmental Racism', *Crossroads/Forward Motion* 11:2 (April).

Myers, Norman (1984) *The Primary Source: Tropical Forests and Our Future* (New York: Norton).

Myers, Norman (1991) *The Gaia Atlas of Future Worlds* (New York: Doubleday).

Newman, Penny (ed.) (1994) *Communities at Risk: Contaminated Communities Speak Out on Superfund* (Riverside, CA: Center for Community Action and Environmental Justice).

Nguiffo, Samuel and Mary Fosi (1995) 'Vérifications des Critères de la Certification dans la Région de Campo' (Yaoundé: SNV).

Nguiffo, Samuel and François Kpwang Abessolo, 'Survey on Local and Traditional Practices in the Management of the Rainforest: Case Study of the Rainforest of Cameroon' (Amsterdam: Both Ends, forthcoming).

North, Douglass (1990) *Institutions, Institutional Change and Economic Performance* (Cambridge: Cambridge University Press).

North, Douglass (1995) 'The New Institutional Economics and Development', *Book of Abstracts of the Fifth International Common Property Conference* (Bloomington, IN: International Association for the Study of Common Property).

Nussbaum, Martha (1995) 'Human Functioning and Social Justice: In Defence of Aristotelean Essentialism', *Political Theory* 20:2.

Oakerson, Ronald J. (1992) 'Analyzing the Commons: A Framework', in Daniel W. Bromley, (ed.) *Making the Commons Work: Theory, Practice and Policy* (San Francisco: ICS Press).

O'Connor, James (1988) 'Capitalism, Nature, Socialism: A Theoretical Introduction', *Capitalism, Nature, Socialism* 1:1.

O'Connor, James, *Natural Causes: Essays on Ecological Marxism* (New York: Guilford Press, 1998).

O'Connor, Martin (ed.) (1994) *Is Capitalism Sustainable?* (New York: Guilford Press).

Olson, Mancur (1965) *The Logic of Collective Action: Public Goods and the Theory of Groups* (Cambridge, MA: Harvard University Press).

Omvedt, Gail (1993) *Reinventing Revolution* (Armonk, NY: M.E. Sharpe).

Ortega, Miguel Angel (1994) 'La Guerilla Anunciada', *El Financiero* 18 November.

Ostrom, Elinor (1990) *Governing the Commons: The Evolution of Institutions for Collective Action* (New York: Cambridge University Press).

Ostrom, Elinor (1994) 'Neither Market nor State: Governance of Common-Pool Resources in the Twenty-first Century', presented at The International Food Policy Research Institute, Washington, DC, June 2.

Ostrom, Elinor (1995) 'Constituting Social Capital and Collective Action' in Keohane, Robert and Elinor Ostrom (eds) *Local Commons and Global Interdependence: Heterogeneity and Cooperation in Two Domains* (London: Sage Publications).

Ovalle Vaquera, Federico and Emilio López Gámez (1994) 'La reestruc-turación de la producción maicera nacional,' presented at Primer Seminario Nacional de Maíz-Tortilla, Centro de Investigaciones Inter-disciplinarias en Humanidades, Universidad Nacional Autónoma de México, Mexico City, November.

Paré, Luisa (1990) 'The challenge of rural democratization in Mexico', *Journal of Development Studies* 26, July.

Peet, Richard and Michael Watts (eds) (1996) *Liberation Ecologies: environment, development, social movements* (London: Routledge).

Peluso, Nancy (1993) 'Coercing Conservation,' in R.D. Lipschutz and K. Conca (eds) *The state and social power in global environmental politics* (New York: Columbia University Press).

Pena, Devon (1992) 'The "Brown" and the "Green": Chicanos and Environmental Politics in the Upper Rio Grande', *Capitalism, Nature and Socialism* 3:1.

Peréz, Matilde (1994) 'Nuevo desarrollo rural, piden 50 mil personas en el Zócalo', *La Jornada* 11 April.

Peters, Pauline (1993) 'Is Rational Choice the Best Choice for Robert Bates? An Anthropologists' Reading of Bates', *World Development* 21.

Peters, Pauline (1994) *Dividing the Commons: Politics, Policy, and Culture in Botswana* (Charlottesville: University Press of Virginia).

Petrere, J. (1989) *Manejo de estoques pesqueiros na Amazonia* (Rio Claro: UNESP).

Petrich, Blance and Elio Henríquez (1994) 'La muerta es nuestra, ahora decidimos cómo tomarla', *La Jornada* February 6.

Plant, Raymond (1978) 'Community: Concept, Conception and Ideology', *Politics and Society* 8.

Platt, Rutherford, Rowan Rowntree and Pamela Mvick (eds) (1994) *The Ecological City: Preserving and Restoring Urban Biodiversity* (Amherst: University of Massachusetts Press).

Plott, Charles R. and Robert A. Meyer (1975) 'The Technology of Public Goods, Externalities, and the Exclusion Principle', in E.S. Mills (ed.) *Economic Analysis of Environmental Problems* (New York: Columbia University Press).

Polanyi, Karl (1944) *The Great Transformation* (Boston: Beacon Press).

Pollack, Sue and Joann Grozuczak (1984) *Reagan, Toxics and Minorities* (Washington, DC: Urban Environment Conference).

Pollan, Michael (1991) *Second Nature: A Gardener's Education* (New York: Atlantic Monthly Press).

Posey, Darell A. and Graham Dutfield (1996) *Beyond Intellectual Property* (Ottawa: IDRC).

Powell, William and Paul DiMaggio (eds) (1991) *The New Institutionalism in Organisational Analysis* (Chicago: University of Chicago Press).

Prakash, Sanjeev (1997) *Poverty and Environment Linkages in Mountains and Uplands: Reflections on the Poverty Trap Thesis*, CREED Working Paper Series No. 12, London: International Institute for Environment and Development).

Price, M.F. and M. Thompson (1997) 'Complexities of human land uses in mountain ecosystems', *Global Ecology and Biogeography Letters* 6 77–90.

Procuraduria Agraria, Delegación Oaxaca (1995) 'Relación de Ejidos Ya incorporados al Procede', mimeo (Oaxaca, Mexico).

Pulido, Laura (1991) 'Latino Environmental Struggles in the Southwest' (PhD dissertation, UCLA).

Putnam, Robert (1992) *Making Democracy Work: Civic Traditions in Modern Italy* (Princeton, NJ: Princeton University Press).

Putnam, Robert (1993) 'Democracy, Development and the Civic Community: Evidence from an Italian Experiment' in R. Keohane et al. (eds) *Proceedings of a Conference on Linking Local and Global Commons* (Cambridge, MA: Center for International Affairs, Harvard University).

RAFI (1993) *Profiting from Diversity: Biological Diversity and Indigenous Knowledge* (Brandon, Manitoba: RAFI).

Rahnema, Majid (1991) 'Global Poverty: A Pauperizing Myth', *Interculture* 24 (2).

Rayner, Steve (1994) 'A Conceptual Map of Human Values for Climate Change Decision Making', presented at the IPCC Working Group III Workshop on 'Equity and Social Considerations Related to Climate Change', Nairobi, Kenya, 18–22 July.

Reid, Walter et al. (1993) *Biodiversity Prospecting* (Washington, DC: World Resources Institute).

Reuters (1995) 'Corn', Anenecuilco, Mexico, October 24, from the Internet.

Ridley, Matt (1996) *The Origins of Virtue: Human Instincts and the Evolution of Cooperation* (London and New York: Viking).

Robberson, Tod (1995) 'Mexican Ranchers Confront Squatters', *Washington Post* September 23.

Rodríguez Cervantez, S. (1993) *Conservation, Contradiction, and Sovereignty Erosion: The Costa Rican State and the Natural Protected Areas, 1970–1992* (PhD thesis, Madison: University of Wisconsin).

Romero Frizzi, María de los Angeles (1988) 'Epoca Colonial (1519–1785)', in Leticia Reina (ed.) *Historia de la Cuestión Agraria Mexicana, Estado de Oaxaca: Prehispanico–1924*, Volumen I (Mexico City: Gobierno de Estado de Oaxaca, Universidad Autónoma Benito Juárez de Oaxaca, Centro de Estudios Históricos del Agrarismo en México).

Ross, John (1994) *Rebellion from the Roots: Indian Uprising in Chiapas* (Monroe, ME: Common Courage Press).

Rotberg, Eugene (1994) 'The Financial Operations of the World Bank', *Bretton Woods: Looking to the Future* (Washington, DC: Bretton Woods Commission).

Ruben, Barbara (1992) 'Leading Indicators: women speak out on the challenges of national grassroots leadership', *Environmental Action* 24:2, Summer.

Ruffins, Paul (1992) 'Defining a Movement and a Community', *Crossroads/Forward Motion* 11:2 (April).

Sachs, Wolfgang (ed.) (1992) *The Development Dictionary: A Guide to Knowledge as Power* (London: Zed Books).

Sachs, Wolfgang (ed.) (1993) *Global Ecology* (London: Zed Books).

Santos, L. and M. Andrade (1988) *As hidrelétricas do Xingu e os Povos Indígenas Comissão Pró-Indio* (São Paulo).

Saxena, N.C. (1988) *Social Forestry in U.P. Hills* (Kathmandu: International Centre for Integrated Mountain Development).

Schapiro, Michael (1988) 'Judicial Selection and the Design of Clumsy Institutions', *Southern California Law Review* 61:6.

Schelling, T.C. (1960) *The Strategy of Conflict* (Cambridge, MA: Harvard University Press).

Schmink, M. (1988) 'Big Business in the Amazon' in J.S. Denslow and C. Paddoch (eds) *People of the Tropical Rain Forest* (Berkeley: University of California Press).

Schmink, M. (1992) 'Amazonian Resistance Movements and the International Alliance', in L. Kosinski (ed.) *Ecological disorder in Amazonia: social aspects* (Rio de Janeiro: Unesco/ISSC/EDUCAM).

Schwarz, Michiel and Michael Thompson (1990) *Divided We Stand: Redefining Politics, Technology and Social Choice* (Hemel Hempstead: Harvester Wheatsheaf).

Schwartzman, S. (1989) 'The rubber tappers' strategy for sustainable use of the Amazon Rainforest' in J. Browder (ed.) *Fragile Lands in Latin America: the Search for Sustainable Uses* (Boulder, CO: Westview Press).

Scott, James (1976) *The Moral Economy of the Peasant: Rebellion and Subsistence in Southeast Asia* (New Haven, CT: Yale University Press).

Scott, James (1985) *Weapons of the Weak: Everyday Forms of Peasant Resistance* (New Haven, CT: Yale University Press).

Shanin, Teodor (ed.) (1971) *Peasants and Peasant Societies* (London: Penguin).

Shiva, Vandana (1993) *Monocultures of the Mind: Biodiversity, Biotechnology and the Third World* (Penang, Malaysia: Third World Network).

Shiva, Vandana (1995) *Captive Minds, Captive Lives, Ethics, Ecology and Patents on Life* (Dehra Dun, India: Research Foundation for Science, Technology and Natural Resource Policy).

Shiva, Vandana and Jayanta Bandyopadhyay (1987) 'Chipko', *Seminar* 330 (February).

Silberling, L. (1990) 'Social Movements and successful common property regimes: the case of the Brazilian Rubber-Tappers' MSc thesis, Cornell University.

Singh, Chhatrapati (1986) *Common Property and Common Poverty* (Delhi: Oxford University Press).

Slater, Candace (1996) 'Amazonia as Edenic Narrative', in William Cronon (ed.) *Uncommon Ground: Rethinking the Human Place in Nature* (New York: W.W. Norton).

Smith, Dorothy (1987) *The Everyday World as Problematic: A Feminist Sociology* (Boston: Northeastern University Press).

SRA (Archive of Secretaría de Reforma Agrara, Delegación de Oaxaca) (1926a) File for Santa María del Tule, 25 de Agosto, 1926. 'Memorandum del Oficio Mayor de la Comisión Nacional Agraria al C. Delegado de la Comisión Nacional Agraria en el Estado de Oaxaca. Ordenándole remíta datos é informes con justificación acerca de la situación de hecho o de derecho guarde asunto agrario del pueblo de Santa María del Tule, Oax'.

SRA (1926b) File for Santa María del Tule, 20 Septiembre 1926. 'Memorandum del Oficio Mayor de la Comisión Nacional Agraria para el C. Vocal Ing. Ignacio M. Cabañas Flores, relativo al estado de tramitación que guarda el expediente de dotación de ejidos promovidos por los vecinos del pueblo de Santa María del Tule'.

SRA (1935) File for Santa María del Tule, 28 Octubre 1935. 'Acta Complementaria de Posesión y Deslinde Relativa a Dotación de Ejidos al Pueblo de Santa Maria del Tule, Municipio del Mismo Nombre, Del ex-dto. del Central, del Estado de Oaxaca'.

Stavenhagen, Rodolfo (1986) 'Collective Agriculture and Capitalism in Mexico: A Way Out or a Dead End?' in Nora Hamilton and Timothy F. Harding (eds) *Modern Mexico: State, Economy, and Social Conflict*, Latin American Perspectives Readers, Volume One (Beverly Hills, CA: Sage Publications).

Stephen, Lynn (1992) 'Women in Mexico's Popular Movements: Survival Strategies against Ecological and Economic Impoverishment', *Latin American Studies* 19 (1) Winter.

Stephen, Lynn (1994) 'Viva Zapata!: Generation, Gender, and Historical Consciousness in the Reception of Ejido Reform in Oaxaca', *Transformation of Rural Mexico*, Number 6, Ejido Reform Research

Project (La Jolla: Center for U.S.-Mexican Studies, University of California).

Stephen, Lynn (1995) 'The Zapatista Army of National Liberation and the National Democratic Convention', *Latin American Perspectives* 22(4).

Stephen, Lynn (1997) 'Pro-Zapatista and Pro-PRI: resolving the Contradictions of Zapatismo in Rural Oaxaca', *Latin American Research Review*, 31(2).

Stephen, Lynn (1998) 'Differentiation, History, and Identity in the Interpretation of Agrarian Reform: Two Oaxacan Case Studies, in Wayne Cornelius and David Myhre (eds) *The Transformation of Rural Mexico: Reforming the Ejida Sector*, (La Jolla: Center for U.S.-Mexican Studies, University of California, San Diego).

Sternberg, E. (1994) *Just Business* (New York: Little Brown).

Streeten, Paul (1991) 'Global Prospects in an Interdependent World', special issue, 'Global Commons: Site of Peril, Source of Hope', *World Development* 19:1 (January).

Stren, Richard, Rodney White and Joseph Whitney (eds) *Sustainable Cities: Urbanization and the Environment in International Perspective* (Boulder, CO: Westview Press).

Swaminathan, M.S. (ed.) (1995) *Farmers' Rights and Plant Genetic Resources: Recognition and Reward – A Dialogue* (Madras: Macmillan India).

Szasz, Andrew (1994) *Ecopopulism: Toxic Waste and the Movement for Environmental Justice* (Minneapolis: University of Minnesota Press).

Taylor, Michael and Sara Singleton (1993) 'The Communal Resource: Transaction Costs and the Solution of Collective Action Problems' in R. Keohane et al. (eds) *Proceedings of a Conference on Linking Local and Global Commons* (Cambridge, MA: Center for International Affairs, Harvard University).

Taylor, William (1972) *Landlord and Peasant in Colonial Oaxaca* (Palo Alto: Stanford University Press).

Tello Díaz, Carlos (1995) *La rebelión de las Cañadas* (Mexico City: cal y arena).

The Ecologist (1992) 'Whose Common Future?', 22:4, July/August.

Thompson, Michael (1979) *Rubbish Theory: The Creation and Destruction of Value* (Oxford: Oxford University Press).

Thompson, Michael (1980) 'The aesthetics of risk: culture or context?', in R.C. Schwing and W.A. Albers (eds) *Societal Risk Assessment: How Safe Is Safe Enough?* (New York: Plenum).

Thompson, Michael (1987) 'Welche Gesellschaftsklassen sind potent genug, anderen ihre Zukunft aufzuoktroyieren? Und wie geht das vor sich?', in L. Burchardt (ed.) *Design der Zukunft* (Köln: DuMont).

Thompson, Michael (1992) 'The dynamics of cultural theory and their implications for the enterprise culture', in S. Hargreaves Heap and A. Ross (eds) *Understanding the Enterprise Culture* (Edinburgh: Edinburgh University Press).

Thompson, Michael (1993) 'The North Starts to Catch Up with the South: The Himalayan Village as a Clumsy Institution and its Lessons for Policy', paper presented to the Workshop on Risk and Fairness, International Institute for Applied Systems Analysis. Laxenburg, Austria, 20–22 June.

Thompson, Michael (forthcoming) 'Cultural Theory and Integrated Assessment', in *Environmental Modelling and Assessment*.

Thompson, Michael, Richard Ellis and Aaron Wildavsky (1990) *Cultural Theory* (Boulder, CO: Westview Press).

Thompson, Michael, M. Warburton and T. Hatley (1986) *Uncertainty on a Himalayan Scale* (London: Ethnographica).

Tiffen, M., M. Mortimor and F.N. Gichuki (1984) *More People, Less Erosion: Environmental Recovery in Kenya* (New York: John Wiley).

Traweek, Sharon (1988) *Beamtimes and Lifetimes* (Cambridge: Harvard University Press).

US General Accounting Office (1983) *Siting of Hazardous Waste Landfills and Their Correlation with Racial and Economic Status of Surrounding Communities* (Washington, DC: General Accounting Office).

US Treasury Department (1995) 'The Multilateral Development Banks: Increasing U.S. Exports and Creating U.S. Jobs' (May).

UNDP, World Bank and UNEP, *GEF Work Program* FY 92 and FY 93, Annexes.

UNEP (1992) *Saving Our Planet: Challenges and Hopes* (Nairobi: United Nations Environment Programme).

United Nations Development Programme (1994) *Human Development Report 1994* (New York: Oxford University Press).

Unmüssig, Barbara (1995) 'Mythos Geld? Zur Finanzierung von Maßnahmen zum Schutz der biologischen Vielfalt', in J. Wolters (ed.) *Leben und Leben lassen* (Giessen: Focus).

Usher, Ann Danaiya (1992) 'After the Forest: AIDS as an Ecological Collapse in Thailand', in 'Women, Ecology and Health: Rebuilding Connections', *Development Dialogue* 1:2.

Van Asselt, M. and J. Rotmans (1995) *Uncertainty in Integrated Assessment Modelling: a Cultural Perspective-Based Approach*, Global Dynamics and Sustainable Development Programme, GLOBO Report Series No 9. (Bilthoven, the Netherlands: RIVM, Netherlands Institute of Public Health and the Environment).

van Wijk, Jeroen (1991) 'Diminishing National Sovereignty in Intellectual Property Rights', presented at the International Symposium 'Property Rights, Biotechnology and Genetic Resources' in Nairobi, Kenya, 10–15 June.

Vavilov, Nicolai I. (1992) *Origin and Geography of Cultivated Plants* (Cambridge: Cambridge University Press).

Verhagen, Herman and Chris Enthoven (1993) 'Logging and conflicts in the Rainforest of Cameroon' (Amsterdam: Milieu Defense and NC-IUCN).

von Weizsäcker, Christine (1993) 'Competing notions of biodiversity', in W. Sachs (ed.) *Global Ecology* (London: Zed Books).

Vondel, Patricia (1987) 'The Common Swamplands of Southeastern Borneo: Multiple Use, Management, and Conflict', in Bonnie McCay and James Acheson (eds) *The Question of the Commons: The Culture and Ecology of Communal Resources* (Tucson: University of Arizona Press).

Wade, Robert (1987) *Village Republics: Economic Conditions for Collective Action in South India* (Cambridge: Cambridge University Press).

Watts, Michael (1994) 'Development II: the privatization of everything?', *Progress in Human Geography* 18:3.

Weber, Thomas (1989) *Hugging the Trees: The Story of the Chipko Movement* (Delhi: Penguin).

Whitt, Laurie Anne and Jennifer Daryl Slack (1994) 'Communities, Environments and Cultural Studies', *Cultural Studies* 8 (January).

Williams, Raymond (1994) 'Selections from Marxism and Literature', in Nicholas B. Dirks, Geoff Eley and Sherry Ortner (eds) *Culture/Power/History* (Princeton, NJ: Princeton University Press).

Williamson, Oliver (1975) *The Economic Institutions of Capitalism: Firms, Markets, Relational Contracting* (New York: Free Press).

Williamson, O. (1979) *Markets and Hierarchies, Analysis and Anti-Trust Implications: A Study in the Economics of Internal Organisation* (New York: Free Press).

Wilson, Edward O. (ed.) (1988) *Biodiversity: Proceedings of the National Forum on BioDiversity* (Washington, DC: National Academy Press, eleventh edn).

Wolf, Eric (1966) *Peasants* (Englewood Cliffs, NJ: Prentice-Hall).

Woodward, David (1992) *Debt, Adjustment and Poverty in Developing Countries*, Volumes I and II (London: Save the Children).

World Bank (1981) *Accelerated Development in Sub-Saharan Africa* (Washington, DC: World Bank).

World Bank (1994) *Adjustment in Africa: Reforms, Results, and the Road Ahead* (New York: Oxford University Press for the World Bank)

World Bank (1995) *Facing the Global Environment Challenge: A Progress Report on World Bank Global Environment Operations*, Washington, DC, March–May, Annex.

World Resources Institute (in collaboration with the United Nations Environment Programme and the United Nations Development Programme) (1990) *World Resources: A Guide to the Global Environment, 1990–1991* (New York: Oxford University Press).

Worldwatch (1994, 1993, 1992, 1991 editions) *State of the World* (New York: Norton).

WRI, IUCN and UNEP (1992) *Global Biodiversity Strategy* (Washington, DC: WRI and UNEP).

Yapa, Lakshman (1993) 'What Are Improved Seeds? An Epistemology of the Green Revolution', *Economic Geography* Vol. 69 (3).

Yokomizo, C. (1989) 'Incentivos financeiros c fiacais na Amazônia; fatos, problemas c soluçiócs' in *Proceedings of the Seminar: Amazônia, facts, problems, and solutions* (São Paolo: USP).

Young, H.P. (1993) *Equity in Theory and Practice* (Princeton, NJ: Princeton University Press).

Young, Oran (1995) 'The Problem of Scale in Human/Environment Relationships', in Robert O. Keohane and Elinor Ostrom (eds) *Local Commons and Global Interdependence* (London: Sage).

Zartman, William (1993) 'Negotiating Justice under Risk', presented to the Workshop on Risk and Fairness, International Institute for Applied Systems Analysis, Laxenburg, Austria, 20–22 June.

Zerner, Charles (1996) 'Telling Stories about Biological Diversity', in Stephen Brush and Doreen Stabinsky (eds) *Valuing Local Knowledge: Indigenous People and Intellectual Property Rights* (Washington/Covelo: Island Press).

Index